New Testament Matters

Also published by Coventry Press for Francis J. Moloney, SDB

Broken For You: Jesus Christ the Catholic Priesthood & the Word of God (2018).

ISBN 9780648360155

New Testament Matters 1 (2024).

ISBN 9781922589545

BIBLICAL & THEOLOGICAL ESSAYS – TWO

New Testament Matters

FRANCIS J. MOLONEY SDB

COVENTRY
PRESS

Published in Australia by
Coventry Press
33 Scoresby Road
Bayswater VIC 3153

ISBN 9781922589637

Copyright © Francis J. Moloney, SDB, 2025

All rights reserved. Other than for the purposes and subject to the conditions prescribed under the *Copyright Act*, no part of this publication may be reproduced, stored in a retrieval system, or transmitted in any form or by any means, electronic, mechanical, photocopying, recording or otherwise, without the prior permission of the publisher.

Apart from the author's own translations, Scripture quotations are from the *New Revised Standard Version Bible*, copyright 1989, Division of Christian Education of the National Council of the Churches of Christ in the United States of America. Used by permission. All rights reserved.

Catalogue-in-Publication entry is available from the National Library of Australia
http://catalogue.nla.gov.au

Cover design by Ian James – www.jgd.com.au
Cover image by Michael Harris, SDB
Text design by Coventry Press
Set in EB Garamond

Printed in Australia 2025

For my Family

Contents

Foreword ix

1. Before I Forget: Fifty Years with the New Testament 1

2. "Interpreters of our own Cultural Tradition".
   The Australasian Catholic Record 1924–2023 21

3. A New Testament Hermeneutic for Divorce
   and Remarriage in the Catholic Tradition 41

4. The Catholic Priesthood: A New Testament Reflection 71

5. The Book of Revelation: Hope in Dark Times 95

6. Tracing a Literary Structure in the Book of Revelation 121

7. The Jews, Israel, and Jerusalem in the Book of
   Revelation 147

8. Postscript: A Review of Christopher Rowland,
   *By an Immediate Revelation: Studies in
   Apocalypticism. Its Origins and Effects* 165

Bibliography 171

Foreword

This second volume of *New Testament Matters* opens with my respectful questioning of several contemporary Roman Catholic interpretative traditions and practices. My choice of the expression "respectful questioning" indicates my deep love and commitment to the Roman Catholic Church and its practices, already shared with my readers in the theological and biographical essay that opened *New Testament Matters – One*.[1] Inspired by the profound return to the sources of the Christian tradition, the Second Vatican Council (1962-1965) sought to bringing into greater light what the Sacred Scriptures and Tradition tell us about institutions and practices that necessarily (as in any institution, however sacred, administered by human beings) tend to become tied to a given period or culture.[2]

The essays on the steady critical engagement with the Word of God that began with Pope Leo XIII's Encyclical *Providentissimus Deus* (1893), through all its fears and difficulties, the current Catholic approaches to the question of marriage, divorce, and access to the life of the Catholic community, and the role and practice of the Roman Catholic Priesthood, deserve our critical attention. Only at this stage of my life and scholarly career do I sense that I can respectfully propose some responses to these issues that have been, and remain, contentious within the life and practice of the Catholic Church. I do not suggest that I have all the answers.

---

1 See "An Irish-Catholic Biblical Scholar," *New Testament Matters I* (Melbourne: Coventry Press, 2024) 1-35.

2 For the ecclesial and political situation in France that played a major role in developing this "return to the sources" (French: *ressourcement*) in a movement often called (initially by its opponents) *la nouvelle théologie*, that impacted upon Vatican II, see Sarah Shortall, *Soldiers of God in a Secular World. Catholic Theology and Twentieth Century French Politics* (Cambridge, MA: Harvard University Press, 2021).

However, my long involvement with the Word of God, side-by-side with my support for the Magisterium of the Catholic Church, has guided me to suggest some alternatives to current thought and practice.³

New Testament Matters – Two closes with my recent fascination with a possible new paradigm for the interpretation of the Book of Revelation.⁴ A brief explanation is called for. Early in my career as a young professor at the Pontifical Salesian University in Rome (April, 1978), I attended a lecture delivered at the Pontifical Salesian University by the then Professor of Early Christian Literature at the University of Turin, Professor Eugenio Corsini.⁵ Saint Augustine's use of the Book of Revelation (especially Rev 20–21) concluded *De Civitate Dei* (City of God) in defence of Christianity after the German Goths sacked the city of Rome in 410 CE. For Augustine, and for the Christian centuries that followed him, this enigmatic New Testament book was a use of a Jewish apocalyptic literary form to indicate a road-map that led to the end of history. Professor Corsini's familiarity with the earliest use of the Book of Revelation by other Christian witnesses (especially the Acts of the Martyrs) led to surprise that they did not reflect an "end-time" reading of the document. They were more concerned with discovering a message of the victorious Jesus Christ. The earliest Christians focused upon the fact that

---

3   I was privileged to me a member of the International Theological Commission of the Holy See for 14 years (1996-2009).
4   See Francis J. Moloney, "The Book of Revelation: Hope in Dark Times," *Religions* 10 (2019) 1–15; Idem, *The Apocalypse of John. A Commentary* (Grand Rapids, MI: Baker Academic, 2020); Idem, *A Friendly Guide to the Book of Revelation* (Mulgrave: Garratt Publishing 2020); Idem, "Tracing a Literary Structure in the Book of Revelation," *The Catholic Biblical Quarterly* 84 (2022) 642–59; Idem, "The Jews, Israel, and Jerusalem in the Book of Revelation," in Robert A. Derrenbacher, Jr., Chrisopher A. Porter, and Muriel Porter, eds., *Many Believed Because of Her Testimony. Essays Celebrating the Scholarship and Service of Dorothy Lee* (Eugene, OR: Wipf & Stock, 2023) 102–115.
5   A summary of that lecture can be found as Eugenio Corsini, "L'Apocalisse di Giovanni nella Catechesi Patristica," *Salesianum* 41 (1979) 419.

resurrection of Jesus is proclaimed throughout the document (see Rev 1:5-6; 5:1-14; 8:1; 11:15-18; 16:17-21; 19:4-8; 21:6). What might this indicate?

For Eugenio Corsini, the Book of Revelation is not about the future coming of Jesus Christ as judge at the end of time, as is almost universally argued. Rather, it affirms the perennial presence of the saving effects of the death and resurrection of Jesus, "from the foundation of the world" (see 5:6; 13:8). The so-called "saints" are not early Christian martyrs, but all those who – from the beginning of time – have accepted the Word of God, especially in the Law, and looked forward to the fulfilment of the messianic promises that took place in and through Jesus. After years of exposure to Corsini's careful analysis of John's text,[6] I became so convinced that he had found the key to the structure and message of the Book that I translated his basic text, and then proceeded to write my own commentary, depending upon (but at times differing from) the theological conclusions that one might draw from Corsini's interpretative paradigm.[7] The studies on the literary structure and the Christian theological contribution of the Book of Revelation that close this volume are the result of this academic and faith journey.

---

6 His two books are Eugenio Corsini, *Apocalisse prima e dopo* (Turin: Società Editrice Internazionale, 1980), and Idem, *L'Apocalisse di Gesù Cristo secondo Giovanni*, Sestante (Turin: Società Editrice Internazionale, 2002). Eugenio Corsini passed away on March 22, 2018, at 94 years of age.
7 Eugenio Corsini, *The Apocalypse. The Perennial Revelation of Jesus Christ*, trans. and ed. Francis J. Moloney (Eugene, OR: Wipf & Stock, 2019). This is a reprint of my original translation, now long out of print, published in Wilmington, DE, by Michael Glazier in 1983. For the details of my commentary on *The Apocalypse of John*, see above, n. 4.

1

Before I Forget
Fifty Years with the New Testament

In 1970, I took entrance examinations in Hebrew and Greek to begin studies at the Pontifical Biblical Institute, Rome. I have shared in various ministries since then, sometimes in positions that distracted from my academic interests (e.g. Dean of the School of Theology and Religious Studies at the Catholic University of America in Washington, DC, 2003–05, and Provincial Superior of the Salesians of Don Bosco in Australia and the Pacific, 2006–11). Nevertheless, I have been a privileged 'insider' to the development of critical studies of the New Testament over the past fifty years.[1] Given my history, the title of this essay shamelessly plagiarises Geoffrey Blainey's delightful recollections of his early years, *Before I Forget*.[2]

---

1 Much published, my major scholarly books have been Francis J. Moloney, *The Johannine Son of Man*, Idem, *Belief in the Word: Reading John 1–4* (Minneapolis: Fortress, 1993); Idem, *Signs and Shadows: Reading John 5–12* (Minneapolis: Fortress, 1996); Idem, *Glory not Dishonor: Reading John 13–21* (Minneapolis: Fortress, 1998); Idem, *The Gospel of John*, Sacra Pagina 4 (Collegeville, MN: Liturgical Press, 1998); Idem, *The Gospel of Mark. A Commentary* (Peabody: Hendrickson, 2002); Idem, *The Gospel of John: Text and Context*, Biblical Interpretation Series 72 (Boston/Leiden: Brill, 2005); Idem, *Johannine Studies 1975–2017*, Wissenschaftliche Untersuchungen zum Neuen Testament 372 (Tübingen: Mohr Siebeck, 2017); Idem, *Gospel Interpretation and Christian Life*, Scholars Collection 3 (Adelaide: ATF Press, 2017); Idem, *The Apocalypse of John*.
2 Geoffrey Blainey, *Before I Forget. An Early Memoir* (Melbourne: Hamish Hamilton, 2019).

I have developed the following overview across four sections that respects the historical development of the New Testament.[3] Paul wrote between 50 and 64 CE. Although written later in the century (and perhaps early in the second century), other deutero-Pauline literature will be considered in this first section. The Gospels and Acts deserve their own section. The Gospel of Mark is closely associated with 70 CE, the Gospels of Matthew and Luke with the late 80s. The Acts of the Apostles followed shortly after. The Fourth Gospel, explicitly aimed at a wider Christian audience in Asia, probably saw the light of day around the turn of the century (100 CE). A group of documents regarded as the Catholic Epistles appeared late in the first Christian century, and early in the second century. Finally, recent attempts to unravel the puzzles of the end-of- the-century Book of Revelation merit their own consideration.[4]

The Pauline Literature

Despite the imaginative presentations of Saul's fall from his horse on the road to Damascus, interpreters nowadays argue that Saul did not experience a "conversion." Luke's report(s) of the event on the road to Damascus in Acts 9:1-22 (see also 23:3- 21; 26:12-18) describe a dramatic intervention of the risen Jesus in his life. Before his encounter on the Damascus road (see also Gal 1:17; 2 Cor

---

[3] It took some centuries to reach consensus on what was "in" and what was "out" of the Christian Scriptures. On this, see Francis J. Moloney, *Reading the New Testament in the Church. A Primer for Pastors, Religious Educators, and Believers* (Grand Rapids, MI: Baker Academic 2015) 45–63. The authoritative voice of St Athanasius generated a definitive list in 367. In the light of a different list that emerged in the Reformation churches, Athanasius' canon was affirmed at the Council of Trent in 1546.

[4] For a more detailed explanation of these four classifications, see Sherri Brown and Francis J. Moloney, *Interpreting the New Testament: An Introduction* (Grand Rapids, MI: Eerdmans, 2019) 90–248. Chronologically, there is considerable overlap in the material considered in the four sections.

11:32), Paul's 'zeal' for the God of Israel led him to persecute any rejection of that God's uniqueness (see 1 Cor 15:9; Gal 1:13, 23; Phil 3:6). His "call" changed his view about the crucified and risen one, but it did not touch his 'zeal' for the God of Israel.

Paul experienced a "call" from God to recognise and proclaim what God had done for humankind, and not only Israel, in and through the death and resurrection of his Son, Jesus Christ.[5] His passion for the God of Israel never wavered, but his acceptance of Jesus' role in God's action in human history, and in creation itself (see Rom 8:18-25), transformed him. As his zeal for the God of Israel sent him on a mission to cleanse a holy people of a heretical Jesus-sect, his experience of the risen Christ developed an equally zealous mission to proclaim what God had done for *all creation* through the death and resurrection of Jesus. As he himself put it: "But whatever gain I had, I counted as loss for the sake of Christ" (Phil 3:7).

Interpreters dispute which New Testament documents came directly from Paul.[6] Traditionally, the apostle Paul has been regarded as the author of 1 and 2 Thessalonians, 1 and 2 Corinthians, Galatians, Philippians, Ephesians, and Colossians, Philemon, and Romans, as well as 1 and 2 Timothy, Titus, and Hebrews.[7] Currently, very few regard Hebrews as Pauline, and most doubt that he wrote 2 Thessalonians. Paul is not mentioned in Hebrews, an elegant theological tract written late in the first century, and 2 Thessalonians takes Paul's thought on the proximate end of the ages into later context. Very few accept that he wrote

---

5 For a summary of this debate, see David G. Horrell, *An Introduction to the Study of Paul*, 3rd. ed. (London: T. & T. Clark, 2006) 29–31.

6 Paul would not have physically "written" every letter. He would have dictated them, as was common at that time. See Rom 16:22: "I, Tertius, the writer of this letter, greet you in the Lord."

7 One reason for this early collection of Pauline letters was the total of fourteen letters (2 x 7), which appeared side by side with the seven so-called "Catholic" Epistles (James, 1 and 2 Peter; 1, 2, 3 John; Jude). In Hebrew thought, the number seven indicates "completion." See below on the Catholic Epistles.

1 and 2 Timothy, and Titus, known as the Pastoral Epistles.[8] It is possible that some authentic memories of Pauline instructions are incorporated in the Pastorals,[9] but they address the later situation of more established Pauline communities.

The origin of Philippians, Colossians, and Ephesians – often discussed together as Paul's Prison Letters – is less certain. Reconstruction of the situation that produced these letters depends upon an imprisonment at Ephesus in the mid-50s. There is no literary trace of such an imprisonment, despite Luke's dedication of a large part of his narrative to Paul's presence in that city (Acts 18:24–19:21). But there was imprisonment in Rome (Acts 28:16-31). Recent scholarship is moving steadily in favour of the suggestion that Philippians was Paul's final (and heartfelt) letter, written not long before his death in the early 60s from Rome.[10]

The Christological hymns of Colossians 1:15-20 and Ephesians 1:3-14 (not without significant Pauline contacts), the description of disorders in the communities (see Col 2:16-19; Eph 5:3-20), and instructions on right order in family life (see Col 3:18–4:1; Eph 5:21–6:9), lead most interpreters to suggest that they were written by Pauline disciples. The similarity between these two beautiful letters suggests that Colossians was written first, and that Ephesians is possibly a "circular letter" based upon Colossians.[11] If either

---

8 An important exception to this is Nicholas T. Wright, *Paul: A Biography* (San Francisco: HarperOne, 2018). Wright accepts an Ephesian imprisonment for the Prison Letters, and a late journey to Spain (see Rom 15:28) to include the Pastorals as Pauline.

9 A suggestion first made by Michael Prior, *Paul the Letter-writer and the Second Letter to Timothy*, Journal for the Study of the New Testament Supplement Series 23 (Sheffield: JSOT Press, 1989), accepted and developed by others since then.

10 Convincingly argued by Paul A. Holloway, *Philippians*, Hermeneia (Minneapolis: Fortress, 2017) 19–24. For the traditional case, see Wright, *Paul*, 271–80. There is no description of Paul's death in the Acts of the Apostles, although hints are given (e.g. Acts 21:13).

11 There are parallels in structure and theme in the two letters, and some early manuscripts have "To the saints who are faithful," rather than "To the saints who are in Ephesus" in Eph 1:1. One manuscript tradition might reflect a "circular," without the name of the audience, while the other might reflect that same circular, directed to the Ephesians.

of these letters came from Paul, it was Colossians, written in the early 60s from a Roman prison. The author of what we know as Ephesians might have developed Colossians to address other audiences as a circular letter.

All interpreters regard 1 Thessalonians, 1 and 2 Corinthians, Galatians, Philemon, Romans, and Philippians as unquestionably Pauline. The search for Pauline thought depends upon the evidence of these letters. I referred earlier to later letters as "deutero-Pauline," rather than "pseudo-Pauline." Whatever modern sensibilities might be about using the name of a past distinguished author, the practice was common in antiquity. The purpose of this form of writing (called pseudepigrapha) was to *continue the Pauline tradition into a later era*. Subsequent authors who adopted Paul's name (and authority) were not cheating. They respected and honoured his foundational significance in emerging Christianity. Pauline thought is alive and well in the deutero-Pauline literature, but it is directed to later audiences. Raymond E. Brown recalls Charles H. Dodd's description of Ephesians as the "crown of Paulinism." He suggests that the author of Ephesians was "Paul's best disciple."[12] The deutero-Pauline letters are important witnesses to what God has done in and through the event of Jesus Christ, and especially to the ethical consequences that flow from that event.[13]

The most important development in Pauline studies over the past fifty years has been a shift away from a so-called "Lutheran" interpretation. Martin Luther's reform was dominated by his personal journey out of scrupulous despair (*Anfechtung*), convinced that God had abandoned him forever, and that God's promises were false. In a tempestuous period, reflecting upon Romans 1:17 – "The one who is righteous will live through faith" – he was overwhelmed by the insight that salvation did not depend upon one's behaviour ("works") but upon faith alone.[14]

---

12 Raymond E. Brown, *An Introduction to the New Testament*, Anchor Bible Reference Library (New York: Doubleday, 1996) 621.
13 See Moloney, *Reading the New Testament*, 155-62.
14 Among many, see Carlos M.N. Eire, *Reformations: The Early Modern World, 1450–1650* (New Haven, CT: Yale University Press, 2016) 133–57. The Augustinian friar was close to Augustine (354–430 CE) in his struggle against

Coupled with a personal antipathy toward Jews, Luther's largely Pauline interpretation of Christianity broke decisively with what could be called "law righteousness." Human beings were made righteous by God's action, "a righteousness that comes from grace." Assisted by the spread of the printed book, Western Christianity divided rapidly into a "Protestant" understanding of salvation by grace alone, and a "Catholic" insistence on the importance of good works. Despite some significant scholarship that bridged the gap,[15] it could be said that until 1977 Catholics tended to devote more attention to the life story of Jesus in the four Gospels, while Protestants looked to the works-free teaching of Paul.

In 1977, Ed Parish Sanders published *Paul and Palestinian Judaism*.[16] According to Sanders, first-century Jews did not relate to God by responding to the demands of the Law. They were not saved by observance of the Mosaic Law. They were gifted by birth into the Abrahamic Covenant, and they showed their belonging to that God-given situation through their obedience to the Law. He claimed that Luther was wrong to caricature Paul's opponents as people seeking righteousness through works. What they did in responding to the Law reflected their being united with God through the covenant granted to Abraham, the father of Israel. He coined the expression "covenantal nomism" to describe first-century Judaism's relationship to God. Sanders opened a new era in Pauline studies.

---

the Donatists. Augustine had passionately argued that everything in the order of salvation was the result of a gift of God, not personal achievement. The Donatists insisted upon a morally perfect clergy.

15 Especially important in this regard was the lifelong work of Stanislas Lyonnet, SJ (1902–1986). His most important essays are found in the posthumous *Études sur l'Epître aux Romains*, Analecta Biblica 120 (Rome: Biblical Institute Press, 1989).

16 Ed Parish Sanders, *Paul and Palestinian Judaism: A Comparison of Patterns of Religion* (London: SCM, 1977).

This was further enriched by J. Christiaan Beker's groundbreaking study of Paul's Jewish apocalyptic worldview, which appeared a short time after *Paul and Palestinian Judaism*.[17] The Christ-event had to be interpreted within an apocalyptic paradigm. The Australian scholar, Brendan Byrne, SJ, among others, has developed an interpretation of Paul that accepts the primacy of God's gracious action in and through Jesus Christ, set within an apocalyptic framework where God-directed "behaviour" is required. He describes it as "living out the righteousness of God."[18]

Before all time and at the beginning of human history, the glory of God was universally present. The disobedience of Adam altered that situation. Sin and death reigned in a history that was destined eventually to be destroyed in the re-establishment of God's glory at the end of time. The Mosaic Law provided Israel with purpose and direction, but it could not free humankind from sin. Only God's gracious action in the Christ-event made that possible. The unconditional obedience of Jesus Christ unto death generated a situation in which the fullness of God's glory, due to be manifested at the end of all time, was anticipated, drawn back into human history (Rom 3:21-26). As well as the story of sin resulting from Adam's disobedience, history now contains an alternative story: that of the righteousness made available through Jesus Christ's obedience (see 5:12-21).

We live in an "overlap time." Entering the Christ story by faith in what God has done, obeying God in imitation of Jesus Christ, we can be freed from the endless frustration of sin (7:1-25). We can enjoy now, in the "overlap time" the freedom that comes from life in the Spirit (8:26-39), while we await the final apocalyptic assize

---

17 J. Christiaan Beker, *Paul the Apostle: The Triumph of God in Life and Thought* (Minneapolis, MN: Fortress, 1980).
18 Brendan Byrne, "Living Out the Righteousness of God: The Contribution of Rom 6:1–8:13 to an Understanding of Paul's Ethical Presuppositions," *The Catholic Biblical Quarterly* 43 (1981) 557-81. On Romans 5–8, see Idem, *Romans*, Sacra Pagina 6 (Collegeville: Liturgical Press, 1996) 162–281.

(8:18-25).¹⁹ The story of sin and disobedience continues to run side-by-side with the story of grace and freedom (see 5:14–17). Our current era of Pauline studies is awash with outstanding studies that manifest a freedom from the straitjacket of Protestant and Catholic disagreements over faith and works.²⁰

New Testament Narratives

A rich interpretation of the four Gospels and the Acts of the Apostles has followed an earlier period that focused intensely upon the sources for the narratives, the historical situations that produced those sources (source and form criticism), and the theological intention of each single author who arranged those sources to form a coherent narrative (redaction criticism).²¹ Interest in sources has not waned. There is near universal agreement that Mark was the first Gospel to appear at the time of the Jewish

---

19 For a more detailed summary of this position, see Brown and Moloney, *Interpreting the New Testament*, 170–8, and the diagram on p. 174. See also Horrell, *Introduction*, 57–88, and the diagram on pp. 70–1.

20 Especially important is Brendan Byrne's major work, *Paul and the Economy of Salvation: Reading from the Perspective of the Last Judgment* (Grand Rapids, MI: Baker Academic, 2021).

21 The nineteenth century was obsessed with the gospel sources, and the discovery of the historical Jesus. It closed with Albert Schweitzer's devastating critique (originally published in 1906, now available in the excellent *The Quest of the Historical Jesus*, ed. John Bowden, 1st complete ed. [Minneapolis: Fortress, 2001]). Influenced by the emerging science of the history of religions, the early form critics (Karl Ludwig Schmidt, Rudolf Bultmann and Martin Dibelius) singled out the individual pericopes assembled to form the narrative and located their development in the life of Jesus or (more commonly) in the life of the early church. See especially Rudolf Bultmann, *History of the Synoptic Tradition*, trans. John Marsh (Oxford: Basil Blackwell, 1968; original German 1921). Using the 'history' uncovered by the Form Critics, the redaction critics asked whether a theological tendency can be located by tracing the way an author strung the pericopes together. The foundation redactional critical work came from Hans Conzelmann, *The Theology of St. Luke*, trans. G. Buswell (London: Faber & Faber, 1961; original German, 1957).

War of 65–70 CE. Matthew and Luke, appearing late in the 80s, used Mark as a major source. However, they also share many words and stories of Jesus not found in Mark. Mainstream Gospel criticism reconstructs a source for this material, given the name 'Q' from the first letter of the German word, *Quelle* ('source').[22] British scholarship tends to have an aversion to 'Q', proposing other relationships between Mark, Matthew, and Luke. They generally falter in providing an explanation for the abbreviated Gospel of Mark, when either Matthew, Luke, or both, are regarded as its source. Helpful in this discussion, however, has been the work of Mark Goodacre, who rightly affirms the priority of Mark, but suggests that Matthew and Luke knew one another's work.[23] This suggestion eliminates the need to "invent" Q, to speculate about its origins, its literary shape, and its theological point of view.[24]

The redaction critics accepted the results of the historical research of the form critics as their starting point. But they took a step back from the historical in their attempts to trace the theological and pastoral concerns of the New Testament narratives. Even here, however, their concern was largely historical: what was the pastoral and theological situation of Mark, Matthew, Luke (for both Gospel and Acts), and John that led each author to tell the story of Jesus and the earliest church *in a different fashion*?[25]

---

22 See especially James M. Robinson, Paul Hoffmann, and John S. Kloppenborg, *The Critical Edition of Q*, Hermeneia (Minneapolis: Fortress, 2000). A most helpful beginner's introduction to Q is John S. Kloppenborg, *Q, the Earliest Gospel: An Introduction to the Original Stories and Sayings of Jesus* (Louisville, KY: Westminster John Knox, 2008).
23 Mark Goodacre, *The Synoptic Problem: A Way through the Maze*, Understanding the Bible and Its World (London: T. & T. Clark, 2004).
24 There is a bewildering amount of "Q" scholarship, even though we do not have any such document. The *Critical Edition* mentioned in note 22 runs to 581 pages.
25 We cannot be certain of the name of any of the authors of the Gospels and Acts. The links with Mark, Matthew, Luke, and John were made late in the second century. Out of respect for the tradition, we continue to use the canonical names, aware that we are not sure who these authors were.

The blossoming of an entirely new approach to narrative texts in the 1980s continued the search for the theological and pastoral interests of the redaction critics. However, rather than delving into the world that created the text (*the world behind the text*) interpreters began to focus upon the narratives as *literature* (*the world in the text*). This led to an increasing interest in the impact the New Testament narratives made upon their audience (*the world in front of the text*). Although some years before the widespread development of the literary interpretations of the narratives, the Spanish biblical scholar and poet, Luis Alonso Schökel, SJ (1920–1998), had long insisted upon the urgent need for such an approach.[26]

Heavily influenced by earlier studies of narrative literature in general, New Testament interpreters devote less attention to who and what might have generated a narrative to focus upon what can be found *in the story itself*.[27] We may not be able to identify a historical 'real author' of a Gospel story, but what is called an 'implied author' can be traced in the rhetoric of the narrative itself. For example, the author of Luke–Acts links his story of Jesus with the story of the earliest church (Luke 1:1-4; Acts 1:1-2). He then sets the agenda for a Spirit-directed and unstoppable spread of the Word from Jerusalem, to Samaria, and to 'the ends of the earth' (1:8). The rest of the narrative is shaped by that journey-agenda,

---

26 Widely published in Spanish, his most influential book in English was Luis Alonso Schökel, *The Inspired Word: Scripture in the Light of Language and Literature*, trans. Francis Martin (London: Herder & Herder, 1965).

27 Important for New Testament interpreters were Seymour Chatman, *Story and Discourse: Narrative Structures in Fiction and Film* (Ithaca, NY: Cornell University Press, 1978) and Gerard Genette, *Narrative Discourse: An Essay in Method*, trans. Jonathan Culler (Ithaca, NY: Cornell University Press, 1980). Frank Kermode, *The Genesis of Secrecy: On the Interpretation of Narrative* (Cambridge, MA: Harvard University Press, 1969) and R. Alan Culpepper, *Anatomy of the Fourth Gospel* (Philadelphia: Fortress, 1983) broke ground as narrative interpretations of Mark and John, respectively.

until the audience leaves Paul preaching without fear in Rome, at 'the ends of the earth' (28:30-31).[28]

We do not know who wrote the Fourth Gospel, but there is a "voice" in the story that manipulates a reader in the story (called the "implied reader"). This rhetorical manipulation strains to produce belief that Jesus is the Christ, the Son of God. That voice is always present, but there are times when it speaks loudly: the Prologue to the Gospel (John 1:1-18), the comment upon the meaning of the blood and water flowing from the side of the crucified Jesus (19:35), and the final verses of the original story (20:30-31).[29] An enduringly significant communication continues to persuade audiences across the centuries.[30] In literary terms, that happens when the "implied reader" *in the text* and the "real reader" *of the text* are one.[31]

Interest in the impact that a narrative makes upon its audience has enabled greater focus upon a variety of readers: reader-response criticism, feminist criticism, postcolonial readings, autobiographical readings, "queer" readings, womanist readings, postmodern

---

28 See Francis J. Moloney, 'Mission in the Acts of the Apostles: "The Protagonist Is the Holy Spirit," *New Testament Matters – One* (Bayswater: Coventry Press, 2024) 149–178.
29 I do not wish to downplay the importance of the epilogue of John 21:1-25. It serves much the same rhetorical purpose. See Francis J. Moloney, "Closure," in *How John Works: Storytelling in the Fourth Gospel*, eds. Douglas Estes and Ruth Sheridan, Resources for Biblical Studies 86 (Atlanta: SBL Press, 2016) 225–39. See also *New Testament Matters – One*, pp. 205–222: "The Final Appearance: Characters in John 20 and 21."
30 See Francis J. Moloney, "Who Is 'The Reader' in/of the Fourth Gospel?" in *The Interpretation of John*, ed. John Ashton, 2nd ed., Studies in New Testament Interpretation (Edinburgh: T. & T. Clark, 1997) 219–33.
31 As David Tracy puts it: "The classic text's real disclosure is its claim to attention on the ground that an event of understanding proper to human beings has here found expression" (*The Analogical Imagination: Christian Theology and the Culture of Pluralism* [New York: Crossroad, 1981] 102).

interpretations, etc.[32] For an interpreter in the Catholic tradition, there is always a need to maintain a relationship with the original community of faith generated by the Christ-event (see *Dei Verbum*, 7–10, 17– 20). It is not satisfactory to develop a postmodern reading that is *entirely* reader-focused. The *text* loses its relevance if *readers* become the determining interpretative principle. Historical questions must still be asked. What aspect of the Christ-event generated narratives written *by believers for believers*? That is found *in the text*, and not only *in the readers*. It can often be uncomfortably countercultural (see, e.g. Mark 8:34–9:1).

Associated with the turn to the audience in contemporary narrative studies is the study of the 'reception' of a story through Christian history. This rich vein has been magisterially developed by the commentary on the Gospel of Matthew by Ulrich Luz.[33] Subsequent to the work of Luz, increasing light is being shone on the richness of the original New Testament narratives by tracing the impact they have made upon subsequent Christian generations. The development and practice of so-called "reception history" promises a rich awareness of the power of the Word of God in the life of the church. It also throws light on moments and periods when the Christian tradition faltered in its response to the Word.

The Catholic Epistles

Seven so-called "Catholic" Epistles are gathered toward the end of a printed New Testament: James, 1–2 Peter, 1–3 John, and

---

[32] For a survey of the strengths and weaknesses of the increasing focus upon the reader, see *The Bible and Culture Collective, The Postmodern Bible* (New Haven, CT: Yale University Press, 1966).

[33] Ulrich Luz, *Matthew: A Commentary*, trans. James E. Crouch, 3 vols., Hermeneia (Minneapolis: Fortress, 2001–2007). The final volume, especially the commentary on Jesus' passion and resurrection, is a masterpiece. It shows how Matthew's version of Jesus' last days has influenced Christian doctrine, history, art, liturgical practice, etc.

Jude. These letters are directed to a more universal ("catholic" in that sense) audience. It is not a precise description as 2 John is directed to a specific church (2 John 1: "the elect lady") and 3 John to a Christian (3 John 1: "Gaius"). James, 1 Peter, and 1–3 John have generated considerable interest over the past fifty years.[34] Jude and 2 Peter are most likely products of the early second century, and 2 Peter is regarded as an adaptation of Jude for a different audience.[35] The apostolic authorship of James and 1 Peter is a matter of ongoing dispute. James' insistence upon works as well as faith (see James 2:14–26) has led many in the past to suggest that the letter is anti-Pauline (perhaps Jerusalem-centred). 1 Peter's call to accept suffering, in imitation of Jesus Christ, has suggested that the letter was written in a time of persecution in Asia (see 1 Pet 4:12-19).

Lack of certainty about the historical author of James has not detracted from its growing importance as an outstanding witness to the practical and moral obligations embraced by Christians. One of the features of James is the high concentration on God and the scant appearance of Jesus Christ. "James offers positive and powerful contributions to the conversation concerning the right relationship of humans to God and to each other that we call theology. James' grounding of its exhortations in *theological* rather than *Christological* principles provides a genuine bridge between Christians and others ... who share belief in one God ... but who do not share the specific gift given in Jesus."[36] A greater appreciation of James' call to social action, along with the contemporary re-evaluation of the traditional 'Lutheran' interpretation of Paul,[37] has largely defused the suggestion that James is anti-Pauline.

---

34 For an overview of the history and message of the Catholic Epistles, see Moloney, *Reading the New Testament*, 155–74.
35 See Sherri Brown, "The Challenge of 2 Peter and the Call to Theiosis," *Expository Times* 128 (2017) 583–92.
36 Luke Timothy Johnson, *The Letter of James*, Anchor Bible 37A (New York: Doubleday, 1995) 164.
37 See the section "The Pauline Literature" above. See especially V. George Shillington, *James and Paul: The Politics of Identity at the Turn of the Ages* (Minneapolis: Fortress, 2015).

The language, theology, and model proposed for Christian life in 1 Peter are striking. There is increasing acceptance that, whoever the author may have been, he is not addressing a situation of systematic persecution, which did not exist late in the first century. The author asks Christians in Asia to accept that they will be marginalised by Greco-Roman society, but they are to respond to this situation by taking on a discipleship that matches the self-sacrifice of Jesus, the suffering servant.[38] "[Jesus'] passion, death, and subsequent resurrection show the way present suffering is related to future glory, and thus provide Christians with a model of the way they are to live a faithful life in the midst of a hostile society."[39] Recent times have led many interpreters to regard 1 Peter as a "little-known jewel of the New Testament."[40]

Many critical issues surround the contemporary interpretation of 1–3 John. They depend upon the relationship between the Gospel of John and the Letters of John. From the time of Irenaeus (c. 130–202), it was taken for granted that John, the Son of Zebedee, wrote the Gospel and the later Letters of John. Very few would nowadays endorse that position. The author of the Gospel

---

38 Two recent fine commentaries afford a good example of the current situation. Johnson, *James*, 89–121, argues for the apostolic James as the author, despite the elegant Greek of the text. His analysis of the text argues that James 1:2–27 serves as an *epitome* (like a table of contents) to the letter and the text is a reverse detailed presentation of the themes raised there. The dominant theme of the letter is "friendship with God" (see 4:1–10). On the other hand, Paul J. Achtemeier, *1 Peter: A Commentary on First Peter*, Hermeneia (Minneapolis: Fortress, 1996) 1–43, does not reject apostolic authorship out of hand. But he suggests that the elegance of the Greek and the advanced Christology point to a date between 80 and 100 CE, too late for Petrine authorship (Peter having been martyred by Nero in the mid-60s).
39 Achtemeier, *1 Peter*, 65.
40 The description of 1 Peter "as a little-known Jewel of the New Testament" comes from the oft-repeated remark of the Australian scholar, Bill Dalton, SJ. Bill was a trailblazer in the renewed interest in 1 Peter. See especially William J. Dalton, *Christ's Proclamation to the Spirits: A Study of 1 Peter 3:18–4:6*, 2nd ed., Analecta Biblica 23 (Rome: Biblical Institute Press, 1989). The first edition appeared in 1965.

of John is identified as "the Beloved Disciple" in John 21:25, but nowhere is this disciple further identified as John the Apostle.[41] The author of 1 John is not named, but the author of 2–3 John is an "elder" (Greek: *presbyteros*. See 2 John 1; 3 John 1). They may or may not be the same person, but not the author of the Gospel. Some suggest that the Letters appeared before the Gospel, or at least contemporaneous with its development over the latter half of the first century.[42] However, the interpretative question that looms large is not authorship; did the Letters influence the writing of the Gospel, or vice versa?[43]

The determining factor is the widespread use of the expression "the Jews" to describe hostility to Jesus and his followers in the Gospel, and the complete absence of reference to them in the Letters. The struggle with people *outside* the community seems to have disappeared by the time the Letters were written. But serious breakdowns are taking place *within* the communities: 'They went out from us, but they did not belong to us; for if they belonged to us, they would have remained with us' (1 John 2:19. See also 2 John 7; 3 John 911). The Letters may be the work of several authors, writing in the first decade of the second century. A figure of considerable authority appears in 1 John. The other Letters are brief 'occasional letters', but reflect the same background, language, and theology as 1 John.[44]

---

41 For more detail, see Moloney, *The Gospel of John*, 6–9.
42 See, e.g. Urban C. von Wahlde, *The Gospel and Letters of John*, 3 vols., Eerdmans Critical Commentary (Grand Rapids: Eerdmans, 2010) 3:12–15. See the survey of R. Alan Culpepper, 'The Relationship between the Gospel and 1 John', in *Communities in Dispute: Current Scholarship on the Johannine Epistles*, eds. R. Alan Culpepper and Paul N. Anderson, Early Christianity and Its Literature 13 (Atlanta: SBL Press, 2014) 95–120.
43 For an up-to-date survey, see Culpepper and Anderson, eds., *Communities in Dispute*.
44 This "similarity" across 1–3 John led to their becoming part of the so-called "Johannine Literature," despite the brevity of 2 and 3 John, and the absence of the name Jesus Christ in 3 John (the only document in the New Testament where this is the case).

Adapting the magisterial commentary of Raymond E. Brown, a majority position argues that the Johannine Letters were written to various members of a "Johannine circle" of communities.[45] They look back to the Gospel of John as their 'beginning' (see 1 John 1:1-2, 14, 18; 2:7, 24; 3:11). The angry divisions in the communities appear to have arisen from differing interpretations of the same gospel "beginnings."[46] Reflection on the breakdown of a community that looks to the Gospel of John for its central call to love one another as Jesus has loved us (see John 13:34-35; 15:12, 17) is salutary. It reminds us that it is easier to *talk about loving* as Christ loved than to *practise* such selfless love.

The Book of Revelation

COVID-19 has led many to have recourse to the Book of Revelation for imagery, and even a theology that explains what God might be doing in our third Christian millennium. Mainstream commentary on Revelation would rightly reject such interpretations. Most argue that John, the author of the book (Rev 1:1, 4, 9; 22:8), has used challenging Jewish apocalyptic language to describe God's final victory at the end of time. The culturally limited and time-bound symbols of Jewish apocalyptic language must not be used to address a contemporary problem.[47]

---

45 Raymond E. Brown, *The Epistles of John*, Anchor Bible 30 (New York: Doubleday, 1982).

46 For a detailed presentation of this case, see Francis J. Moloney, *Letters to the Johannine Circle: 1–3 John*, Biblical Studies from the Catholic Biblical Association of America 2 (New York: Paulist, 2020) 1–27.

47 The end-time interpretation, asking the faithful to resist in time of persecution as they wait for God's final intervention, remains the dominant paradigm. See esp. Craig R. Koester, *Revelation*, Anchor Yale Bible 38A (New Haven, CT: Yale University Press, 2014).

However, a "new look" in Revelation studies has been emerging since the 1990s that suggests another "key" to this puzzling book.[48] It challenges the interpretation of Revelation as a series of symbolic representations of the end of all time, almost unquestionably accepted since the time of St Augustine's *City of God* in 426 CE.[49] Patmos was not a penal settlement. The emperor Domitian (81–96 CE) did not systematically persecute Christians in Asia. Nor were Christians being forced to participate in the emperor cults. Babylon is a symbol of unfaithful Jerusalem, not of the city of Rome. More positively, Revelation was written to Christians who are 'a kingdom, priests serving his (Christ's) God and Father' (1:6. See 5:10). The victory of the death and resurrection of Jesus over the perennial presence of evil is proclaimed throughout the document (5:6, 9-14; 7:12–8:1; 11:15-19; 16:17-21; 18:20-24; 19:1-8, 17-21; 21:11-15; 21:1–22:5). Rampant evil is powerfully and frighteningly described with biblical and apocalyptic language. But the same language is used to claim that evil has been definitively overcome in and through the death and resurrection of Jesus.

The "saints" are all those in Israel, described in Daniel 7:23-27 (and elsewhere), who have lived by the Word of God and accepted the messianic promises of the prophets (see 8:34; 11:18; 13:7, 10; 14:12; 16:6; 17:6; 18:20). They already have life, fruit of the saving effects of the death and resurrection of Jesus "from the foundation of the world" (13:8). John presents the model of those saints from Israel's history to guide Asian Christians, tempted by the allure of the Greco-Roman world and its pagan way of life.[50] He invites them away from their mediocrity (2:1–3:22. See 18:4: "Come out

---

48 Leonard L. Thompson, *The Book of Revelation: Apocalypse and Empire* (New York: Oxford University Press, 1990), rejected that Domitian persecuted Christians. Steven J. Friesen, *Imperial Cults and the Apocalypse of John* (New York: Oxford University Press, 2001), questioned that Christian persecution resulted from refusal to participate in the emperor cult.
49 The following synthesis is argued in detail in Moloney, *Apocalypse of John*.
50 This is one of several features that Revelation shares with 1 Peter (see esp. 1 Pet 1:19-20), also written to Christians at the end of the first century.

of her, my people") into the life and light of the New Jerusalem, the Christian Church (22:1-5).

Times and literary practices have changed since the 90s of the first Christian century. But the conflict between ambiguous and destructive evil and the light of God's saving presence among us is alive and well. We are experiencing it in our own challenging times. John tells us where we should place our trust.

Conclusion

New Testament interpretation in the nineteenth century was often marked by rationalist and anti-establishment polemic that perplexed the leaders of the churches, both Catholic and Protestant. Catholic leadership was ill equipped to cope with the brilliance of Albert Loisy (1857–1940) and the critical but unswerving loyalty of Marie-Joseph Lagrange (1855–1938).[51] In 1893, Pope Leo XIII addressed that situation with *Providentissimus Deus*, an encyclical that insisted upon the importance of the Word of God in the life of the church, and the need to strengthen Catholic biblical scholarship. Difficult years followed, as Pius X (1903–14) attacked the so-called "Modernists."[52] In 1943, Pius XII published *Divino Afflante Spiritu*, an encyclical commemorating the fiftieth anniversary of *Providentissimus Deus*. He explicitly reaffirmed the

---

51 Loisy was a leading Catholic priest and intellectual who focused intensely upon the human and social factors that produced the New Testament. He was excommunicated by Pius X in 1908. His grave in Ceffonds is marked: "Albert Loisy. Prêtre Catholique." Lagrange was a Dominican scholar, the founder of the École Biblique et Archéologique de Jérusalem. Warned by the Holy See on his views about the possibility of sources in the Pentateuch, he remained firm in his loyalty to the teaching office of the church. His cause for beatification has been introduced.

52 These years produced the aggressive decree *Lamentabili Sane Exitu* (1907), formally condemning sixty-five propositions, many of them associated with biblical research. This was followed by the encyclical *Pascendi Dominici Gregis*, a condemnation of modernism.

teaching of Leo XIII, asking Catholic biblical scholarship to engage in international critical biblical scholarship that would eventually locate Catholics among the best scholars and teachers in the world.[53]

The spirit of Leo XIII and Pius XII has vigorously supported the last fifty years of New Testament scholarship. The challenge of placing the Scriptures at the heart of the life of the church was articulated at Vatican II in *Sacrosanctum Concilium* and *Dei Verbum*. This was followed by the 1993 document from the Pontifical Biblical Commission, *The Interpretation of the Bible in the Church*, and the 2008 Synod of Bishops on the theme, "The Word of God in the Life and Mission of the Church." Benedict XVI released his brilliant postsynodal exhortation, *Verbum Domini*, in 2010. Pope Francis has focused upon the Word of God in *Evangelii Gaudium*, nn. 110–175 (2013). He has recently declared that each year the Second Sunday of Ordinary Time is to be dedicated to honouring the Word of God (2019).[54] Pastoral experience shows that believing communities are moved and enlightened by well-prepared biblical homilies. Group reflections on the Bible, when well run, are life-giving.

Despite this, contemporary Catholicism is manifesting a return to ritual and mystery, and a neglect of the centrality of the Word of God in the life of the church. The hopes of Leo XIII, Pius XII, Vatican II, Benedict XVI, and Francis are not being realised. A long-term, coordinated and committed engagement of

---

53 Proof of this statement can be found in two significant contemporary volumes, edited and written by Catholic scholars: José Enrique Aguilar Chiu, Richard J. Clifford, Carol J. Dempsey, Eileen M. Schuller, Thomas D. Stegman, and Ronald D. Witherup, eds., *The Paulist Biblical Commentary* (New York: Paulist, 2018); John J. Collins, Gina Hens-Piazza, Barbara Reid, and Donald Senior, eds., *The New Jerome Biblical Commentary for the Twenty-First Century* (London: T. & T. Clark, 2022).

54 See Francis J. Moloney, 'Pope Francis and the Word of God in the Catholic Tradition', in *Broken for You: Jesus Christ, the Catholic Priesthood & the Word of God* (Bayswater, VIC: Coventry Press, 2018), 53–64.

the Catholic Church is either not happening or has not borne fruit. Although regularly mentioned in preparation for the Plenary Council of the Australian Catholic Church, due to meet in 2021–22, there was no "Thematic Paper" dedicated to biblical renewal, upon which so much else depends.

In these aggressively secular times, bishops, priests, religious, and active Catholics are understandably worried by matters they consider more urgent for the survival of the church than understanding the role of the Scriptures in the life of the church. But we must not give up hope. Fifty years is a short time in the history of the Catholic Church. It took centuries to articulate what was meant by believing in the Father, the Son, and the Holy Spirit (First Council of Nicaea, 325), and more than another century to arrive at agreement on the union of the human and divine in Jesus Christ (Council of Chalcedon, 451).[55] Only now, after five hundred years of bitter conflict, are Catholics experiencing the richness that comes from sharing with the Christian communities born in the Reformation of the sixteenth century. So might it also be for the dreams of those of us who have had the privilege of fifty intimate years with the New Testament. Isaiah 40:8 gives us reason for hope: "The Word of God will stand forever" (see also 1 Pet 1:25).

---

55 Familiarity with the history of those centuries instructs that even after Nicaea and Chalcedon, these epoch-making "agreements" were rather shaky!

2

"Interpreters of our own Cultural Tradition" The Australasian Catholic Record 1924–2023

One of Pope Francis' lesser-known pontifical interventions was released in Rome, at the Basilica of Saint John Lateran, on 30 September 2020. Entitled *Scripturae sacrae affectus* ("Devotion to Sacred Scripture"), this brief Apostolic Letter (17 pages, including notes) was written to commemorate the sixteenth hundred anniversary of the death of Saint Jerome (30 September 420). Toward the end of the letter, Pope Francis turns from the figure of Jerome to address the current lack of involvement with the biblical Word of God. In a worrying assessment of the contemporary situation of bible interpretation in the Catholic community, he laments that "[o]ne of the problems we face today, not only in religion, is illiteracy: the hermeneutic skills that make us credible interpreters and translators of our own cultural tradition are in short supply."[1]

Pope Francis suggests that we strive to overcome this problem by imitating Jerome's passion for books. "For him, study was not limited to the years of his youthful training, but a continual commitment, a daily priority. We can say that he became himself a library and a source of knowledge for countless others."[2] As we mark the one hundredth volume of *The Australasian Catholic*

---

[1] The English version of the text is available at: vatican.va/content/Francesco/ed/apost_letters/documents/papa-francesco-lettera-ap_20200_scripturae-sacrae-affectus.html. The above citation comes from pp. 13–14 of the online English text from the Vatican website.

[2] Pope Francis, *Scripturae sacrae affectus*, 13 (online text).

Record (ACR), gratitude and recognition must be directed to the many, deceased, and alive, who have served as the editors of the journal, and the numerous dedicated figures who have made their contributions as members of the editorial board. The ACR has provided an Australian "Catholic library" where teachers and scholars have been able to publish their research, and where large cohorts of Bishops, Priests, and Religious Men and Women have been nourished.[3]

Truth and History

The cultural and ecclesial contexts shaping the interpretation of the Bible across the decades that closed the nineteenth Century and opened the twentieth Century twisted and turned. I have no access to the reasons why a decision was made to produce an Australian Catholic journal in the first decades of the twentieth Century, but one of them may have been to provide a steadying hand in those complex times. What follows is a brief sketch of the last one hundred years of biblical studies with a focus upon the unhelpful Catholic tendency to tie the "truth" of the Word of God to its "historical accuracy."[4]

The beginning years of *ACR* unfolded under the shadow of the declaration of Papal Infallibility at Vatican I (1870),

---

[3] The bulk of *ACR*'s readership has been from these groups in the Australian Church across its one hundred years. As theological education has become more available to lay men and women, and as they play a more active leadership role in the Australian Catholic Church, several of them publish in the journal and use it as a resource. The *ACR* also has a widespread presence in international libraries.

[4] For recent studies of this period, see Ronald D. Witherup, "The Bible in the Life of the Church," in Aguilar Chiu, Clifford, Dempsey, Schuler, Stegman, and Witherup, eds., *The Paulist Biblical Commentary*, 1615–621, and especially Donald Senior, "Interpreting the Scriptures. The Church and the Modern Catholic Biblical Renewal," in Collins, Hens-Piazza, Reid, and Senior, eds., *The Jerome Biblical Commentary for the Twenty-First Century*, 1923–949.

followed by the Leo XIII's positive insistence upon the central role of the Word of God in the life and practice of the Catholic Church in his Encyclical *Providentissimus Deus* (1893). Pope Leo insisted that that Catholic scholars and teachers become qualified biblical interpreters and that all theology and preaching must be based upon a sound understanding of the Sacred Scriptures (*Providentissimus Deus* 16). Herein lies the seeds of a dilemma. On the one hand, there could be no questioning anything that came from an authority-based leadership.[5] On the other, Priests were to be well instructed on the complexities of a biblical Word of God that has a variety of faces and could – at times – raise awkward questions: "You know that among the Gentiles those whom they recognise as their rulers lord it over them, and their great ones are tyrants over them. But it is not so among you, ... But the Son of Man also came not to be served but to serve, and to give his life as a ransom for many" (Mark 10:43–45).

Confusion followed as those Catholic scholars and teachers who had begun to adopt contemporary critical approaches to the Word of God were reined in by Pius X's *Lamentabili sane exitu* (July 1907). The Pope listed a "Syllabus of Errors," condemning the interpretative stance of some contemporary Catholic biblical scholars. The "Syllabus of Errors" was closely followed by the Encyclical *Pascendi Dominici Gregis* (September 1907) repeating the warnings about critical approaches to the Word of God.

A *Motu Proprio*, a document from a Pope with papal authority that signifies the Pope's special personal interest in an issue, appeared in 1910: *Sacrorum Antistitum*. From that point on, all teachers in Catholic higher institutes had to take an oath widely known as the anti-Modernist oath. Although a few decades prior

---

[5] Although not intended, and indeed a misunderstanding of what was taught at Vatican I, one of the results of a focus upon "infallibility" was an association of authoritative truth with all Catholic leadership. Popular Catholic culture took it for granted that anything said or done by Bishops, Priests, and Religious was infallible!

to the birth of *ACR* in 1924, this was the cultural and interpretative context within which the journal first appeared.

There were good reasons for a Catholic response to some biblical criticism of the late nineteenth and early twentieth century. The Renaissance of the fifteenth and sixteenth centuries led to a rebirth of interest in the achievements of the classical world. In its turn, it produced a Reformation of the European Church in the sixteenth century, followed by the so-called Enlightenment, also called the Age of Reason, a period that exalted the achievements of the human spirit and the capacity of the human mind.[6] Unless philosophical or religious affirmations could be shown to be true by means of experimentation and the strict application of logical principles, they should be regarded as uncertain and unprovable. Baruch Spinoza (1632–1677) applied these principles to the biblical narratives, especially the miracle stories. David Hume (1711–1776) followed. Religions based upon a book that received its authority from an improbable affirmation that it was divinely inspired came under threat.[7]

This new spirit was accompanied by an intellectual movement that did not reject the practice of religion as such but asked that it be articulated according to principles of human reason. English scholars (e.g. Lord Herbert of Cherbury [1583–1648], John Toland [1670–1722], and Mathew Tindal [1657–1733]), influenced the French (e.g. Voltaire [1694–1778], Jean-Jacques Rousseau [1712–1778], and Denis Diderot [1713–1784]), Germans (King Frederick II [1712–1786], Gotthold Lessing [1729–1781]), and US Americans (e.g. Benjamin Franklin [1706–1790], Thomas Jefferson [1743–1826]). In the late nineteenth century, a group of scholars at the University of Göttingen began to compare the religions of Israel and Christianity to other religions. Known as the History of Religions School (*Religionsgeschichtliche Schule*), they

---

6 See Eire, *Reformations*, 43–129.
7 For a detailed survey, see John Barton, *A History of the Bible. The Book and Its Faiths* (Milton Keynes: Allen Lane, 2019) 387–435.

pointed out that biblical religion shared many characteristics with other religions. The books of the Old Testament were strongly influenced by the religions and cultures of the ancient Near East. Christianity reflected Hellenistic Judaism, the mystery cults, and Gnosticism. Skepticism about the originality, the use and usefulness of biblical religion was widespread in intellectual circles.

In response, creative Catholic interpretations proliferated. An insistence upon traditional historical views was sternly imposed. The "truth" of the Bible was attached to the "historicity" of the traditional authors (Moses, David, Solomon, Matthew, Mark, Luke, John, Paul, Peter, James, etc.), and the historicity of the narratives within each book. Catholic Old Testament scholars and teachers strained to defend the Mosaic authorship of Genesis, Exodus, Leviticus, Numbers and Deuteronomy, founded in the experience of the Exodus and the gift of the Law at Sinai (the Jewish Torah). It had long been noticed that the narratives of the historical books of the Bible – Joshua, Judges, 1–2 Samuel and 1–2 Kings – steadily repeated a pattern of God's graciousness, a prosperity that led to disloyalty and failure, followed by disaster and destruction. Most read these books as objective histories of ancient Israel from the conquest of Israel and the establishment of King Saul at the turn of the second and first millennium BCE to the restoration of Israel after the Babylonian Exile in the fifth Century BCE, and the struggle for survival against the Hellenistic Empires in the second Century BCE.

Similar difficulties surrounded the interpretation of other texts. The Prophet Isaiah was the work of a single figure, the "historical Isaiah." But the text has clear relationships to three different situations and audiences. Isaiah 1–39 addresses people in Jerusalem prior to the Babylonian Exile [740–687 BCE]. Isaiah 40–55 supports Jews from the southern kingdom in exile in Babylon [540–537]. Isaiah 56–66 encourages those who have returned to Israel from exile [587–538]. Catholics were discouraged from adopting the widespread recognition that these "books" were most likely the product of an "Isaian school," recognised as First, Second, and Third Isaiah.[8]

Examples from the New Testament abound.[9] A few notorious examples must suffice. The apparent contradiction between the location of Jesus' first major sermon on a mountain (Matt 5:1-2) and on a level place (Luke 6:17-19) was resolved by the suggestion that there was a level location somewhere on the way down the side of the mountain (see Luke 6:17: "He came down with them and stood on a level place"). The fact that Jesus explicitly addressed the sermon to his disciples (Matt 5:1-2), yet when he finishes "the crowds were astounded at his teaching" (7:28) indicated that some had crept up the hill and joined the disciples as Jesus delivered the sermon. 1 Thessalonians, 1-2 Corinthians, Galatians, Romans, Philippians, and Philemon are certainly from the Apostle Paul. The remaining documents, including the glorious Colossians and Ephesians, are all post-Pauline. They reflect a later Christian world. But for most they were all from Paul (even though he was long deceased by the time some of them appeared).

It is impossible to construct a "life of Paul" from the Acts of the Apostles. His movements and message in the Acts differ too seriously from the biographical information that can be gleaned from his letters.[10] A blanket rejection of modern critical methods

---

8 These are but a few Old Testament "historical" issues. There are many others: e.g. the historicity of Job, Tobit, Esther, the complexities of the Prophet Daniel (a book written in Hebrew and Aramaic, set in the sixth Century BCE but addressing problems of the second Century BCE), and the original text of the Prophet Jeremiah. See below, n. 17. For an outstanding survey, see Rolf A. Jacobson and Michael Chan, *Introducing the Old Testament. A Historical, Literary, and Theological Survey* (Grand Rapids: Baker Academic, 2023).

9 For more detail, see Francis J. Moloney, "Whither Catholic Biblical Studies?" *The Australasian Catholic Record* 65 (1988) 83-93. See above, pp. 00-00: "Before I Forget. Fifty Years with the New Testament."

10 The Acts of the Apostles continues the Gospel of Luke's witness from Nazareth (Luke 1:26-38), via Jerusalem (Luke 24:13-35) to "the ends of the earth" (Acts 28:16-31. See Luke 24:46-49; Acts 1:1-11). See *New Testament Matters – One*, 149-178: "Mission in the Acts of the Apostles: The Protagonist is

ran the danger of "throwing out the baby with the bathwater," subjecting uncritical Catholic biblical interpretation to ridicule and (more importantly) a tendency for Catholics to regard the Bible as "a Protestant book."

Overall, the emergence of critical biblical scholarship was well-intentioned. It struck back at disregard for the central role of the biblical Word of God in the establishment and articulation of the Christian Tradition. But to do this effectively, Catholic biblical scholarship had to accept the scientific methods used by those who wished to weaken the significance of the Bible. Dialogue rather than confrontation was called for. That process took some time. Given the Lutheran and Protestant dependence upon the principle of *sola Scriptura* (Scripture alone) as the source for all that was Christian, German Lutheran scholars led the way, but some Catholics were also trail-blazers.

Initial Catholic Approaches

Richard Simon (1638–1712), a French Oratorian Priest, suggested that the repetitions and the changes of literary style and structures across the Book of Genesis were the fruit of the assembling of different sources from different times and circumstances. He was suspended from the Oratory for his efforts. Slightly later, another Catholic, Jean Astruc (1684–1766), a significant professor of medicine in Montpellier and Paris, traced sources in Genesis based on the different Hebrew names used for God: IHWH and ELÔHIM.[11] More than a century later, a French Dominican Priest, Marie-Joseph Lagrange (1855–1938), restated the case for the use of sources in the first five books of the Bible (the Pentateuch). His

---

the Holy Spirit." For a "life of Paul" built upon his letters, with support from Acts, see Jerome Murphy-O'Connor, *Paul: His Story* (Oxford: Oxford University Press, 2004).

11 Astruc's father was a Huguenot, but converted to Catholicism and his son was raised a Catholic.

work was condemned by Vatican authorities. He was forbidden to teach and research in the Old Testament.[12]

Another Catholic Priest, Albert Loisy (1857-1940), argued that the methods of secular criticism were to be applied to the New Testament. Driven by a desire to provide a more rational basis for the inherent historical and literary tensions within the biblical text, he focused intensely upon the human and social factors that had influenced the development of the New Testament. Many of the "errors" listed in Pius X's "Syllabus of Errors" (1907) came from Loisy's work. Too much was granted to human causes, and not enough to the divine origins and nature of the Word of God. He was excommunicated in 1908. Appointed Chair of History at the Collège de France in 1909, he served there till he retired in 1931.[13]

Too little attention had been devoted to the practical applications of Leo XIII's *Providentissimus Deus*. It would not be corrected until Pope Pius XII published the Encyclical *Divino afflante Spiritu* in 1943 to mark the occasion of the fiftieth anniversary of *Providentissimus Deus* (1893). Pope Pius XII insisted that Catholic scholars use all the archeological, linguistic, literary, and historical tools available to analyse the Word of God. A new era began for Catholic biblical studies. Gradually, thanks to the work of pioneering Catholic scholars, several sources – some of them quite late as the collection was put together after the Babylonian Exile of (597-538 CE) – were recognised as the explanation for the tensions

---

12 He obediently accepted the ruling of the Vatican authorities and spent the rest of his life at the École Biblique et Archéologique de Jerusalem (which he founded in 1890) working on the New Testament, producing major commentaries, especially on the Four Gospels, that retain their importance. His cause for beatification has been introduced. The prayer-card for his canonisation describes him well: "Il a voué son existence à l'étude de la foi et de la raison afin de sauver des âmes perturbées par la critique scientifique" (*Association des Amis du Père Lagrange*).
13 Loisy never recanted his views, and always regarded himself as a Catholic intellectual. His gravestone in the village cemetery of Ceffonds (Haute Marne, France) is marked "Albert Loisy. Prêtre Catholique."

across the combination of narratives and legal instructions of the Torah.[14] It was accepted that a single theological agenda with its roots in the destruction of the Northern Kingdom in the seventh Century BCE, lay behind the bulk of Israel's historical books,[15] that there were at least three stages in the development of the text that appears in the Bible as the prophecy of Isaiah,[16] that many of the books that "tell a story" (e.g. Job, Tobit, Esther, and parts of Daniel [Daniel in the lions' den; Susannah, etc.]) are primarily didactic, and not reports of historical events.[17]

---

14 The fruit of the groundbreaking work of Julius Wellhausen, *Prolegomena to the History of Ancient Israel*, trans. J. Sutherland Black and Allan Menzies, preface by William Robertson Smith (Cambridge: Cambridge University Press, 2013; original German, 1878). An outstanding recent work on the sources of the Pentateuch comes from two Australian Catholic scholars, Anthony F. Campbell and Mark A. O'Brien, *Sources of the Pentateuch. Text, Introduction, Annotation* (Minneapolis, MN: Fortress, 1993).

15 Martin Noth, *The Deuteronomistic History*, Journal for the Study of the Old Testament Supplement Series 15 (Sheffield: Sheffield University Press, 1981; original German 1957). For an up-to-date and comprehensive study of Israel's historical books (including Chronicles, Ezra and Nehemiah), see Brad E. Kelle and Brent A. Strawn, eds., *The Oxford Handbook of the Historical Books of the Hebrew Bible* (New York: Oxford University Press, 2021).

16 First argued by a member of the History of Religions School, Bernard Duhm, *Das Buch Jesaja, übersetzt und erklärt* (Göttingen: Vandenhoeck und Ruprecht, 1892). See Richard I. Schulz, "The Origins and Basic arguments of the Multi-author View of the Composition of Isaiah. Where Are We Now and How Did We Get there?" in Daniel I. Bock and Richard I. Schulz, eds., *Bind Up the Testimony. Explorations in the Genesis of the Book of Isaiah* (Peabody, MA: Hendrickson, 2015) 7–31.

17 The story of Susannah is not found in the Hebrew or Aramaic (chaps. 8–12) text of the Book of Daniel. It made its way into the Catholic Bible via Greek versions as Dan 13. Daniel in the lions' den (Dan 6) is in Aramaic, as is the famous presentation of the one like a Son of Man in 7:13–14. This remark introduces the complex issue of the Catholic "canonisation" of Jerome's Latin Vulgate translation of the Greek version of the Old Testament (the Septuagint), allied with the canonical status of the Septuagint in the Orthodox tradition. The Reformers rejected books (and parts of books) that cannot be found in the Hebrew Bible (our only complete source being the twelfth century St. Petersburg Codex): Tobit, Judith, parts of Esther, Wisdom, Ben Sirach, parts

Even after *Divino afflante Spiritu* tension continued. Old prejudices die hard. In 1961 a *Monitum* (warning) was issued by Vatican authorities against the teaching of two outstanding Jesuit scholars at the Pontifical Biblical Institute, Fathers Maximilian Zerwick and Stanislaus Lyonnet. Accused of an over-reliance on secular history in their application of form-critical criteria (see below), they stood aside from their teaching duties for some years. At the opening of the Second Vatican Council in 1962, a pamphlet written by Monsignor Francesco Spadafora, a professor of Biblical Studies at the Lateran University, condemning the two Jesuits, and the Biblical Institute's use of modern critical methods, was given to all participants at the Council.[18] In more recent times, the outstanding Catholic biblical scholarship of the now deceased Raymond E. Brown (1928–1998) and Joseph A. Fitzmyer (1920–2016) met consistent rejection and accusations of heresy in the United States of America and elsewhere.[19]

A New Era

The Catholic Church's leadership stood by its biblical scholars. The Pontifical Biblical Commission issued a supportive and nuanced statement on the historicity of the Gospels as the Council began ("The Historical Truth of the Gospels" [1964]), an elegant affirmation of serious faith-filled critical scholarship appeared in

---

a Daniel, and 1-2 Maccabees. There are many textual variations the Hebrew Bible's Jeremiah, the Septuagint, and Jeremiah scripts found at Qumran. See Esther Eshell, "Jeremiah, Book of," in Lawrence H. Schiffman and James C. VanderKam, eds., *Encyclopedia of the Dead Sea Scrolls*, 2 vols. (New York: Oxford University Press, 2000) 1:397–400. On the theological consequences of this situation, see Barton, *The Word*, 212–25, and especially Timothy Michael Law, *When God Spoke Greek. The Septuagint and the Making of the Christian Bible* (New York: Oxford University Press, 2013).

18 On this disturbing debate, see Joseph A. Fitzmyer, "A Recent Roman Scriptural Controversy," *Theological Studies* 22 (1961) 426–44.

19 On these attacks, see Donald Senior, *Raymond Brown and the Catholic Renewal* (New York: Paulist, 2018) 199-230.

the Council's Decree on Revelation (*Dei Verbum* [1965]), and the Pontifical Biblical Commission produced a fine statement on the use of the Bible in the life and practice of the Church (*The Interpretation of the Bible in the Church* [1993]).[20] Under Benedict XVI, an Episcopal Synod dedicated to the role of the Word of God in the Life and Mission of the Church (2008), was followed by the Papal Post–Synodal Apostolic Exhortation, *Verbum Domini* (2010).[21] Catholic biblical scholarship and the use of the best fruits of its research in the day-to-day life of the Catholic Church is now second to none. This situation is reflected in Pope Francis' *Evangelii Gaudium* (2013) and *Scripturae sacrae affectus* (2020).

Doubts and accusations still occur because of an unwillingness to separate "truth" from "history." In Australia, this stance has been recently stated by Greg Sheridan, a significant Catholic journalist: "It is part of the distinctiveness of Christianity that it locates God in history, *history* 2000 years ago, and *history* today. ... I have a particular reason for recommending the Gospels. They validate accurate reporting even if the editing varies from edition to edition .... Or, to put it another way, they are *true*."[22] They are indeed *true*, but that does not depend upon their *historical*

---

20 In 1971–72, I was the student representative on the Academic Senate of the Pontifical Biblical Institute, Rome. In early 1972, we were visited by Paul VI, the Rector Magnificus of the Institute. He instructed me: "Tell the students that biblical scholars will always have difficulties in the Catholic Church. Many do not appreciate the richness of a critical approach to the Word of God. But let the students know that the Holy Father supports them in their work and teaching." At that time, Frs Lyonnet and Zerwick, due to become "emeritus" because of their age, were granted further years as full-time professors in recognition of their earlier enforced unjustified withdrawal from teaching. The charismatic Fr. Carlo M. Martini, SJ, was the then Rector of the Institute.
21 For a concise and well-annotated presentation of Vatican support for critical biblical scholarship, see Senior, "Interpreting the Scriptures," 1930–1947.
22 Greg Sheridan, Christians. *The Urgent Case for Jesus in our World* (Sydney: Allen & Unwin, 2021) 78. Stress mine.

accuracy which cannot be maintained.²³ The Gospels are not various "editions" of the same data. To suggest that they are misunderstands the theological importance of *each Gospel* and flies in the face of the teaching of Vatican II:

> Holy mother church has firmly and with absolute constancy maintained and continues to maintain, that these four Gospels, whose historicity it unhesitatingly affirms, faithfully hand on what Jesus, the Son of God, while he lived among men and women, really did and taught for their salvation until the day he was taken up (see Acts 1:1–2). For after the ascension of the Lord the apostles handed on to their hearers what he had said and done, *but with that fuller understanding which they, instructed by the glorious events of Christ, and enlightened by the Spirit of truth, now enjoyed.* The sacred authors, in writing the four Gospels, *selected certain of the many elements which had been handed on, either orally or in written form; others they synthesised or explained with an eye to the situation of the churches.* ... [T]*heir purpose in writing was that we might know the "truth" concerning the things of which we have been informed (see Lk 1:2–4)*" (*Dei Verbum* 19. Italics mine).²⁴

---

23 This does not mean that we cannot make firm conclusions about matters historical, including the historical history of Israel or the historical life of Jesus, through a careful analysis of biblical sources. For an example, see Francis J. Moloney, "Jesus of Nazareth. A Biographical Sketch," in *Reading the New Testament in the Church*, 64–90. The Gospels are far more than "different editions." Did Jesus only travel to Jerusalem once (as in Mark, Matthew, and Luke), or was he there regularly (as in John)? Was he born in Joseph's home in Bethlehem (as in Matthew), or on a journey between Nazareth and Bethlehem (as in Luke). These are significant "historical" (not "editorial") questions Each Gospel narrative is a bearer of crucial Christian "truth" about Jesus' origins and destiny and what his life, teaching, death and resurrection achieved "for our salvation" (*Dei Verbum* 19), however they might differ in their storylines.

24 The reference to Luke 1:1–4 is telling. The author has received traditions from "eyewitnesses" (v. 2). As a second-generation believer he writes an "orderly account" (v. 1) to Theophilus, a third generation (v. 3), "so that you may know the truth" (v. 4), "taught for their salvation" (*Dei Verbum* 19). The Greek word for "truth" in v. 4 (*asphaleia*) is not in defence of "historical

From History to Audience

The "historical" issue is modern. Profound Jewish and Christian interpretations of the Bible across the centuries are reflected in the methods used by the Rabbis, the Fathers of the Church, and the Medieval period.[25] These scholars and teachers communicated "the truth" about God and God's relationships with humankind, proclaimed by the narratives, the poetry, the wisdom literature, the letters, and other literary forms found in the Bible. They were not obsessed with the modern search for "historical truth." Centuries of interpretation were guided by variations of Medieval biblical readings as (1) literal (2) allegorical (3) moral and (4) anagogical. This agenda was summed up in a verse attributed to a Dominican friar in Denmark (Augustine of Dacia, died in 1282): "The literal sense teaches historical truths; the allegorical what you are to believe; the moral what you are to do; the anagogical what you are to strive for."[26]

This rich blend of approaches to the biblical texts provided a lively and faith-filled use of the Word of God. The Reformers of the sixteenth Century continued this interpretative heritage, adding a preparedness to use the Word of God to criticise the Church's teaching (e.g. papal primacy, priestly ministry, the seven sacraments, indulgences, relics, etc.), and to even subject some books of the Bible to criticism. Luther famously regarded the Letter of James as of little worth because it stressed the need for

---

facts," but affirming that Theophilus is being instructed in a "secure way" to salvation by means of Luke's "orderly account." See Frederick William Danker, *A Greek English Lexicon of the New Testament and Other Early Christian Literature*, 3d ed. (Chicago: University of Chicago Press, 2000) 147, s.v. ασφάλεια §§ 1-2. On the unique literary and theological nature of each single Gospel, see Francis J. Moloney, *The Living Voice of the Gospel. The Gospels Today*, 2nd ed. (Mulgrave: Garratt Publishing, 2006).

25 See Barton, *A History of the Bible*, 331–86.

26 The Latin original of the verse is: Littera gesta docet, quid credas allegoria, moralis quid agas, quo tendas anagogia. See Barton, *A History of the Bible*, 520 n. 11.

good works as well as faith (see James 2:14-19), and, in the preface to his translation of the Book of Revelation, he commented "I can in no way detect that the Holy Spirit produced it ... there are many far better books for us to keep" (1522).

Historical questions emerged from the determination of the literal sense, but they were adroitly mollified through the use of allegorical, moral, and anagogical readings. Whether they were "historical" or not became a minor concern. This rich tradition came under fierce criticism and was unfairly damaged once the Age of Reason insisted that "truth" depended upon "historicity."[27] Tensions and even contradictions across the narratives were easy to find. Did miracles happen as they are described? Exactly what did Jesus say at Caesarea Philippi (Mark 8:27-33, Matthew 16:13-23, and Luke 9:18-22 report it differently)? Did Jesus deliver a major sermon at the beginning of his ministry on a mountain (Matt 5:1-2), or on a level plain (Luke 6:17)? How is it possible that the two birth narratives of Matthew 1-2 and Luke 1-2 are so different? The same question can be asked of the accounts of Jesus' death and resurrection. Was Jesus a regular visitor to Jerusalem (John) or was he there only at the end of his life (Mark, Matthew, and Luke)?[28] Is it possible to build a faith-tradition upon such historically dubious reports? Under intense "historical" scrutiny, long-assumed "truths" were questioned.

The Reformer's development of a critical approach to the Bible – that had origins in the biblical scholarship of Martin Luther himself – rendered the Protestant tradition more open to a considered response to the attack on the Bible. Although not free from inner-church controversy, German Protestant scholars were better equipped to accept the questions being asked, and to

---

27 It is an anomaly that the contemporary conservative insistence upon "historicity" as the agent of "truth" returns to the aggressive rejection of the "truth" of the Bible that emerged from the Enlightenment era.

28 See "Revisiting the Temple: Mark 11:15-16 and 13:2," in *New Testament Matters - One*, 89-106.

respond to them by adopting the same critical methods, although many were harshly judged by church leadership.[29] Their initial focus was upon an identifiable portrait of Jesus (especially David Friedrich Strauss [1808–1874]) and the story of early Christianity (especially Ferdinand Christian Baur [1772–1860]). In 1863, Heinrich Holtzmann published an epoch-making source critical study. He argued for the priority of the Gospel of Mark, the most reliable point of access to Jesus and to a portrait of the gradual development of his messianic consciousness.[30] Decades of research into the historical Jesus followed, ended by the remarkable work of Albert Schweitzer in 1906. Schweizer showed that attempts to recover the historical founder of Christianity produced a Jesus that reflected the religious and social views of the researcher, rather than an objective view of the Jesus of history.[31]

Once dissociated from a reliable history of Jesus, it was but a short step to recognise that the Four Gospels were products of their own time, cultural and social setting, largely determined by their audiences. With the aid of the findings of the History of Religions School, this recognition led to the establishment of the discipline of Form Criticism, a study of the individual pericopes of the narratives, attempting to identify the source of their literary form in the cultures of their time, and deciding what life-setting (*Sitz im Leben*) had produced the form in which they appear in

---

29 For a vivid description of the factions and inner-church conflicts (often leading to the dismissal of leading scholars) of one of the great centres of German Protestant criticism, see Horton Harris, *The Tübingen School* (Oxford: Clarendon Press, 1975). Major figures, including Baur and his student Strauss (see below), lost their church-supported academic positions at the University.
30 Heinrich J. Holtzmann, *Die synoptischen Evangelien: Ihr Ursprung und geschtlicher Charakter* (Leipzig: Wilhelm Engelmann, 1863).
31 Albert Schwetizer, *The Quest of the Historical Jesus*. This is the same Albert Schweitzer (1875–1965), musicologist who catalogued Johann Sebastian Bach's prodigious output, and who ended his days as a missionary medical doctor in Lambarene, Gabon, East Africa. See his unforgettable *On the Edge of a Primeval Forest & More from the Primeval Forest* (London: Adam and Charles Black, 1951).

the Gospels. While some may go back to Jesus (*Sitz im Leben Jesu*), most narratives are best explained as emerging from the life and practices of the early Church (*Sitz im Leben der Kirche*). The final shape of each Gospel account reflected the work of an editor rather than an original author.[32] Rudolf Bultmann's assessment of Mark as an editor was not encouraging: "Mark is not sufficiently master of his material to be able to venture on a systematic construction himself."[33]

But was that true? The so-called Redaction Critics began with the historical data provided by the Form Critics but gave more credit to the evangelical, theological, and literary acumen of each Evangelist. Their agenda was well described by Hans Conzelmann in his ground-breaking study of the Gospel of Luke:

> Our aim is to elucidate Luke's work in its present form, not to enquire into the possible sources or into the historical facts that provide the material. A variety of sources does not necessarily imply a similar variety in the thought and composition of the author. How did it come about that he brought together these particular materials? Was he able to imprint on them his own views?[34]

The Redaction Critics continued to lean upon historical investigation, but they used investigation into the *world behind the text* to focus more carefully upon the pastoral-theological motivation for the narrative sequences of the *world in the text*.

It was but a short step to consider what an author might want to communicate to the *world in front of the text*. Adopting the methods of contemporary literary critics, Narrative Criticism

---

32 Wilhelm Wrede, *The Messianic Secret*, trans. J. C. G. Grieg (Cambridge & London: James Clark, 1971; original German, 1901) argued that Jesus' claims to Messiahship in Mark reflects the situation in the Church that produced Mark, not Jesus. The fundamental form-critical study remains Bultmann, *History of the Synoptic Tradition*.
33 Bultmann, *Synoptic Tradition*, 350.
34 Conzelmann, *The Theology of St. Luke*, 9.

traced the techniques used by biblical storytellers to speak to an audience.[35] Recent biblical scholarship (of both the Old and the New Testament) has turned toward an appreciation of the "reception" that biblical texts have had by audiences over the centuries,[36] even to the recreation of the context and form in which they were originally delivered. Jews and early Christians did not read their sacred texts. Books were a rarity and very few people could read. They experienced oral "performance." Performance Criticism has become part of the interpreter's armoury.[37] Rudolf Bultmann claimed in 1921 that the Evangelists were not much more than editors, and that Mark had lost control of his sources. Today's focus upon a believing community "receiving" and "experiencing" its sacred texts indicates that the exact opposite was the case.[38]

---

35 See Francis J. Moloney, "Narrative Criticism of the Gospels," *Pacifica* 4 (1991) 181–201.
36 The most thorough study of a biblical book that portrays its "reception history" in Luz, *Matthew*. His pages on the cultural, historical, artistic, theatrical [the passion plays] and theological "reception" of Jesus' passion and resurrection (Matthew, 3:297–644) are a superb example of the wealth of such an approach.
37 See Kelly R. Iverson, *Performing Early Christian Literature. Audience Experience and Interpretation of the Gospels* (Cambridge: Cambridge University Press, 2021).
38 This sketch hints at the fruits that might come from a faith-filled application of all the newer approaches to biblical texts, from Source Criticism (Holzmann in 1863) to Performance Criticism (Iverson in 2021). For a study that attempts to do this, see Francis J. Moloney, "Teaching the Most Difficult Text in the Gospel of Mark: Mark 9:42–50," in Elizabeth E. Shively and Geert Van Oyen, eds., *Communication, Pedagogy, and the Gospel of Mark, Resources for Biblical Study* 83 (Atlanta: SBL Press, 2016) 129–50. Even more impressive is Jennifer Knust and Tommy Wasserman, *To Cast the First Stone: The Transmission of a Gospel Story* (Princeton: Princeton University Press, 2019), a stunning study of John 7:53–8:11 (the *Pericopa de Adultera*) from every angle (text critical, exegetical, canonical, reception history, etc.).

Consequences

A feature of the current shape of *ACR* is the series of Reflections on the Readings of Sundays and Feast days that closes each number. They continue the journal's long recognition of the importance of the Word of God in the Church that began in 1947 (Volume 24) under the rubric "Homiletics." This contribution ran until 1973 (Volume 50) after which period anonymous authors provided "Homilies for Sundays." The current "Reflections on the Readings for Sundays and Feasts" began in 1988 (Volume 65) and is the most sought-after section of each issue of the journal. Many contributions are anonymous, but major figures across the Australian Catholic Church's intellectual and ecclesial life (including a Cardinal, two Archbishops, and two Bishops) have contributed (e.g. Edward Clancy, Walter Baker, William Leonard, Bede Heather, Kevin Walsh, Harry G. Davis, Thomas Veech, William Dalton, SJ, John Hill, David Coffey, Patrick Murphy, Timothy J. Costelloe, SDB, Denis Stanley, Mark O'Brien, OP, Geoffrey Dunn, Chris Monaghan, CP, and Joseph Sobb, SJ).

The passage from biblical scepticism (1924) to a current positive appreciation of the reception of the Word of God (2023), sketched above, suggests that we are in a good place to continue this contribution of "credible interpreters and translators of our own cultural tradition."[39] Might I suggest the following process as we look forward to the next one hundred years?

1. Begin with the conviction that any biblical text is a formative part of the Christian Tradition, a source of inspiration to early Christians to such an extent that Saint Athanasius included it in his canonical list 367 CE.[40] The documents that formed that list meant something to a believing community. It is a "sacred text" – part of the ongoing saving revelation of God within the Catholic Tradition (see *Dei Verbum* 9–10). Its status as

---

39 Pope Francis, *Scripturae sacrae affectus*, 13 (online version).
40 See Moloney, *Reading the New Testament*, 57–61.

revelation of the divine interest in the human condition does not depend upon the "historicity" of the events reported or the authors to whom the documents are attributed (often attached more than a century after the document first appeared).[41]
2. Interpret each text as part of a larger literary utterance. An awareness of the shape and message of the whole utterance (e.g. Genesis, Job, the Gospel of Matthew, the Gospel of Luke and the Acts of the Apostles as one work, the Letter to the Romans, etc.) guides any attempt to make sense of its respective parts.[42]
3. Use all available critical methods to trace the situation in the life of Jesus or the life of the Church that produced the text that arose in the bosom of a Christian world.[43] As members of a believing Christian community, we find in them inspired reflections upon the great truths, sometimes articulated in a variety of hostile circumstances (e.g. Mark, Galatians, 2 Corinthians, 1 Peter, 1-3 John, Revelation), at other times solemnly proclaimed (e.g. John 1:1–18; Phil 2:6–11; Col 1:15–20; Eph 1:3–14; Rev 5:8–14). Theological, Christological, community, and ethical messages address contemporary believers through our shared canonical texts in circumstances that parallel the worlds that produced them.
4. A healthy theology, Christology, sense of community, and ethics can be gleaned from biblical documents. But we must allow the Word of God to be "foreign." It does not always present its case the way we would.[44] Why does the Gospel of Mark close with the flight of frightened women who do

---

41 For detail, see Schmid and Schroter, *The Making of the Bible*, 222–79.
42 See the helpful pages on this feature of biblical literature in Barton, *The Word*, 191–97.
43 The availability of high-quality single volume commentaries upon the whole Bible is most helpful in this regard. Most recently, see *The Paulist Biblical Commentary* (2018) and *The Jerome Biblical Commentary for the Twenty-First Century* (2022).
44 On the "foreignness" of the biblical text, see Barton, *The Word*, 57–85.

not report their Easter experience (Mark 16:8)?[45] What caused Matthew's opposition to Synagogue Judaism (Matt 23) and even a condemnation of Israel's posterity (Matt 27:25)? Why does Jesus limit his mission and the mission of the disciples to "the lost sheep of Israel" (15:24; 10:5–6)? John rejects Jesus' opponents, "the Jews," all the while insisting on the centrality of love (13:34-35; 15:12, 17; 17:21, 23, 24–26). Does the idyllic situation of the earliest community in Acts 2:44–5:42 report exactly how things were? What about the deaths of Ananias and Sapphira (5:1–11)? Does Paul support the institution of slavery (Philemon)? The author of the Letters of John advocates mutual love (1 John 3:13–17; 4:4:7–21) but regards those who do not agree with him as the Antichrist (1 John 2:18–22; 2 John 7). It is one thing to proclaim Christological belief (see Matt 16:13-23; John 1:1–18) but another to insist that others have irretrievably lost their way (Matt 27:25; 1 John 2:19). What can we learn from these apparent roadblocks?

In this centenary year of the *ACR*, the oft-conflicted journey of the Catholic approach to the Word of God challenges us to listen to Pope Francis: "How can we not heed, in our day, the advice that Jerome unceasingly gave to his contemporaries: 'Read the divine Scriptures constantly; never let the sacred volume fall from your hand'" (*Epistola* 52,7)?[46]

---

45 Mark 16:9-20, found in most printed Bibles, was one of several later additions to the original ending (16:8). See Francis J. Moloney, *The Gospel of Mark. A Commentary* (Grand Rapids, MI: Baker Academic, 2002) 355–62.
46 Pope Francis, *Scripturae sacrae affectus*, 14 (online version). Jerome's Latin text can be found in *Corpus Scriptorum Ecclesiasticorum Latinorum* 54 (Vienna/Leipzig: F. Tempsky/G. Freitag, 1910) 426: Diuinas scripturas saepius lege, immo numquam de manibus tuis sacra lectio deponatur.

3

A New Testament Hermeneutic for Divorce and Remarriage in the Catholic Tradition

Jesus' teaching on divorce is a question of central importance to the Christian churches.[1] The ministry of Pope Francis, and the agenda of the Synod of Bishops on the Family, has again drawn attention to the issue. Given the paucity of material on marriage and divorce in the entre Bible, it is not surprising that very little material in the New Testament is dedicated to Jesus' attitude to the issue. But what is found in Paul, Mark, Matthew, and Luke is confronting to contemporary sensitivities, and calls for clear analysis. An uncritical affirmation that Jesus prohibited divorce does not do justice to what is recalled in our inspired Scriptures. The fact that he did so must be given its due importance, but Jesus' prohibition of divorce and remarriage is not the only word on marriage and divorce in the pages of the New Testament.[2] A neglect

---

1 John P. Meier, *A Marginal Jew. Rethinking the Historical Jesus*, 5 vols., Anchor Bible Reference Library (New York: Doubleday; New Haven, CT: Yale University Press, 1992–2016) 4:128-39 provides twelve densely printed pages of "sample of representative works." I will limit my consultation of secondary literature to the detailed work of Meier, Raymond F. Collins, *Divorce in the New Testament*, Good News Studies 38 (Collegeville, MN: The Liturgical Press, 1992), and David Instone-Brewer, *Divorce and Remarriage in the Bible* (Grand Rapids, MI: Eerdmans, 2002), as well as classical and recent commentaries on 1 Corinthians, Mark, and Matthew.
2 The recent study of William R. G. Loader, "Did Adultery Mandate Divorce? A Reassessment of Jesus' Divorce Logia," *New Testament Studies* 61 (2015) 67-78, raises a doubt about Jesus' prohibition of divorce. For Loader, Jesus' prohibition of divorce may only appear to be absolute. As a person of his time and tradition, Jesus took it for granted, on the basis of Genesis 2:24, that adultery necessarily led to divorce. He did not need to say it. As Loader recognises, the weakness of this suggestion is its argument from silence.

of the subtleties expressed across the pastoral and theological re-interpretations of Paul, Mark, and Matthew, accepted by the Church as the inspired Word of God, call for close attention.

In terms of the texts, Jesus' teaching on divorce and remarriage appears in 1 Corinthians 7:10-11; Mark 10:1-12; Matthew 5:32; 19:1-12, and Luke 16:18. The material itself, however, comes from three sources:

1. Paul (1 Corinthians 7:10-11)
2. "Q" (Matt 5:32 and Luke 16:18)
3. Mark (Mark 10:11-12// Matthew 19:9)

On the basis of these three sources, the following reflection on the teaching of the New Testament on divorce and remarriage responds to four questions:

1. Can we claim with certainty what Jesus said about marriage and divorce, based on our earliest traditions: Paul, "Q," and Mark 10:11-12?
2. Using that tradition, what does Paul say about the question in 54 CE, as he speaks to the situation of the Greco-Roman Christian community at Corinth in 1 Corinthians 7:8-16?
3. How does Mark use that same Jesus-tradition, in the context of the Roman Empire about 70 CE, as he reports Jesus' debate with the Pharisees, and in his subsequent discussion with his disciples in Mark 10:1-12?
4. Finally, how does Matthew use it, both in his adaptation of his "Q" source, and in his rewriting of Mark 10:1-12 in Matthew 19:3-12, in the latter half of the 80's CE?

A New Testament Hermeneutic

The Gospels bear witness to what Jesus did and said during his lifetime; they also reflect the pastoral and theological agenda of the inspired Scriptures that have been accepted by the Church as its New Testament. The earliest Christian writers looked back to Jesus and inform their audience about Jesus of Nazareth; but they go further.³ They also instruct a Christian audience about what God has achieved for humankind in and through the event of Jesus. One leads to the other, but the latter very regularly develops the traditions that come from Jesus to speak to the needs of the community for which any single author is writing. These "writings" subsequently became part of the Christian Sacred Scriptures because they were recognised as speaking to the ongoing history of the Church as a "Word of God" (see *Dei Verbum* 11-13).

This simple affirmation hides a very important principle of interpretation for a Church that takes the New Testament as part of its inspired Scriptures (see *Dei Verbum* 17-20). The Word of God in the New Testament is not *only* to be identified with the words of Jesus that we can confidently find within its pages. The Word of God is *also* the ongoing interpretation and application of those words developed within the teaching of the earliest and inspired Christian authors to address the Church.

It is universally accepted that the Gospel of John, that appeared about 100 CE, is the most theologically developed document in the New Testament. Without hesitation, it proclaims that Jesus of Nazareth was the Christ, the pre-existent Logos of God (John 1:1-2), the only begotten Son of God (1:14), I AM HE (8:24, 28, 58; 13:19, etc.), the Son of Man (1:51; 3:13-14, 5:27; 6:27, 53; 8:28, etc.) and the Messiah (20:30-31), who was always aware of his oneness with God, and thus made God known in an authoritative and unique fashion (6:25-59, etc.). Having come from a oneness with God that the Logos has occupied since before all time (John 1:1-2, 14), Jesus returns to the Father (17:5; 20:18), to send the gift

---

3 No document called "Q" is found in the New Testament. It is a sigla used by critics to indicate early material, common to Matthew and Luke, but not found in Mark, that would have been earlier than Mark. See Kloppenborg, *Q, the Earliest Gospel*, 1-40, and Ivan Havener, *Q: The Sayings of Jesus*, Good News Studies 19 (Wilmington, DE: Michael Glazier, 1987). The most complete treatment of "Q," is Robinson, Hoffmann, and Kloppenborg, *The Critical Edition of Q*.

of the Paraclete (14:15-17, 25-26; 15:26-27; 16:7-11, 12-15; 19:30; 20:21-23). The Christology of John's Gospel became the backbone for the eventual articulation of the Christian Church's faith at the Councils of Nicea (325 CE), Constantinople (381 CE), Ephesus (431 CE), Chalcedon (451 CE), and again at Constantinople (553 CE).[4] As Christians make their confessions of faith, they do so in a language that has been shaped by the Gospel of John, not by what we can be determine about what Jesus of Nazareth *actually said* between 28-30 CE.

The same must be said for the formative role of the Letters of Paul, written in the 50s of the first Christian century, in the development of the later Christian Tradition. Jesus understood his forthcoming death as in some way "for others," but the inspired writings of Paul the Apostle make the saving significance of the death and resurrection of Jesus Christ so central to his thought and teaching that it has shaped all subsequent Christian teaching – and practice.[5] The revelation of God to the world is not found in *either* the Word of God in the Bible, *or* the formal teaching of the Councils. It is found in *both*. Indeed, without John and Paul, there would be very little in the teaching of the Councils. Scripture and Tradition "flow from the same divine well-spring" (*Dei Verbum* 9). "Tradition and scripture make up a single sacred deposit of the word of God, which is entrusted to the Church" (*Dei Verbum* 10).

Obviously, therefore, God's revelation is not only found in those words of Jesus that can be reliably traced to the life and teaching of Jesus and Nazareth. What follows will initially trace what Jesus of Nazareth taught about divorce and remarriage. Once

---

4 Most, but not all, mainstream Christian Churches have continued the use of the pre-Reformation Creeds, originally forged through vigorous debate at the early Councils, as an essential statement of what they believe.

5 On Jesus' approach to his death, see Dale C. Allison, Jr., *Constructing Jesus. Memory, Imagination, and History* (Grand Rapids, MI: Baker Academic, 2010) 387-433. On the centrality of the saving effects of Jesus' death and resurrection in Paul, among many, see James D. G. Dunn, *The Theology of the Apostle Paul* (Grand Rapids, MI: Eerdmans, 1998) 207-65.

that is in place, we must examine what the earliest Church (Paul, Mark, and Matthew) passed on to their own communities in their letters and gospels, accepted as an integral part of the Word of God to the Church. As with the example of the use of the Christologies of the Gospel of John and the Letters of Paul for the eventual formation of the Catholic Tradition, so also with the Church's understanding and practice of marriage and divorce, we must *see the entire picture*.

Jesus of Nazareth and Divorce

Jesus of Nazareth was a product of traditional Palestinian Jewish thought and practice. He would have been shaped by the teaching of the Mosaic Torah.[6] Adultery was a capital crime. According to Leviticus 20:10 and Deuteronomy 22:22, both offending parties involved must die; and its prohibition is found in the Decalogue (Exodus 20:19; Deuteronomy 4:10; 5:20-21).[7] Surprisingly, however, the question of divorce and remarriage was not a major concern for the Jewish legal tradition. It was taken for granted that divorce and remarriage would take place. The tradition ensured that the male partner was always in command of the situation. There is only one passage in the Torah that deals with the question in any detail: Deuteronomy 24:1-4.[8] The text itself is one long single Hebrew sentence. Its major concern is to ensure that a woman who is dismissed from the household by the male, not be permitted to return to the intimate situation of man and wife by returning to the husband who dismissed her. This is regarded as bringing "sin upon the land" (v. 4). "That, remarkably, is the extent of

---

6 For much of what follows, I am indebted to the work of Meier, *A Marginal Jew*, 4:74-181.
7 See the discussion in Elaine A. Goodfriend, "Adultery," in *The Anchor Bible Dictionary*, ed. David N. Freedman, 6 vols. (New York: Doubleday, 1992) 1:82-86.
8 See Collins, *Divorce*, 89-91.

the divorce laws in the Pentateuch."⁹ The same basic approach to the question is found in the Prophets (already part of Israel's Sacred Scripture at the time of Jesus) and the Wisdom literature (an important pseudo-philosophical reflection reflecting Israel's gradual integration with its surrounding Hellenistic world, but with ancient roots in Israel's tradition).¹⁰

Recourse is often had, by Christian scholars, to the prophet Malachi 2:10-16. The NRSV renders v. 16: "For I hate divorce, says the Lord, the God of Israel." It has come down to us in a corrupted Hebrew text and does not make sense the way it stands. Using an image found elsewhere in the prophets (e.g. Isaiah, Jeremiah, Ezekiel, and Hosea),¹¹ Malachi 2:10-16 criticises Jerusalem and Judah for their unfaithfulness to God by paralleling their behaviour with husbands unfaithful to their wives. After careful consideration of the Hebrew of v. 16, however, John Meier states categorically that the text does not say: "I hate divorce." The closest he can come to generating a confusing English translation for the confused Hebrew is "For [or: 'if'; or 'when'; or 'indeed'] he hated [or possibly: 'hating'], send away! [or possibly "to send away"].¹² The same confusion is found in the Greek translations, and the Latin Vulgate for 2:16 is "cum odio habueris dimitte"

---

9 Meier, *A Marginal Jew*, 4:80.
10 See Meier, *A Marginal Jew*, 4:81-86; Instone-Brewer, *Divorce and Remarriage*, 34-58. One anomaly needs attention. Archaeologists have uncovered documents from a Jewish community in Elephantine in Egypt that reflects the thought and practice of a diaspora Jewish military community from the 5th century BCE. The practice of divorce is taken for granted, but the documents indicate, for the first time, that a "bill of divorce" had to be prepared, and that it was not only possible for the man to divorce the woman, but also for the women to divorce the man. This was a quite unique diaspora situation and should not be given too much weight in trying to establish divorce practices in first century Palestinian Judaism. See Meier, *A Marginal Jew*, 4:83-84.
11 See Instone-Brewer, *Divorce and Remarriage*, 34-58.
12 Meier, *A Marginal Jew*, 2:82. For the discussion, see pp. 81-82, and the associated footnotes on pp. 144-49. The options in the square parentheses generate a translation: "Indeed he hated to send away."

("when [or: since] you hate [her], send [her] away." Later Christian interpreters and Rabbinic thought have turned to Malachi 2:16 for biblical support for the absolute prohibition of divorce. But this is a misuse of the original text (which remains confused) and would not have influenced Jesus of Nazareth in any way. When Jesus comes to discuss divorce, he turns to the Torah texts of Deuteronomy and Genesis. He never mentions Malachi.

There are other witnesses to Jewish thought that come from the same period, notably Philo of Alexandria (20 BCE – 40 CE), a Jew who worked strenuously to make Jewish traditions relevant to a Hellenistic world, and Josephus (37-100 CE), a Jewish historian who wrote significant commentaries on the Jewish War and the history of Jewish life and practice. They both demonstrate minimal interest in the matter of marriage and divorce and repeat the legislation of Deuteronomy 24:1-4.[13] The texts found at the Dead Sea raise further questions about the attitude of a first century Jewish sect that produced those documents, generally recognised as the Essenes. Much has been made of two texts that suggest a prohibition of divorce, the Damascus Document (CD 4:20-21) and the Temple Scroll (11QTemple 57:15-19). The former is a difficult text to interpret. It has been widely translated as a condemnation of those who take two wives in their lifetime, but it may be better understood as the prohibition of multiple wives. The second envisions the way things will be when the ideal king rules in the near future.

One of the telling arguments against the prohibition of divorce at Qumran is that there is no suggestion of any such practice in the Community Rule (1QS). The Damascus Document was written for Essene communities at large; the Community Rule determines the life of the Essene community at Qumran.[14] Regularly regarded

---

13 See Meier, *A Marginal Jew*, 4:84-87.
14 For excellent treatments of CD 4:20-21 and 11QTemple 57:15-19, and wide-ranging scholarship that surround the interpretation of these texts, see Meier, *A Marginal Jew*, 4:87-93, and the associated notes on pp. 155-62.

as a minority sectarian group that advocated the prohibition of divorce, reflecting a sectarian strain within Judaism to which Jesus also belonged,[15] recent detailed analysis of the situation at Qumran is more reserved. While such a view of divorce and remarriage at Qumran is not ruled out, majority position is nowadays that "[t]he Essenes did forbid polygamy; their position on divorce remains a question mark."[16]

This is the cultural, religious, and legal setting for Jesus' teaching on divorce. Our earliest witness is 1 Corinthians 7:10-11. Addressing this enthusiastic community, Paul regularly opens his reflections with the expression "now concerning ..." (περὶ δέ: 7:1, 25; 8:1; 12:1; 16:1). He responds to queries concerning the Corinthians' state of life, now that they live in new existence generated by the death and resurrection of Jesus.[17] His general principle is that they should stay as they are,[18] and this is what he tells them to do concerning their marital state in 7:1-9. To this point in his argument, he is expressing his own opinion. He will resume giving advice on these ground in vv. 12-16 (see v. 12: "I say, not the Lord"). However, in vv. 10-11, he leaves his own opinion to one side, and gives a word of Jesus on divorce:

---

15 See, for example, Joseph A. Fitzmyer, "The Matthean Divorce Texts and Some New Palestinian Evidence," *Theological Studies* 39 (1976) 221-23.
16 Meier, *A Marginal Jew*, 4:93. But see Joseph A. Fitzmyer, "Marriage and Divorce," in *Encyclopedia of the Dead Sea Scrolls*, ed. Lawrence H. Schiffman and James C. VanderKam, 2 vols. (Oxford/New York: Oxford University Press, 2000), 1:512, who interprets these same documents as the prohibition of divorce, and not only polygamy. Meier's uncertainty is shared by Luz, *Matthew*, 2:494. William R. G. Loader, *The Dead Sea Scrolls on Sexuality in Sectarian and Related Literature at Qumran* (Grand Rapids, MI: Eerdmans, 2009) 107-19, argues that the availability of all the Qumran material now makes it clear that "the cited prohibition is best taken as referring not to divorce but to polygyny."
17 See Benjamin A. Edsall, *Paul's Witness to Formative Early Christian Instruction*, Wissenschaftliche Untersuchungen zum Neuen Testament 2.365 (Tübingen: Mohr Siebeck (2014) 99-109; Collins, *Divorce*, 11-13.
18 On this principle, see Joseph A. Fitzmyer, *First Corinthians*, The Anchor Yale Bible 32 (New Haven, CT: Yale University Press, 2008) 305-307.

To the married I give charge, not I but the Lord, that the wife should not separate from her husband (but if she does, let her remain single or else be reconciled to her husband) – and that the husband should not divorce the wife.

There are two remarkable aspects to these words that Paul claims come from Jesus. Most significantly, Paul reports that Jesus forbad divorce. The wife was not to leave her husband (v. 10), and if she does, she must return to him (v. 11a). No husband should divorce his wife (v. 11b). Secondly, unlike anything we find in Jewish tradition, Paul takes it for granted that a woman could leave her husband on her own initiative.

There may be several possible explanations for the latter element from the teaching of Jesus (the initiative of the woman),[19] but our concern is with the former. We have no verbatim use of the words of Jesus of Nazareth. But Paul's consistent claim that he is teaching on his own authority (vv. 1-9 and vv. 12-16), and the dramatic change to a "charge" that comes from the Lord (v. 10) when he prohibits divorce, is early evidence of Jesus' prohibition of divorce and remarriage.[20] Paul has not provided a setting for this "word of the Lord." The early evidence of Matthew 5:32, paralleled in Luke 16:18 (thus "Q" material), provides two different narrative settings for a tradition that looks back to the words of Jesus.[21]

In the Gospel of Luke, Jesus addresses the question of divorce only once: in Luke 16:18. These words are found in a rather loosely connected series of teachings poised between Jesus' parable on the

---

19 The possible remembrance in the tradition of the new world that Jesus created for women could be one of the motivations. Most explain it by indicating the Corinthian situation in the Roman colony of Corinth. See Richard A. Horsley, *1 Corinthians*, Abingdon New Testament Commentaries (Nashville, TN: Abingdon Press, 1998) 98-99; Collins, *Divorce*, 13-22; Meier, *A Marginal Jew*, 4:165-66 n. 92.
20 See Collins, *Divorce*, 29-39; Idem, *First Corinthians*, Sacra Pagina 7 (Collegeville, MN: The Liturgical Press, 1999) 263-65.
21 For the discussion of possible links between 1 Corinthians 7:10-11 and Synoptic sayings, see Collins, *Divorce*, 32-38.

dishonest steward (16:1-9) and the parable on the rich man and Lazarus (vv. 19-30). Most of these teachings are connected in some way with the theme of wealth and possessions that is present in the two parables (see vv. 10-13, 14-15), while vv. 16-17 touches upon important Lukan concerns: the place of John the Baptist, and the law and the prophets in God's design. Oddly, v. 18 follows: "Everyone who divorces his wife and marries another commits adultery, and he who marries a woman divorced from her husband commits adultery."[22]

The issue of divorce appears twice in Matthew.[23] In 19:1-12, Matthew reports, in his own way, an encounter between Jesus and the Pharisees originally found in Mark 10:1-12. Although Matthew reports this discussion of divorce between Jesus and the Pharisees by using Mark 10:1-12 as his source, he does so in his own way. In a fashion that fits its narrative context more coherently than Luke 16:18, Matthew deals with the question of divorce in 5:32, in the series of ethical instructions located in the antitheses of 5:17-48. Commenting on the words of Decalogue

---

22 For a discussion of the problems surrounding Luke's narrative composition at this point of his Gospel, see Collins, *Divorce*, 175-79.
23 In fact, as Dale C. Allison, Jr, "Divorce, Celibacy and Joseph (Matthew 1.18-25 and 19.1-12)," *Journal for the Study of the New Testament* 49 (1993) 3-10, points out, Matthew raises the issue of divorce three times: Joseph's decision to divorce his wife "quietly" is recorded in 1:19. Allison's main concern is to show that πορνεία in 19:9 means adultery, and that Joseph's celibacy in 1:24-25 clarifies what is meant by the eunuch saying in 19:10-12. However, he makes an important point when he suggests that the description of Joseph as a "righteous man" (Greek: δίκαιος) demands that there be an exception to Jesus' absolute prohibition of divorce. It is "righteous" to divorce the unfaithful wife. Not to do so would bring "sin upon the land" (see Deut 24:4). Joseph "is to be regarded as a model of behaviour in accord with God's will" (p. 5). Coherently, therefore, Matthew *must* add the exception clauses to Matthew 5:32 and 19:9. If divorce was necessary for Joseph, the just man, it must be fine for the followers of Jesus. Loader, "Did Adultery Mandate Divorce?" 68-69, understands Joseph's "righteousness" as a judgment of his decision to divorce Mary, rather than execute her. But he agrees that this decision is closely linked to the addition of the exception clauses in 5:32 and 19:9.

forbidding divorce (Exodus 20:14 and Deuteronomy 5:18), Jesus extends his commentary to the legislation of Deuteronomy 24:1-4. He comments: *"But I say to you that* everyone who divorces his wife, *except on the ground of unchastity,* makes her an adulteress; and whoever marries a divorced woman commits adultery" (Matt 5:32).

The closeness between the two teachings is clear. Once the Matthean redactional additions, "But I say to you that," and "except on the ground of adultery," are removed, then the possibility that Luke 16:18 and Matthew 5:32 come from the same source ("Q") is very real.

Matthew 5:32	**Luke 16:18**
(a) Everyone who divorces his wife *except on the ground of unchastity*	Everyone who divorces his wife and marries another
(b) makes her an adulteress	commits adultery
(a) and whoever marries a divorced woman	and the one who marries a woman woman divorced by her husband
(b) commits adultery.	commits adultery

Allowing for stylistic and slight changes of content made by the two authors using the same source (Luke clarifies, while Matthew takes the details of divorce between a husband and a wife for granted), the literary structure and the message of this passage indicates that Matthew and Luke are using the same source. The passage (from "Q") points back to a very early record of a word from Jesus that prohibited divorce, prior to Matthew and Luke, but not found in Mark. Unlike Paul's words, "from the Lord," the "Q" passage makes no allowances for the initiative of the woman. At least in that respect, it continues Jewish tradition.

Calling upon the data provided by 1 Corinthians 7:10-11, where Paul appears to be paraphrasing a word of Jesus, Matthew

5:32, and Luke 16:18 ("Q"), scholars are able to suggest the probable "primitive form" of this word of Jesus that had its origins on the lips of Jesus of Nazareth during the course of his ministry. Reflecting a Semitic balance, intricacy, and a density worthy of the importance of the subject being dealt with, a two-part saying emerges:

Part 1a: Everyone who divorces his wife and marries another

Part 1b: commits adultery.

Part 2a: And the one who marries a divorced woman

Part 2b: commits adultery.[24]

Whether or not one accepts this "reconstruction" as words of Jesus himself, there is no doubt that Jesus of Nazareth forbade divorce and remarriage.[25] Our glance at the society and religious practice of Jesus' time and Jewish society, indicates that such teaching stands alone. "Jesus the Jew clashes with the Mosaic Torah as it was understood and practiced by mainstream Judaism before, during, and after his time."[26]

---

24 See Meier, *A Marginal Jew*, 4:107-108 for the reconstructed text, and reflections upon its structure and meaning. This is also the reconstruction of Robinson, Hoffmann, and Kloppenborg, *The Critical Edition of Q*, 470.

25 See also Collins, *Divorce*, 214; Fitzmyer, *First Corinthians*, 290-91. However Loader, "Did Adultery Mandate Divorce?" 67-78, has indicated his serious doubt. He claims that, on the basis of Genesis 2:24 (see pp. 75-76), Jesus took it for granted that divorce would follow adultery. "[T]he exception now found in Matt 5.32 and 19.9 was already presupposed in Mark 10.11-12, Luke 16.18 and 1 Cor 7:10-11. Matthew, rather than uncharacteristically softening Jesus' demand, simply spelled out what has always been assumed" (p. 74).

26 For an application of the usual "criteria" used by historians to detect the historicity of material found in such sayings, see Meier, *A Marginal Jew*, 4:112-19. The citation comes from p. 114. Not all would be so clear-cut. See, among many, Collins, *Divorce*, 178, who suggests that Moses did not mandate divorce, so therefore there is some "room" for Jesus' hard line in these debates. See also Gerhard Lohfink, *Jesus of Nazareth. What He Wanted,*

Although centuries and worlds apart, there is a certain parallel between the challenge of Jesus' teaching then and now. Modern society is structured, legally and socially, to accept and even encourage (in certain circumstances) the practice of divorce and remarriage. Although the practice of divorce and remarriage was not as widespread at the time of Jesus, Deuteronomy 24:1-4 indicated that a man could dismiss his wife and marry another (see Mark 10:3-4; Matt 19:7).3 Jesus contradicted this teaching and practice.

John Meier indicates how Jesus' prohibition of divorce and remarriage must have appeared to his contemporaries.

> Jesus consciously presented himself to his fellow Jews as the eschatological prophet, performing Elijah's task of beginning the regathering of Israel in the end time while also performing miracles like Elijah's. These miracles were interpreted as signs of the kingdom that was coming and yet that, in a way, was already present in Jesus' ministry. In this highly charged context of future-yet-realised eschatology, the eschatological prophet named Jesus may have inculcated as already binding certain types of behaviour that pointed forward, as did his whole ministry, to the final period of Israel's restoration as God's holy people.[27]

1 Corinthians 7:8-16: God has called us to peace

In 1 Corinthians 7:1, Paul turns his attention to several issues related to marriage, with his usual indication of "now concerning these matters ..." (περὶ δέ ...). Writing to his over-enthusiastic new Christians, in vv. 1-7 he informs them that there should not be anything "new" in the way husband and wives should relate, although expressing his personal support for his own way of life, most likely celibate, admitting that not all have this gift from God

---

Who He Was, trans. Linda M. Maloney (Collegeville, MN: Liturgical Press, 2012) 202-204.
27 Meier, *A Marginal Jew*, 4:127. See also Collins, *Divorce*, 218-22.

(v. 7).²⁸ He then addresses, in sequence, the issues face by the unmarried and the widows (vv. 8-9), the married (vv. 10-11), and the situation of a woman married to an unbeliever (vv. 12-16). On the first and the third question he provides his own opinion: "I say" (v. 8); "I say, not the Lord" (v. 12). In dealing with the married, he indicates: "I give charge, but not I but the Lord" (v. 10), taking us back to our earliest record of Jesus' prohibition of divorce.

As he has done in his general discussion of matters sexual (vv. 1-7), in vv. 8-9 he asks that people maintain their current status. But in vv. 12-16, he moves on to discuss what must have been a common enough reality in Pauline Corinth: a man (v. 12) or a woman (v. 13) married to an unbeliever.²⁹ Paul recommends that they too remain in their current sexual situation. He provides reason for this recommendation: the potential for mutual consecration of a couple through marriage, and the subsequent consecration of the children (see v. 14).³⁰ Critically, however, "if the unbelieving partner desires to separate, let it be so; in such a case your brother or sister is not bound" (v. 15abc). He again provides reason for this decision: there can be no certainty that such a mixed marriage will lead to salvation (v.

---

28 The likely background to Paul's insertion of this thought is that some of the Corinthians, who were not able to live such a life (see v. 9), aspire to live as Paul lives. This would not be appropriate. See Pheme Perkins, *First Corinthians*, Paideia Commentaries on the New Testament (Grand Rapids, MI: Baker Academic, 2012) 109-110.
29 It was only natural that adult conversion to Christianity (which was the norm in this founding period) brought women and men into Christianity who already had non-Christian spouses.
30 On the idea of the mutual "sanctification" of spouses and children in the biblical and Jewish tradition, see Collins, *First Corinthians*, 266-67. See also Fitzmyer, *First Corinthians*, 299-301. See p. 301: "God's sanctifying power is greater than any unbelief."

16).³¹ The fundamental principle of human relationships must be maintained: "it is to peace that God has called you" (v. 15d). Immediately after reporting Jesus' word that there be no separation between married couples, Paul addresses the difficult situation of couples and families in Corinth where the union of a believer and an unbeliever is damaging an essential elements in God's calling (see the Greek of v. 15d: κέκληκεν) the Christians to live in peace (Greek: ἐν δὲ εἰρήνῃ).³² He reads that situation in the light of God's call of the Christian to peace and salvation, and instructs the Christians in Corinth that a separation should take place.

Paul sees the necessity to *accommodate* the special circumstances of a mixed marriage between a pagan and a Christian, and *reverses* Jesus' decision to prohibit divorce. However, Paul does not permit the believing partner, no doubt instructed and committed to the word of the Lord recalled in vv. 10-11, to initiate the process of separation.³³ Jesus has *reversed* the traditional Jewish understanding of the possibility of divorce; Paul now does the same thing with the teaching of Jesus (vv. 10-11) in *allowing* separation between Christian and non-Christian partners. There were no

---

31 The interpretation of v. 16 concerning a wife or a husband's knowledge of the eventual salvation of their respective partner is divided. A positive interpretation supports the permanence of the union, in the hope that the partner might come to salvation. A negative interpretation suggests that there is no point staying in the marriage hoping that salvation will come to one's spouse. That is beyond anyone's knowledge of control; it belongs to God. See Collins, *First Corinthians*, 272, for the discussion.
32 I have drawn attention to the Greek verb "to call" (Greek: καλέω) as this became a technical expression in early Christianity for God's initiative in calling people to the following of Jesus Christ: "vocation." See Collins, *First Corinthians*, 267. Following NTG28 and the NRSV, I have used the second-person plural pronoun: "you" (ὑμᾶς). This is textually doubtful. The original may be the first-person plural: "us" (Greek: ἡμᾶς). Although the "us" is more clearly associated with the inner group of the Christian community, the use of "you" does not alter the argument. The reference to "any brother" (Greek: τις ἀδελφός) in v. 12 makes it clear that Paul is addressing the inner dynamics of a Christian community.
33 See, among many, Horsley, *1 Corinthians*, 99.

doubt outstanding pastoral reasons for making this decision in support of the God-given peace of Corinthian community.[34] Paul does not appear to be in any anguish over this decision. Juxtaposed with the word of the Lord (vv. 10-11), in vv. 12-16, he gives instructions that are not consistent with vv. 10-11, but which clearly *accommodate* the situation of the Church in Corinth.[35] There is no indication from Paul whether or not the Christian spouse would be permitted to remarry; what he said about remarriage in v. 11 ("remain single") may well continue to apply.[36] Pheme Perkins wisely suggests that Paul might expect them to be guided by v. 7: "I wish that all were as I myself am. But each one has his own special gift from God, one of one kind and one of another."[37]

There are several puzzles associated with the interpretation of 1 Corinthians 7:12-16.[38] What is crucial for this essay, however, is that *within the Sacred Scriptures of Christianity* we find an accommodation of Jesus' absolute prohibition of divorce.[39] But Paul is not alone in instituting an exception.

---

34 Perkins, *First Corinthians*, 110, points out that Paul is speaking to "the social goal of harmony within the household is the divine intent for all marriages."
35 For an awareness of the sharpness of the contrast, see Fitzmyer, *First Corinthians*, 301-302.
36 Collins, *Divorce*, 63-64, rightly claims that there is a lack of clarity in what Paul thinks about remarriage. Meier, *A Marginal Jew*, 174 note 126, suggests that the texts reflect Paul's own lack of certainty as to "what the Christian caught in this difficult situation can or should do." Fitzmyer, *First Corinthians*, 301-302 is more optimistic: "Paul says nothing against further marriages" (p. 302).
37 Perkins, *First Corinthians*, 110.
38 They are expertly dealt with by Collins, *Divorce*, 40-64.
39 The Catholic Church recognises this "exception" in its law. Naming Paul, it claims that it has the authority to "dissolve" a marriage between two non-believers (not baptised), when one of the parties subsequently becomes a Catholic. This so-called *privilegium paulinum* (the Pauline privilege), is legislated in Canons 1143-1150. Fitzmyer, *First Corinthians*, 302-302, comments: "That is a development in Canon Law that goes beyond the limits of the case envisaged by Paul."

Mark 10:1-12 // Matthew 19:1-12 (Matthew 5:32 again)

Matthew regularly uses Mark as one of his major sources. But he generally has something of his own to say and does not re-write Mark *verbatim*. The reporting of Jesus' debate with the Pharisees over divorce is a good example of this.[40]

Mark 10:1-12	**Matthew 19:1-12**
¹And he left there and went to the region of Judea and beyond the Jordan,	¹Now when Jesus had finished these sayings, he went away from Galilee and entered the region of Judea beyond the Jordan;
and crowds gathered to him again; and again, as his custom was, he taught them.	²and large crowds followed him, and he healed them there.
²And Pharisees came up and in order to test him asked, "Is it lawful for a man to divorce his wife?"	³And Pharisees came up to him and tested him by asking, "Is it lawful to divorce one's wife for any cause?"
³He answered them, "What did Moses command you?"	
⁴They said, "Moses allowed a man to write a certificate of divorce, and to put her away."	[**Transposed**: ⁷*They said to him, "Why then did Moses command one to give a certificate of divorce, and to put her away?"*

---

40 The following parallel presentation of the Markan and Matthean texts provides the order of the Markan text. Both texts are presented in full, in regular type. However, passages that Matthew has relocated are presented in *italics*, so that the reader will more easily be able to follow the parallels. They also show Matthew's creative freedom with his source.

Mark 10:1-12	Matthew 19:1-12
	⁸*He said to them, "For your hardness of heart Moses allowed you to divorce your wives,*
⁵But Jesus said to them, "For your hardness of heart he wrote you this commandment.	
	but from the beginning it was not so.]
⁶*But from the beginning of creation,* 'God made them male and female.'	⁴He answered, "Have you not read that he who made them from the beginning made them male and female,
⁷'For this reason a man shall leave his father and mother and be joined to his wife, ⁸and the two shall become one flesh.' So they are no longer two but one flesh.	⁵and said, 'For this reason a man shall leave his father and mother and be joined to his wife, and the two shall become one flesh'? ⁶So they are no longer two but one flesh.
⁹What therefore God has joined together, let not man put asunder."	What therefore God has joined together, let not man put asunder."
	⁷They said to him, "Why then did Moses command one to give a certificate of divorce, and to put her away?" ⁸He said to them, "For your hardness of heart Moses allowed you to divorce your wives, but from the beginning it was not so.

Divorce and Remarriage in the Catholic Tradition

Mark 10:1-12	Matthew 19:1-12
[**Transposed**: ¹¹*And he said to them, "Whoever divorces his wife and marries another, commits adultery against her;* ¹²*and if she divorces her husband and marries another, she commits adultery."*]	⁹And I say to you: whoever divorces his wife, *except for unchastity* (Greek: μὴ ἐπὶ πορνείᾳ), and marries another, commits adultery."
¹⁰And in the house the disciples asked him again about this matter.	
	The disciples said to him, "If such is the case of a man with his wife, it is not expedient to marry."
¹¹And he said to them, "Whoever divorces his wife and marries another, commits adultery against her; ¹²and if she divorces her husband and marries another, she commits adultery."	¹¹But he said to them, "Not all men can receive this saying, but only those to whom it is given. ¹²For there are eunuchs who have been so from birth, and there are eunuchs who have been made eunuchs by men, and there are eunuchs who have made themselves eunuchs for the sake of the kingdom of heaven. He who is able to receive this, let him receive it."

Mark 10:1-9 is shaped like a traditional rabbinic discussion. The question of divorce is posed. Mark indicates the hostility of the Pharisees; they asked the question "in order to test him" (v. 2). Jesus responds with a further question, asking the Pharisees to locate their query within the teaching of the Law (v. 3). They respond by citing the general meaning of Deuteronomy 24:1-4 (v. 4), but

Jesus counters with a correction of the Pharisees' understanding of Torah by showing that this was not God's original design. It was allowed, through Moses, only because of the hardness of hearts in Israel. The *original* design of God, *from the beginning of creation*, is found in Genesis 1:27 and 2:24 (vv. 5-8). It provides his response to the original question (see v. 2) with the words, "What therefore what God has joined together, let no man put asunder" (v. 9).[41] Jesus has answered Torah with Torah, and the Pharisees fall silent. But "in the house" as the disciples who ask him about this matter, he shifts the argument from divorce to adultery.[42] Mark regularly uses "the house" as the location for teaching the disciples (see 3:20; 7:17-23; 9:28, 33). A man or a woman who divorces and remarries "commits adultery" (vv. 11-12). Although adultery has been introduced in Jesus' discussion with the disciples, there is a logical link with what Jesus has taught the Pharisees. The Torah legislates against adultery (Exod 20:19; Deut 4:10; 22:22; Lev 20:10). Jesus teaches his disciples (and they are the object of all that is found across 10:1-31) that the practice of the Pharisees leads to a breach of Torah, as divorce and remarriage is adultery.[43] Jesus' absolute prohibition of divorce in Mark 10:1-12, echoes the earlier record of 1 Corinthians 7:10-11. Writing in the Roman world, Mark addresses the possibility of divorce and remarriage (and subsequent adultery) on the part of both the man and the woman.

Matthew does not have the parrying back-and-forth that shapes rabbinic discussion. The Pharisees test Jesus by asking if it

---

41 A crucial distinction is drawn between what God (ὁ θεός) has done, and what "man" (ἄνθρωπος) attempts to undo in v. 9.

42 See, for example, Adela Y. Collins, *Mark*, Hermeneia (Minneapolis, MN: Fortress, 2007) 469-70.

43 On the focus upon teaching the disciples across 10:1-31, see Moloney, *The Gospel of Mark*, 192-203.

is lawful to divorce one's wife *for any cause* (v. 3).[44] Matthew has Jesus respond immediately in terms of Genesis 1:27 and 2:24 (vv. 5-6). Only when the Pharisees are cornered by Jesus' use of the Torah do they turn to Deuteronomy 24:1-4 (v. 7). Jesus replies in terms of Israel's hardness of heart, catching up his earlier response from Genesis by telling them that "from the beginning it was not so" (v. 8). Mark's location of the link between divorce and adultery (Mark 10:11-12) is used to end the Matthean encounter between Jesus and the Pharisees (v. 9), rather than to the disciples (Mark 10:11-12). Matthew, reflecting a more Jewish tradition, regards the man as the one who might initiate divorce, and thus commit adultery. The woman is not considered. As in Mark (10:10-12), Matthew closes the episode with an explanation to the disciples in 19:10-12, but the discussions are very different. Matthew uses his own special traditions, not found anywhere else in the New Testament.[45] The disciples cannot imagine how such a prohibition could work. If one cannot divorce, then the institution of marriage is to be avoided (v. 10). Jesus' responds that the never-failing gift of loyalty in marriage is "a special gift from God" (v. 11; recalling 1 Cor 7:1) and closes with the famous saying about being a eunuch because of the kingdom of heaven (v. 12).[46]

---

44 It has long been argued that Matthew's addition of "for any cause" reflects the difference of opinion between the school of Shammai, who only allowed divorce on the basis of moral disorder on the part of the woman, and the school of Hillel, who allowed divorce "for any cause." This debate is widely recorded in Rabbinic documents. See, among most, Fitzmyer, "The Matthean Divorce Texts," 197-226. This position is strenuously opposed by Meier, *A Marginal Jew*, 94-95, 163 n. 80. He claims the Rabbinic texts are too late (written early in the third century) to be used in the interpretation of a first century document.

45 See Collins, *Divorce*, 119-20.

46 It is beyond our scope to discuss the history and meaning of Matthew 19:10-12. For more detail, see Francis J. Moloney, "Matthew 19,3-12 and Celibacy: A Redactional and Form Critical Study," *Journal for the Study of the New Testament* 2 (1979) 42-60.

Within these parallel narratives in Mark and Matthew, there are two significant issues that call for closer attention:
1. Matthew's report of Jesus' prohibiting divorce, "except for unchastity" in his encounter with the Pharisees (19:9: μὴ ἐπὶ πορνείᾳ). This exception must have been important for Matthew and his Christian community. It was not present in Mark 10:11-12, that Matthew is using as a source. He also inserts the same sentiment, "except for unchastity" in 5:32 (παρεκτὸς λόγου πορνείας), where the original "Q" passage (see Luke 16:18) did not allow any such possibility (see Luke 16:18).
2. Jesus' use of Genesis in both accounts, and his explanation that the prohibition of divorce is based upon God's design "from the beginning of creation" (Mark 10:6a) and "from the beginning" (Matthew 19:4b, 8c).

1. *"Except for Unchastity" (Matthew 5:32; 19:9)*

When Matthew uses two of his major sources, "Q" (see Luke 16:18) and the Gospel of Mark (see Mark 10:1-12), he *accommodates* the absolute prohibition of divorce found in both. What is perhaps more remarkable, for the contemporary interpreter of the New Testament, he uses the same expression to describe the motivation for this exception. The Greek word used, πορνεία, is a notoriously difficult word to translate with any precision. This is so because a number of different Greek expressions are used with reference to specific sexually immoral acts, but πορνεία is a more generic word that can refer to any one of them, or to all of them.[47] In his use of "Q", he softens Jesus' absolute prohibition by adding "except in the case of πορνεία," and his rewriting of Mark is similarly softened by the words "except for πορνεία."

---

47 For a very good survey, see William R. G. Loader, *The New Testament on Sexuality* (Grand Rapids, MI: Eerdmans, 2012) 244-50.

Understandably, given the importance of these two exceptions, what Matthew meant by his use of πορνεία has long been the source of debate and discussion.[48] A decision need not be made here, and what I am about to suggest is one possibility among many. The situation of the early Christian community addressed by the Gospel of Matthew would have been marked by the presence of both Jews and Gentiles. No doubt the inner-community marital situation addressed by Paul in 1 Corinthians 7:12-16 would have again been present, even though the cultural and religious settings of Corinth and Antioch were different. In the newly founded Christian community, there would have been marriages that had been entered into by the pre-Christian *Gentile* members of some of the new Christians. For the Christian community, and especially for the Matthean community where an observance of the Law was required (see 5:17-19), some of these pagan marriages were regarded as πορνεία.

We need not decide precisely what that meant, and the generic word used by the NRSV, "unchastity," serves well. I suspect that Paul's use of the expression πορνεία to refer to the incestuous relationship between a man and his father's wife in 1 Corinthians 5:1 is a pointer to its meaning in Matthew 5:32 and 19:9.[49] Whatever one makes of that suggestion, Matthew asks that marriages marked by what the Christian community considered πορνεία be ended. In rewriting Mark 10:1-12, he adds vv. 10-12, found only in Matthew, to his Markan source instructing his disciples (again in a way that echoes 1 Corinthians 7:8-9) that, once freed from this unacceptable marriage situation, they should remain single.[50] Such a request, however, is recognised as extremely

---

48 For a survey of this discussion see Luz, *Matthew*, 1:250–59.
49 As we have seen, Loader, "Did Adultery Mandate Divorce?" 67-78, challenges this suggestion. He claims that πορνεία certainly meant adultery, and that it was taken for granted, even by Jesus, that divorce would follow adultery.
50 This case is argued at length in Moloney, "Matthew 19:3-12 and Celibacy," 44-60. In support of the meaning of "incestuous relationship," see also Fitzmyer, "Matthean Divorce Texts," 221.

difficult. It is not possible for everyone to live that way, and only those gifted for such a lifestyle should practice it (v. 12d. See 1 Cor 7:7-9).[51]

Whatever the precise situation addressed by Matthew, and whatever the exact meaning he wishes to give to the word πορνεία, the decisive matter is that he uses two sources that record the memory of Jesus' absolute prohibition of divorce and remarriage ("Q" and Mark), and he modifies *both* (Matt 5:32; 19:9). We are dealing with another moment in the developing theological and pastoral consciousness of the earliest Church that quite freely *and consistently* accommodates a teaching of Jesus. This is a further indication *within the inspired pages of our Christian Sacred Scriptures* that shows the need for the Church to rethink Jesus' fiercely eschatological teaching, in the light of the long-term pastoral situation of the developing Christian Church. As Craig Keener has pointed out: "In practice, the early Christians immediately began to qualify Jesus' divorce saying; other principles of Jesus, such as not condemning the innocent (12:7) or the principle of mercy (23:23), would have forced them to do so in some circumstances. ... Paul and Matthew's exceptions (Mt 5:32; 19:9; 1 Cor 7:15, 27-28) constitute two-thirds of the extant first-century Christian references to divorce."[52]

2. From the Beginning (Mark 10:6; Matthew 19:4, 8)

The dispute between Jesus and the Pharisees over divorce and remarriage in Mark 10:1-12 swings upon the use Jesus makes of the Torah texts of Genesis 1:27 and 2:24 to overcome their use of the Torah text of Deuteronomy 24:1-4 as the reason for allowing

---

51 The verb used by Matthew in 19:12d, translated in the NRSV in the command "He who is able to *receive* this, let him *receive* it," is χωρέω. Its primary meaning is not "receive," but "make space" (see Mark 2:2). It carries the idea of being open to a gift, and thus "accept."

52 Craig S. Keener, *A Commentary on the Gospel of Matthew* (Grand Rapids, MI: Eerdmans, 1999) 191.

divorce. Whether or not this use of a text that comes "before" the legislation handed down through Moses in Deuteronomy 24:1-4 because of the hardness of heart of Israel closes the issue, Jesus' explanation of why the Genesis texts close the discussion is provided with words "from the beginning of creation" (ἀπὸ δὲ ἀρχῆς κτίσεως) that open his citations from Genesis (Mark 10:6. See also Matt 19:8). A crucial theological point needs to be made here: Mark (followed by Matthew) presents Jesus' teaching as the reconstitution of God's original design: "from the beginning (ἀρχή) of creation" (Mark), "from the beginning" (ἀρχή) (twice in Matthew).

Jesus' appeal to texts from Genesis, and his explicit reference to "the beginning," situates Jesus' description of the situation between a woman and a man in the Garden of Eden! Genesis 1:27 and 2:24 describe the situation between a man (Adam) and a woman (Eve) before the introduction of sin into the human story (see Gen 3:1-24). As Joel Marcus has correctly commented, "Jesus and the Markan Christians are people who rejoice in the dawning light of the new age – which is also the recaptured radiance of Eden."[53] But sin has entered the world, and we now claim that only Jesus of Nazareth has embodied the perfect human condition designed by God. That perfection has been represented in the biblical account of Adam and Eve, but such perfection has been lost to the human condition (Genesis 3). The loss of the glory of these beginnings through the sin and disobedience of Adam has been overcome by the universal significance of the obedience of Jesus, revealed in his death and resurrection. But the story of Adam and the story of Jesus Christ continue to run side by side throughout the human story. Nowhere has this been more eloquently stated than in the close contrasting parallels that Paul draws between Adam and Christ in Romans 5:12-21. The Christian must live the in-between-time, called to join the

---

53 Joel Marcus, *Mark*, The Anchor Yale Bible 27-27A, 2 vols. (New York/New Haven: Doubleday/Yale University Press, 2000-2009) 2:710.

Christ story and reject the Adam story.[54] As history eloquently demonstrates, humankind is "in process": the ideal of God's original creative plan has never been fully present in the ambiguity of that history.[55]

The introduction of Pauline thought on the "new creation" (see Gal 2:15; 2 Corinthians 5:17) raises a further question. Reflecting upon Jesus' bold rejection of Torah in forbidding the practice of divorce, we earlier saw John Meier arguing that Jesus understood himself and was understood by his followers as the eschatological prophet.

> In this highly charged context of future-yet-realised eschatology, the eschatological prophet named Jesus may have inculcated as already binding certain types of behaviour that pointed forward, as did his whole ministry, to the final period of Israel's restoration as God's holy people.[56]

Both Paul (in the 50's CE) and Mark (about 70 CE) continue to portray Jesus in this fashion. However, they not only continue Jesus' teaching by looking to "the end" as the explanation for the uniqueness of Jesus and his teaching.[57] They reach back to the beginnings of all creation. This tendency develops as the early Church developed an ever-deepening understanding of Jesus' significance.[58] Paul refers to a pre-existent Christ in Philippians

---

54 On Paul's concept of the Adam story, and the "new creation" of Jesus' death and resurrection, see Moloney, *Reading the New Testament in the Church*, 97-102.
55 Some may query this statement in the light of the saints, and especially the Mother of Jesus, in Catholic teaching. Such holiness, which is a restoration of God's original design, is only possible because of a positive response to the gift of God's grace. It is not *natural*.
56 Meier, *A Marginal Jew*, 4:127.
57 Jesus' looking to "the end" as the basis for an understanding of his person and message has been splendidly shown by Allison, *Constructing Jesus*.
58 There is considerable contemporary interest in the relationship between Pauline and Markan theology, initiated by Joel Marcus, "Mark – Interpreter of Paul," *New Testament Studies* 46 (2000) 473-87.

2:6-11, but this development finds its highest expression in the Prologue to the Gospel of John, where Jesus is described as the Logos of God, who dwelt in a unique oneness of time "in the beginning" (John 1:1-2: ἐν ἀρχῇ).

Mark 10:1-12 and Matthew 19:1-12 are bearers of this theological tradition. The strength of Jesus' prohibition of divorce comes from his indication that there was no divorce in the Garden of Eden. Christians do not live in the Garden of Eden, but within the ambiguity of the contemporary human story. Contemporary Catholic legislation prohibits divorce because of the fact that Jesus did so. This position misses an important theological truth in its presupposition that the "ideal" of God's original creation is in place from the very first moment of the long, and often complex, "real" journey of Christian marriage. It transfers what was primarily a christological intuition of the early Church into an essential element of its marriage legislation (Canon 1141). The confusion of the "ideal" with the "real" in the lives of imperfect people, striving (and sometimes failing) in their Christian lives, calls for re-examination by the Church's highest authority.

Conclusion

The Christian Church does not base its teaching and practice only on what can be shown as the authentic teaching and practice of the historical Jesus. The foundational Councils that produced much of the Christian Tradition ranged widely across *everything in the New Testament*, especially the Gospel of John and the Letters of Paul, to establish its rule of faith, and to articulate it in the Creeds. There should be no "picking and choosing" with the Word of God. These debates are often coloured by the suggestion that the Church is selective in what it chooses from the teaching of Jesus and point to such requirements as cutting off the hand, the foot, and plucking out the eye (see Mark 9:43-47). They are not legislated in Canon law, but Jesus' prohibition of divorce (found only in 1 Cor 7:10-11 and Mark 10:1-12) is found there (see Canon 1055). Such debates can sometimes be superficial, but they contain a challenge. Martin Hengel has devoted detailed attention to a saying of Jesus, found in "Q," that he argues lies at the heart of Jesus' personal sense of his charism: "Leave the dead to bury their own dead; but as for you, go and proclaim the kingdom of God" (Luke 9:60//Matt 8:22).[59] Living the Word of God in the Christian Church is no easy matter.[60]

An important hermeneutic has always been at play in the development of Christian tradition, and in the Church's necessary commitment to play an effective role in an increasingly informed world. It has never been a simple process. It generates tension and misunderstanding, as the story of the Ecumenical Councils, from Nicea (325 CE) to Vatican II (1962-65 CE), indicate.[61] But the Church does not simply look back to the identifiable words of Jesus to establish its doctrinal and moral bedrock truths; it reflects upon its biblical and ecclesial tradition in dialogue with an ever-expanding body of knowledge and experience.

The Church's treatment of the divorced and the remarried must consider *the entire picture*. As the early Church recognised that Jesus had begun a "new creation," it challenged believers to resist and overcome sin, guided by the example of Jesus, enlivened by the pardoning and life-giving grace generated by his death and resurrection (see Rom 5:12-21; Mark 10:6; Matt 19:4, 8).

---

59 Martin Hengel, *The Charismatic Leader and His Followers*, trans. James C. G. Greig, Studies of the New Testament and Its World (Edinburgh: T. & T. Clark, 1981). This study rightly points to the importance of Jesus' intense eschatological understanding of his mission, shared by his followers.

60 This statement could lead to a discussion of the need for all the Christian Churches to reflect a "shared wisdom and experience" when they face such difficult questions. This is not the place for such a debate, but the Catholic Church stands alone among Christian Churches that also look to the Word of God for their founding and formative Traditions in the matter of divorce and remarriage. This calls for some self-examination.

61 The tensions surrounding Vatican II have been graphically documented by Yves Congar, *My Journal of the Council*, trans. Dennis Minns, and Others (Adelaide: ATF Theology, 2012).

The earliest Tradition recognised that only Jesus incarnated the "new creation." The rest of humankind strives to live a Christian life caught in the ambiguity of the ongoing presence of both the Adam and the Christ story (see Rom 5:12-21), confident that "where sin increased, grace abounded all the more" (Rom 5:20). Consequently, Paul and Matthew, without compunction, accommodated Jesus' absolute prohibition of divorce for its fragile members (1 Cor 7:14-16; Matt. 5:32; 19:9).

This is the *authentic Tradition* generated within the Spirit-filled formative decades of Christianity. It should direct us as we read the entire New Testament, seeking the guidance that is found there.[62] No one has stated this more authoritatively than Joseph Fitzmyer:

> If Matthew under inspiration could have been moved to add an exceptive phrase to the saying of Jesus about divorce that he found in an absolute form in either his Marcan source or in 'Q,' of if Paul likewise under inspiration could introduce into his writing an exception on his own authority, then why cannot the Spirit-guided institutional Church of a later generation make a similar exception in view of problems confronting Christian married life of its day or so-called broken marriage?[63]

Recognising this *authentic Tradition*, the Church's leadership should see that its current legislation is based on a late, biblically unfounded, *tradition*. The Church must face the confusing challenges of contemporary society through an examination of its Tradition, and not purely based on mercy and compassion – however precious these hallmarks of Francis' papacy might be.

---

62 This hermeneutic was hesitatingly proposed to the teaching authority of the Church 45 years ago by Pierre Benoit, "Christian Marriage according to Saint Paul," *The Clergy Review* 65 (1980) 309-321. See especially pp. 320-21.
63 Fitzmyer, *First Corinthians*, 298. Fitzmyer first made this suggestion in 1976 ("The Matthean Divorce Texts," 224-26).

4

The Catholic Priesthood: A New Testament Reflection

A New Testament reflection upon the Catholic priesthood must face complex historical and hermeneutical problems. At the heart of these problems lies the fact that the New Testament authors' response to the experience of Jesus, his teaching, his death, his resurrection and the beginnings of a believing community does not *directly* consider "the Catholic priesthood." In a vain search for something to provide a biblical word on the institution of the Priesthood, at least since the time of Cyril of Alexandria (*In Johannis Evangelium* XI, 8; PG 74:545), made popular in the sixteenth century by David Chytraeus (1530-1600), scholars have focused upon John 17:18 as "priestly consecration." In this interpretation, some view Jesus' prayer that his disciples be "made holy" (*hēgiasmenoi*) as he is holy as an act of priestly consecration.

Although some scholars have attempted to resurrect this view,[1] the sense of "consecration" of Jesus followers is nowadays almost universally rejected. Indeed, the most thorough rejection of this position comes from the significant Catholic Johannine specialist, Ignace de la Potterie. He insists that the language is associated with holiness, and not consecration.[2] For many, the absence of

---

[1] See especially André Feuillet, *The Priesthood of Christ and His Ministers*, trans. Matthew J. O'Connell (Garden City, NY: Doubleday, 1975).

[2] See especially Ignace de la Potterie, "Consécration ou sanctification du Chrétien d'après Jean 17?" in *Le Sacré: Etudes et Recherches. Actes di Colloque organisé par le Centre International d'Etudes Humanistes et par l'Institut d'Etudes Philosophiques de Rome*, ed. E. Castelli (Paris: Aubier-Montaigne, 1974) 339-49. For a fuller documentation of the discussion, see Moloney, *Glory not Dishonor*, 117 n. 46. More recently, see Harold Attridge, "How Priestly is the 'High Priestly Prayer' of John 17?" *The Catholic Biblical Quarterly* 75 (2013) 1-14.

any reference to the institutionalised Priesthood in the New Testament suggests that we Catholics should look elsewhere for the Christological and Ecclesiological inspiration for our Priesthood. From within a Catholic theological and hermeneutical world, such a position is quite acceptable. The significant theological assessment of the Word of God and the Sacred Tradition as forming "flowing from the same divine wellspring" in the process of revelation, made at Vatican II (*Dei Verbum* 9),[3] legitimates a Catholic understanding of the ongoing presence of the inspiring and foundational presence of the Holy Spirit that led to the eventual emergence, perhaps late in the second Christian century, of the institution of the sacrament of Holy Orders, and the institution of a Christian Priesthood, as we know it today.[4]

The Problem

What follows will argue that the prophetic nature of the Gospel narratives enables us to bridge the gap between the Gospel-values so clearly articulated there, to pose questions to the institution of the Priesthood that certainly postdates the last book of the New Testament.[5] I wish to associate myself with the seminal work of

---

3 On this major development in the history of Catholic understanding of the sources of revelation, see Joseph Ratzinger, "The Transmission of Divine Revelation," in *Commentary on the Documents of Vatican II*, ed. Herbert Vorgrimler, 5 vols. (London: Burns & Oates/Herder & Herder, 1967-1969) 3:190-96.

4 As is well known, the absence of the ordained ministry in the pages of the New Testament led to the attack on the Catholic Priesthood by the Reformers. They were sometimes assisted in their attacks by the poor formation of the clergy and laxity in the monasteries of the time. Most of these Reformers were once ordained Priests (e.g. Luther, Müntzer, Zwingli, Sattler, Melanchthon, Bucer). On this, see Eire, *Reformations*, 3-4; 44-47.

5 The precise date of the latest books of the New Testament is hard to pin down. We can be reasonably confident that 2 Peter and Jude may come from late in the first or early in the second Christian century. See Moloney, *Reading the New Testament in the Church*, 166-68.

The Catholic Priesthood: A New Testament Reflection

Raymond E. Brown, *Priests and Bishops*, published more than fifty years ago,[6] returning to the question Brown raised as he embarked on that study: "[G]ranted the existence of these institutions, what light do the Scriptures cast upon what should be expected of them by both Catholics and non-Catholics?"[7] However, writing of the Catholic Priesthood in 2025 I must face issues and ask questions that Brown had no call to consider. Brown's study recalls the conflicts that surrounded the search for the identity of the Catholic Priesthood at that time, in the immediate aftermath of Vatican II. The Priesthood had to be understood within the context of the radically new vision of the Church, the Liturgy, the presence of the Church in the World, its relationship to the other great religions, and the unprecedented teaching on religious freedom that emerged from the Council.

Today the contemporary Catholic Priesthood is facing further problems. I deliberately chose to say "further problems," as Brown's list of challenges has not gone away! In my culturally determined Western society of Australia, young people manifest little interest in priestly life. The Priesthood has lost its privileged status in society for many reasons. At the heart of this loss of status is the lessening of the sense of religion, spiritual values, and the importance of the transcendent. Modern western society is self-sufficient, although such celebrations as Baptism, Easter, Marriages and Funerals remain embedded in the culture.

Priests today find themselves serving within a community where they have lost the high moral ground they once occupied, a necessary consequence of the scandalously widespread sexual abuse of minors that has come to light across all the Churches in the Western World, generating major national investigations in Ireland and Australia. The passionate pursuit of errant Priests,

---

6 Raymond E. Brown, *Priest and Bishop. Biblical Reflections* (New York: Paulist Press, 1970). It was reprinted in Eugene, OR, by Wipf & Stock, in 1999. I am using the reprinted edition.
7 Brown, *Priest and Bishop*, 4.

Bishops and Cardinals, the cover-up tactics of many Bishops, loyally but illegally attempting to defend the public image of the Church, have repeatedly placed this problem on the front pages of the secular media. Because of the behaviour of a few, all priests sense that they are "under a shadow."[8] These are but the most notorious problems that provide the contemporary context for a New Testament reflection on the Catholic Priesthood.

Some History

The Jewish and Greco-Roman worlds and cultures that provided the categories, languages, socio-cultural, religious and political background for earliest Christianity, were familiar with the figure and function of the priest. Israelite religion had a long tradition of priesthood, members of the tribe of Levi who served in the Jerusalem Temple. They were set apart from the people at large, performed cultic functions, acting as intermediaries between God and the people, financially supported by Temple-taxes. These functions have been described in Deuteronomy 33:8-10: consult the Urim and Thummim (sacred lots that had been cast to discover God's response to major questions), teaching, and offering cultic sacrifices. It is more difficult to describe the role and identity of the priests who served the various Greco-Roman religious and cultic traditions. The many mainstream Greek religions had been taken over by the Romans. Rome also developed its own cultic practices, especially the expansion of the Imperial cults.[9]

---

[8] Apart from the findings of the various commissions, the most helpful study of the problem I have read is Marie Keenan, *Child Sexual Abuse and the Catholic Church. Gender, Power, and Organizational Culture* (New York: Oxford University Press, 2012). For some brief thoughts on the failure of my own Congregation, the Salesians of Don Bosco in Australia and the Pacific, see Francis J. Moloney, *Don Bosco in Australia and the Pacific 1923-2023* (Mulgrave: Garratt Publishing, 2022) 50–51.

[9] On these cults in Asia, see Friesen, *Imperial Cults*, 25-131. On the personnel who officiated at the cults, see pp. 104-21.

The Catholic Priesthood: A New Testament Reflection

Subsequent to the campaigns of Alexander the Great and the steady hellenisation of the Mediterranean world, eastern religions were gradually influencing mainstream Greco-Roman religions. Across the widespread and varied search for the divine, there were many "priests" who played an intermediary and representative role between non-priestly members and the divine. Their function was largely, but not only, cultic. The Greek term used to describe these figures, both Jewish and Greco-Roman, was *hiereus*. The Latin word was *sacerdos*.

Despite the widespread presence of "priests" in the first century, there is no figure in the New Testament, apart from Jesus Christ, who is described as a priest (*hiereus*). Even the New Testament's notion of the priesthood of Jesus Christ must be understood within its literary and historical context. In the Epistle to the Hebrews, the author compares the priestly action of Jesus, whose death and resurrection led to his entry into heaven, with the action of the Jewish High Priest who into the Holy of Holies of the Temple once a year to make a blood offering for himself went and for the sins of the people (Heb 9:6-7). This makes the once-and-for-all sacrifice of Jesus (see Heb 10:12-14) a priestly act that surpasses the cultic priestly actions of the Jewish High Priest, repeated year by year. New Testament scholars agree that the Epistle to the Hebrews was written after the Jewish War of 66-70 C.E. and the destruction of the Jerusalem Temple. As both Jews and Christians struggled to work out their identities in the confusion that this loss produced for *both* religious traditions, Christians readily pointed to Jesus as the fulfilment and perfection of all that had been merely a sign and a shadow of God's design in the Jewish Institutions.[10]

---

10 This idea is expressed in many ways in the early Church, and in the Patristic tradition. But it is already a major theological theme in the Gospel of John, as he presents Jesus in the setting of the Jewish feasts of Sabbath, Passover, Tabernacles and Dedication in John 5:1-10:42. See Moloney, *Signs and Shadows*.

This is the *only* reference in the New Testament to any individual as a "priest" (apart from references to the Jewish priests), and it is associated with Jesus. It appears in a late document that established the superiority of the mediation between God and humankind through Jesus Christ (see Heb 1:1-2) over the mediation effected by the Jewish High Priest (Heb 9:6-22). The New Testament provides no evidence of any individual who functioned as a "priest," a person set apart by God to preside over the cult of the Christian community, or to act as an intermediary between God and the believers (a *hiereus*).

However, in the authentic Pauline Letters, the Acts of the Apostles, the Pastorals (1 and 2 Timothy and Titus, widely accepted as continuing the Pauline tradition, but written some time after the death of Paul) and the Catholic Epistles (the Letter of James, 1 and 2 Peter, 1, 2 and 3 John, and Jude), one finds reference to overseers, elders and deacons (Greek: *episcopoi, presbyteroi* and *diakonoi,* respectively). These expressions appear for the first time in the early 60s in Philippians 1:1. They are sometimes translated as "bishop, priest and deacon." Some suggest that we find already in Paul who was martyred in the mid-60s of the first century, the first indications of the three-tiered sacerdotal hierarchical "order" that became central to the Catholic Church's later hierarchical structure of its Priesthood and its priestly ministry to the community. The reasonably widespread use of these expressions (see Phil 1:1; Acts 6:1-6, 14:23; 20:17; 20:28; 1 Tim 3:1-7; 5:17-19; Titus 1:5. 7-11; 2 John 1; 3 John 1) indicates an emerging sense of a hierarchy. But no one figure acts as a *hiereus*, like the priests of the Jewish and the Greco-Roman religions.[11]

---

11 The adjective "priestly" is associated with the Christian believers, drawn into a relationship with God in and through their faith in Jesus. See 1 Peter 2:5; Rev 1:6; 5:10; 20:6. This is the sound biblical background to the important understanding of the community of Christian believers as a "priestly people." See *Lumen Gentium* 9-11. See Moloney, *The Apocalypse of John*, 46–47, 101.

The Catholic Priesthood: A New Testament Reflection

A careful reading of these passages indicates that these "offices" within early Christian communities are not associated with a cultic ministry. They are never associated with the celebration of the Eucharist, and they are described or instructed in a way that suggests they were the senior administrators of a single community. In the Johannine Letters, there may have been several communities involved, but the Johannine "elder" (2 John 1; 3 John 1; Greek: *presbyteros*) is above all a teacher, attempting to protect fragile early Christians from understandings of God, Jesus and the Christian life that he regarded as erroneous. The early use of "bishop and elder" probably had its roots in the Jewish practice, witnessed to in both the Synagogue and at Qumran, of supervising or "overseeing" (the meaning of the Greek noun *ho episkopos* means "the overseer") the life of the community. The diaconal role was to see to the practical needs of members of the community, especially the poorer members, or those most neglected (see Acts 6:1-6).

As a priestly ministry emerged in the second century, the performance of *hieratic* (priestly in the sense of performed by a *hiereus*) ministry was different from the picture one receives of the activities of the overseers, elders and deacons described in the New Testament. It is fair to say that a *hierarchical structure* appears very early in the reflection of the Christian Church. But this characteristic of early Christian communities must be distinguished from the presence of a priestly ministry. This important distinction must be kept in mind in these debates. The figure of Peter, and Jesus' choice of twelve disciples whom the later Church, especially Luke and Paul, named "apostles" are vital keys to an understanding of a very early hierarchical structure.[12] However, while there appears to have been a sense of *hierarchy* in the earliest Church, and reflected in its literature that eventually became our Christian New Testament, there does not appear to be any *hiereus* ("priest") in the early Church, apart from Christ, the

---

12 Much has been written on this. For a comprehensive discussion, supporting the claims made above, see Meier, *A Marginal Jew*, 3:125-97, 221-45.

perfect and everlasting high priest in his communication between God and humankind.

Eucharist: From Jesus to the Early Church

There is strong literary evidence for gatherings of early Christian communities to celebrate the Lord's Supper. The three Synoptic Gospels report a final meal, shared by Jesus and the disciples, during which Jesus takes elements from a traditional ritual meal (and possibly a Passover Meal), bread and wine (Mark 14:17-31; Matt 26:20-35; Luke 22:14-38). Instead of looking back to the past to explain the significance of the elements (the bread as a memory of the manna in the desert and the wine as a memory of the opening of the Reed Sea), Jesus points forward to his death: the bread is his broken body and the wine is his spilt blood "for" others. All the records of this meal indicate, by means of the preposition "for/for the sake of" (Greek: *hyper*) that this death is in some way "for others." This is not only the case for the three Synoptic Gospels (Mark 14:24; Matt 26:28; Luke 22:19), but it is also found in words that probably reflect the Johannine Eucharistic tradition (John 6:51c), and the tradition found in Paul (see 1 Cor 11:24; see also Luke 22:19). There are accounts of such meals celebrated in the Jerusalem Church in the early chapters of the Acts of the Apostles (see Acts 2:42-47; 20:7-11; 27:33-36), but these reports were written by Luke some time in the 80s of the first century and reflect an idealised portrait of the Jerusalem Community.

The situation Paul addresses in Corinth, while not very flattering, is the earliest written evidence we have of the practice of celebrating the Eucharist. It was written some time in the early 50s of the first century, some 20 years after the death of Jesus, and already at that early stage is regarded by Paul as a *Jesus tradition*: "For I received from the Lord what I also handed on to you, that the Lord Jesus on the night when he was betrayed took a loaf of bread ..." (1 Cor 11:23). Unlike the Gospels, where the report of Jesus' final meal with his disciples is set within a broader narrative of his life, death and resurrection, Paul's only reference to Jesus' words on that night is: "This is my body that is for you. Do this in remembrance of me" (1 Cor 11:24) and "This cup is the new covenant in my blood. Do this, as often as you drink it, in remembrance of me" (11:25).

As well as these explicit "meal contexts," during which Jesus shares bread and wine with his disciples, there are other scenes in the Gospel traditions that reflect a Eucharistic background. Not all scholars agree, but the multiplication of the loaves and fishes in the Synoptic (Mark 6:31-44; 8:1-9; Matt 14:13-21; 15:32-39; Luke 9:10-17) and the Johannine (John 6:1-15) traditions, as well as Jesus' gift of the morsel to the disciples, including Judas, in John 13:21-30 reflect the early Church's easy use of language and symbolism that came from a practice central to their emerging uniqueness: the celebration of the Eucharistic meal.[13] The evidence for the origins of this early Christian cultic practice in the life of Jesus is overwhelming. The various forms of Christianity, reflected in the different traditions found in Paul, Mark, Matthew, Luke, and John took the celebration of the Lord's Supper for granted.

There is no evidence for a specifically Christian Priesthood in the New Testament; but the New Testament communities celebrated the Eucharist. This leads to a final, and crucial, historical note, leading to the development of a ministry in the early Church. While the Jerusalem Temple and its Priesthood existed, Judaism and Christianity lived side by side, no doubt with their difficulties, but the Priesthood was linked with the Religion of Israel and the cultic practices of the Jerusalem Temple. Once this situation changed with the destruction of the Temple and the disappearance

---

13 I was privileged to develop this theme at some length as part of the Theological Symposium that prefaced the 51st International Eucharistic Congress, held at Cebu in the Philippines on 24-31 January 2015. See Francis J. Moloney, "'He Loved Them to the End.' Eucharist in the Gospel of John," *The 51st International Eucharistic Congress. Lectures and Catecheses* (Cebu: University of San Carlos Press, 2017), 11-29.

of the Temple Priesthood, after 70 CE early Christians necessarily developed an awareness of their uniqueness, as did the Jews. The latter group turned more and more to the centrality of Torah in their life, given that they could no longer offer cultic sacrifice in the Temple. This movement led to what came to be known as Rabbinic Judaism. Christians focused more intensely upon the Eucharist "as an unbloody sacrifice replacing bloody sacrifices no longer offered in the now-destroyed Temple."[14]

This developing understanding of the Eucharist can be traced in Christian literature from the second century. The author of the *Didache*, which some suggest may have come from the last decade of the first century,[15] instructs Christians: "Assemble on the Lord's Day, breaking bread and celebrating the Eucharist; but first confess your sins that your *sacrifice* (Greek: *thusia*) may be a pure one ... for it was of this that the Lord spoke. 'Everywhere and always offer me a pure sacrifice' (Mal 1:10-11)." As well as speaking of the Eucharist in sacrificial terms, *Didache* 13:3 says that the charismatic prophets are the Christian "high priests." This is possibly the earliest indication of a link between designated individuals and the celebration of the Eucharist (see also *Didache* 10:7). About the same time, writing from Rome to Corinth, Clement draws a parallel between the now defunct Old Testament structure of High Priest, Priest and Levite. A contrast is drawn between the Christian sacrificial practice of the celebration of Eucharist and the rejected cultic practices of the Jerusalem Temple

---

14 Brown, *Priest and Bishop*, 19.

15 For a thorough summary of the discussion of the original place and date of the *Didache*, see Kurt Niederwimmer, *Die Didache*, 2nd ed., Kommentar zu den Apostolischen Vätern 1 (Göttingen: Vandenhoeck & Ruprecht, 1993) 64-80. Niederwimmer convincingly argues for an early second Century date, based on traditions that come from late in the first Century. For a briefer introduction, and the Greek and English text, see Michael W. Holmes, *The Apostolic Fathers. Greek Texts and English Translations*, 3rd ed. (Grand Rapids: Baker Academic, 2007) 334-69. See also the excellent introduction of Clayton N. Jefford, *Reading the Apostolic Fathers. An Introduction* (Peabody, MA: Hendrickson, 1996) 33-51.

(*1 Clement* 40-41).[16] A little later, Justin Martyr (100-165 CE) describes the basic order of the Eucharistic celebration, referring to the minister of the Eucharistic celebration as "he who presides" (*Apologia* 1, 65-67).[17]

Once the celebration of the Eucharist is seen as the central sacrificial cult of the Christian religion, the emergence of a notion of a Christian Priesthood followed rapidly. At the turn of the second and third centuries, Tertullian (160-220 CE) can speak of the bishop as the "high priest" (*summus sacerdos; De Baptismo* 17; CCSL 1, 291) and Hippolytus of Rome (170-235 CE) can refer to the "high priestly spirit" of the bishop (*Apostolic Tradition* 3.5).[18] The evidence points to priestly role being regularly associated with designated office-bearers in the Christian community, and associated with its cultic life.

Over the centuries, the Roman Catholic tradition has looked back to the New Testament accounts of the Last Supper as the moment when Jesus "ordained" the Twelve Apostles. Attractive as this association appears to contemporary Christians, especially the liturgical link made between commemoration of the institution of the Eucharist and the foundation of the Priesthood on Holy Thursday, there is no literary or historical evidence for this tradition. The New Testament largely reflects Jewish communities

---

16 The First Letter of Clement is also dated from late in the first century to early in the second. It was written from Rome to address various issues, especially disunity, in the Christian community in Corinth. For an introduction and the text, see Holmes, *The Apostolic Fathers*, 33-131. See also Jefford, *Reading the Apostolic Fathers*, 98-116. Both the Didache and 1 Clement are regularly found in very early manuscripts containing the books of the New Testament. They were highly regarded in the Western Church.

17 For the full text in English, see Thomas B. Falls, *Saint Justin Martyr. The First Apology, The Second Apology, Dialogue with Trypho, Exhortation to the Greeks, Discourse to the Greeks, The Monarchy or the Rule of God*, The Fathers of the Church (Washington, DC: The Catholic University of America Press, 1948) 104-107. For the citation, see p. 105.

18 For the text, see Gregory Dix, *The Apostolic Tradition of Hippolytus of Rome* (London: SPCK, 1937) 5.

struggling to cope with the loss of land, Temple and Priesthood on the one hand, and the "parting of the ways" between the Jews and the Christian communities on the other. Christians were no longer welcome within Jewish worship (thus, the use of the Greek expression *aposungagōgos* in John 9:22; 12:42; 16:2).[19] These socio-religious dynamics generated the gradual move among Christians to the establishment of its own priesthood, paralleling the priests who served the cultic activities of Greco-Roman and Jewish traditions.

A Eucharistic Priesthood

The Catholic Tradition has rightly caught the *symbolic and sacramental importance* of the relationship between the Eucharist and the Priesthood. But a *historical link* between the Jesus' participation in a meal with his disciples "on the night before he died," and the ordination of the Apostles and Bishops and Priests is impossible. I am sharply aware that Christians, and Christian leadership, find it difficult to accept that such a central Christian belief and practice did not begin in the life and teaching of the Jesus.[20] Not even Jesus could imagine and establish *everything* that has unfolded across the two thousand years of Christian history in three brief years! We are subliminally unwilling to accept the ongoing presence of the Spirit guiding, teaching and enlightening the Church in an ever-unfolding understanding of God: "I have yet many things to say to you, but you cannot bear them now. When the Spirit of truth comes, he will guide you into all truth"

---

19 There is still a hefty debate surrounding how, when, where, and why "the parting of the ways" took place. For a collection of contemporary views, see R. Alan Culpepper and Paul N. Anderson, eds., *John and Judaism. A Contested Relationship in Context*, Resources for Biblical Study 87 (Atlanta: SBL Press, 2017).

20 Unfortunately, this historically indefensible point of view is maintained in *The Catechism of the Catholic Church* (Homebush: Society of Saint Paul, 1994) 1137 §610, citing the Council of Trent.

(John 16:12-13). "And lo, I am with you always, to the close of the age" (Matt 28:20). Jesus Christ gave us a meal that we celebrate in his memory. He did not ordain Priests. A New Testament reflection on the Priesthood must look through the lens of the New Testament's Eucharistic teaching. There we will find what a eucharistically-oriented Priesthood looks like.

The Catholic Priesthood, because of its age-old association with the celebration of the Eucharist, has emerged as a special caste of distinct and much-respected men. This has led to the gradual adoption of distinctive forms of dress, the practice of celibacy, administration of the Sacraments (except for Baptism and Marriage [Baptism can be celebrated by anyone, and the couple celebrate Marriage]), and a strong association with the hierarchy and governance of the Catholic community. The Priesthood has developed into a unique socio-cultural phenomenon. Priests are men, set apart, supported financially by their communities, privileged and powerful intermediaries between human beings and God, between bishops and people, authoritative counsellors in matters that run from political decisions to sexual morality. They have become the unique dispensers of the graces that flow from the Church's Sacramental life and the bearers of authoritative teaching. At least in the Western world, this socially and culturally elite group of men, so long accepted and respected in the Catholic Church and beyond, has fallen upon hard times. A *New Testament Reflection* on the Catholic Priesthood, looking back to the presentation of the Eucharist in the New Testament as its source, suggests an alternative paradigm.

The earliest Christian witness to the practice of the Lord's Supper is found in 1 Corinthians 11:17-34.[21] Throughout 1 Corinthians, Paul addresses problems which have arisen in the community at Corinth. In Paul's discussion of the Corinthians' problematic

---

21 For a more extensive treatment of what follows, see Francis J. Moloney, *Body Broken for a Broken People. Divorce, Remarriage, and the Eucharist* (Mulgrave: Garratt Publishing, 2015) 41-69.

celebration of the Lord's supper, he first attacks the nature of their abuse of the Eucharistic table in 11:17-22. He then reports his tradition of the Eucharistic words (vv. 23-26). More theological conclusions and recommendations close his treatment (vv. 27-34). In vv. 27-28, Paul warns against eating the bread and drinking the cup of the Lord in an "unworthy manner," drawing conclusions from the abuses he described in vv. 17-22. "I hear that there are divisions among you" (v. 18). These divisions are described as follows: "For when the time comes to eat, each of you goes ahead with your own supper, and one goes hungry and another is drunk. What! Do you not have homes to eat and drink in? Or do you show contempt for the Church of God, and humiliate those who have nothing? What should I say to you? Should I commend you in this? In this matter I do not commend you!" (vv. 21-22).

The Lord's supper was supposed to be a common meal, but Paul has heard that this has become impossible at Corinth because such divisions between the wealthy and the poor have arisen that no one was concerned about the other. It would be better for the Corinthians to eat in their own homes, rather than pretend a unity in their Eucharistic celebration which their behaviour belies. In addition to humiliating "those who have nothing," they show they hold true community in contempt. This is the "unworthy manner" of participating in the Eucharist chastised by Paul in v. 27, and the reason for the request that the Corinthians should "examine yourselves" expressed in v. 28.

Within this context of instruction and warning, Paul inserts his tradition of the Eucharistic words of Jesus (vv. 23-26). They are highlighted by the command, repeated over both the bread and the wine, to perform the action of breaking the bread and sharing the cup "in remembrance of me" (vv. 24 and 25). While this twice repeated command may have its origins in the earliest liturgies, it is also a challenge to an appreciation of the Eucharistic nature of the Christian life. To celebrate Eucharist is to commit oneself to a discipleship which "remembers" Jesus – not only in the breaking of the ritual bread and sharing the ritual cup – but also in "imitation" of Jesus, in the ongoing breaking of one's own body and spilling of one's own blood "in remembrance" of Jesus. For this reason, Paul adds: "You proclaim the Lord's death until he comes" (v. 26). It is in the broken body and the spilt blood of a Church of disciples who live the Eucharist which they celebrate that the Lord's death is proclaimed in the world, until he comes again.

Paul's call for unity in 1 Corinthians 11:17-22 is a summons motivated by the need for the Corinthian community "to remember," to practise at the level of life what they proclaims at the level of ritual (vv. 23-26). To continue in their present practice would be to eat the bread and drink the cup "unworthily" (v. 27). Thus they must examine themselves carefully on these issues before approaching the Eucharistic meal (v. 28). In v. 29, Paul warns the Corinthians: "For all who eat and drink without discerning the body eat and drink judgment against themselves." Not to discern the body is to fail to recognise the Lord's presence in the Eucharist in the sense of the Lord who died for us (see v. 24: "This is my body which is for [*hyper*] you)." But "body" also means the context of the community. Ignoring the "body" of Christ, present in the "body" of the community in their Eucharistic meals, the Corinthians proclaim the presence of the Lord in a lie that offends against the "rhythm" of the offering of Christ which they claim to be "remembering" in their celebration. Christians are called to repeat the self-gift of Christ in his memory both in cult and in life. Not to celebrate Eucharist in this way is to "eat and drink judgment" against oneself (v. 29). Not recognising the sacrificed "body" of Jesus in the Eucharist, they offend against the "body" which is the Church, called to repeat that sacrifice in its own life.

The Gospels, written decades after Paul's letter to the Corinthians (Mark: c. 70; Matthew and Luke: c. 85; John: c. 100), continue to develop a rich understanding of Jesus' self-gift in love in narratives that presuppose the celebration of the Eucharist. A brief selection from some well-known narratives will illustrate this.

Mark 14:17-31, the account of the Last Supper in this Gospel, is an example of the practice of framing episodes.[22] Jesus shares a meal with his disciples (14:22-25), but the episodes before and after the meal tell of his disciples' betrayal, denial and flight. (vv. 17-21; 26-31). In vv. 17-21 Jesus "came with the twelve," a group appointed in 3:14 "to be with him." (v. 17). The setting for Jesus' prediction of his betrayal is the meal table, a sacred place among friends. Jesus explains that the betrayer will be "one who is eating with me" (v. 18). Intimacy is heightened by the words of Jesus: "It is one of the twelve, one who is dipping bread in the same dish with me."

A similar attention to the closeness that exists between Jesus and his future betrayers is found in vv. 26-31. He predicts they "will all become deserters" (v. 27). He uses the image of the shepherd and his sheep (v. 27), and his predictions lead to expressions of love and devotion. Peter swears an unfailing loyalty, better than all the others who may fall away (v. 29). He even claims that he is prepared to lay down his life for his master (v. 31). Peter is not alone in swearing loyalty and love: "And all of them said the same."

In the centre of the passage, 14:22-26 reports Jesus' last meal with the disciples, who will betray, deny and abandon him (14:22-26). The theme of table fellowship with the betrayers opens the passage: "While *they* were eating, he took a loaf of bread, and after blessing it he broke it, and *gave it to them*." (v. 22: AT). This theme is continued in the sharing of the cup, where the same recipients are again specified: "Then he took a cup, and after giving thanks, he *gave it to them*, and *all of them drank from it*" (v. 23). The words over the bread and the cup point to the Cross: a body given and blood poured out (vv. 22 and 24), but they also point to something beyond the day of crucifixion. The blood is to be a covenant (v. 24), and he comments that he will "never again drink of the vine until that day when I drink it new in the kingdom of God" (v. 25).

---

22 For a more extensive treatment of what follows, see Moloney, *Body Broken*, 82-97.

The word "until" rings out a message of trust and hope that looks well beyond the events of Good Friday. There is to be a body given and blood poured out which will set up a new covenant reaching beyond the Cross into the definitive establishment of the Kingdom. A covenant with whom? The body broken and the blood poured out sets up a new covenant with *the fragile disciples* who were the first recipients of that bread and cup. Mark has given us an account of Jesus' gift of himself unto death to set up a new and lasting kingdom with the characters in the story. Jesus loves his failing disciples with a love which is in no way matched by the love which they bear him.

The theme of a "journey" is important across the Gospel of Luke and the Acts of the Apostles.[23] Throughout the Gospel, a journey leads to Jerusalem, where the paschal events take place (see especially Luke 9:51). At the beginning of Acts, the first Christian community is still in Jerusalem. In Jerusalem, the Spirit is given to the community, and a second journey begins, reaching out to the ends of the earth. The city of Jerusalem is the center of God's history. The early Church was founded in that city, the Holy Spirit was given there, and from there a mission began which would reach out to the ends of the earth (see Luke 24:46-49; Acts 1:8). In the opening remarks of the journey to Emmaus (24:13-35), in the midst of the paschal events, two disciples are going to Emmaus, "about seven miles *away from Jerusalem*" (v. 13: AT). They are walking away from Jerusalem, the central point of God's story, away from God's design of the journey of the Son of God from Nazareth to Jerusalem, and of the Christian community from Jerusalem to the ends of the earth. They tell him of their expectations: "We had hoped that he was the one to redeem Israel" (v. 21). Jesus' way of responding to the design of God (see vv. 25-27) has not fulfilled their expectations of the one who would redeem Israel.

---

23 For a more extensive treatment of what follows, see Moloney, *Body Broken*, 144-65.

They know of his life: Jesus of Nazareth, a prophet mighty in word and deed (v. 19). They know of his death: "Our chief priests and leaders handed him over to be condemned to death and crucified him" (v. 20). They know of the events at the tomb: "it is now the third day" (v. 21), women have been at the tomb early in the morning, but they did not find his body (v. 23). They have even heard the Easter proclamation: there has been a vision of angels who said: "He is alive" (v. 23:AT). The two disciples know everything ... but him they did not see, and thus they have had enough. They continue their walk away from Jerusalem.

Jesus "interpreted to them the things about himself in all the scriptures" (v. 27). At the meal they recognised him in the breaking of the bread (vv. 30-31). Jesus followed, joined, and journeyed with these failing disciples, as they walked away from God's design. He has come to meet them, to make himself known to them and to draw them back to the journey of God through opening the word of God to them, and through the breaking of the bread. Touched in their failure, the immediate reaction of the failed disciples is to turn back on their journey: "That same hour they got up and returned to Jerusalem" (v. 33). Once they arrive back, they are told: "The Lord has risen indeed, and he has appeared to Simon!" (v. 34). They have come back home, but only because the Lord has reached out to them in their brokenness, and made himself known to them in the breaking of the bread. As with Mark, and also with Matthew who has repeated Mark's story (Matt 26:17-35), the Evangelist Luke has no hesitation in setting the Eucharistic presence of the Lord in the midst of the broken disciples.[24]

In John 13:1-38, Jesus' unconditional self-gift to fragile broken disciples reaches its most theological expression.[25] The footwashing

---

24 Matthew is even more forthright. His only substantial addition to his Markan source is his indication that the blood of the covenant is poured out "for the forgiveness of sins" (Matt 26:28).
25 See Moloney, "Eucharist in the Gospel of John," 11-29. See also Idem, *Body Broken*, 175-203.

and its aftermath (vv. 1-17), lead to words from Jesus (vv. 18-20). These words are followed by the gift of the morsel and its aftermath (vv. 21-38). In the footwashing (vv. 1-17), Jesus shows his love for his disciples in his gift of himself for them and in the gift of his example to them (v. 15). The passage highlights his knowledge of the ways of God (v. 3), and his knowledge of all that is about to happen (v. 11). This series of gracious gifts of Jesus to his disciples is contrasted by the themes of the betrayer (vv. 2, 10-11), and the ignorance of the disciples (vv. 6-10). The gift of the morsel (vv. 21-38) reflects the gifts of the Eucharist and the new commandment (vv. 34-35). There is the repeated reference to the betrayer (vv. 21-26a), the theme of the ignorance of the disciples (vv. 26b-29), the exit of Judas for the betrayal (v. 30) and the prophecy of the denial of Peter (vv. 36-38). Repeating the argument of vv. 1-17 in vv. 21-38, we find Jesus' love for his disciples in the gift of the Eucharistic morsel, and the gift of the new commandment of love, set in the midst of the ignorance of the disciples, the denial of Peter and the betrayal of Judas. To failing disciples Jesus has insisted: "For I have set you an example, that you should do as I have done to you" (v. 15), and "I gave you a new commandment, that you love one another. Just as I have loved you, you should also love one another" (v. 34).

It is at the centre of this context of unconditional love given to failing disciples that we situate the centre-piece of 13:1–38: vv. 18-20:

> I am not speaking of you all; I know whom I have chosen. But it is to fulfil the scripture, "The one who ate my bread has lifted his heel against me."
> I tell you this now, before it takes place, so that when it does occur you may believe that I AM HE.
> Very truly, I tell you, whoever receives one whom I send receives me; and whoever receives me receives him who sent me.

The Fourth Evangelist has deliberately set vv. 18-20 between two flanking passages (vv. 1-17 and vv. 21-38). In v. 18, Jesus speaks of having no illusions about the ones whom he has chosen. One of them will become the betrayer who has shared in the Eucharistic morsel and another will deny him. Nevertheless, in v. 20, Jesus speaks of his intention to send forth his disciples. John 13:1-38 is marked by the extraordinary love of God, revealed in Jesus, who gives himself in the footwashing and the eucharistic morsel. He knows whom he has chosen; he is aware that one who shares his table will betray him, another will deny him and that all the others are unable to understand him, yet he loves them and sends them out to proclaim both himself and his Father.

The theological significance of this message is summed up in the central statement of the whole of 13:1-38: " I tell you this now, before it takes place, so that when it does occur you may believe that I AM HE." (v. 19). Jesus loves his own so much that he chooses them (v. 18a), and sends them out as his presence (v. 20). Yet, these very loved ones are responsible for his death on a Cross (v. 18b). It is precisely in this unconditional gift of himself to people who do not love him that he reveals who he is.

The Fourth Evangelist uses the expression "I am," an expression with a long history in the literature of Israel, to refer to the living presence of a God who is made known among the people, and applies it to the person of Jesus. John informs his readers that only when love reveals itself in such an extraordinary fashion, loving "to the end" (13:1) those who do not love, him, can one begin to understand the God whom Jesus has come to make known. When these things happen, when his disciples have betrayed, denied and abandoned him, and he is "lifted up" on the Cross (see 3:13; 8:28; 12:32), then his disciples of all times will know that Jesus is the revelation of God: "I tell you this now, before it takes place, that when it does take place you may believe that I AM" (v. 19).

Conclusion

This sketch of some New Testament presentations of the Eucharist does not pretend to exhaust all the nuances. Even less does it pretend to touch upon the rich theological, liturgical, symbolic, cultural and ritual developments of the Church's understanding and celebration of the Eucharist, as it has developed and emerged over two thousand years of Christian history. What has been outlined in Paul, the Synoptic Gospels and John, however, might serve as a suitable point of departure in our search for the discovery of a genuinely New Testament understanding of the Catholic Priesthood. The current crises now present in every corner of the Catholic Church demands that we look at ourselves again, and engage in a genuine "conversion," a *metanoia* as the New Testament would call it – a "turning away" from much current thought and practice.

The New Testament's use of pre-existent Eucharistic thought and practice reflects *at least* the following convictions:

- The Eucharist is a gift of God, given in and through the death and resurrection of his Son, Jesus Christ (Mark 14:22-24; Matt 26:26-28; Luke 22:19-21; John 6:51c; 1 Cor 11:24-25).

- It is never an end in itself. In all New Testament traditions, the Eucharist is "for" (*hyper*) others.

- The Eucharist provides access to the saving power of the death and resurrection of Jesus, something that is needed by all who frequent the Lord's table. All the New Testament narratives insist that the Eucharist is for the fragile and the broken, the unique symbol of Jesus' manifestation of God's endless love (John 13:1).

- The celebration of the Eucharist summons participants to break their own bodies and spill their own blood "in memory" of Jesus. "As often as *you* eat this bread and drink the cup, *you* proclaim the Lord's death until he comes" (1 Cor 11:26).

- It serves as the lived experience of two great gifts: Jesus' example of self-gift that all who claim to be followers of Jesus are to follow (13:15) and the gift of the new commandment of mutual love (13:34-35).

If the Priesthood emerged in the Christian tradition as a Eucharistic ministry, perhaps the contemporary socio-cultural model of the Catholic Priesthood that is undergoing such crisis needs to be rethought in those terms. A paradigm emerges, different from the one outlined as I opened these reflections on the Priesthood. This form of life within the Church is part of the universal call to the perfection of love, to which all the baptised, whatever their socio-cultural and political status, have been called (see *Lumen Gentium* 39-42, especially 40; Pope Francis, *Gaudete et Exsultate* 6-24).

There is no place within a Eucharistic community for a privileged caste. Priests, like everyone else who prays that God's will be done and God's kingdom come, as Jesus taught us (see Luke 11:2; Matt 6:10), are called to recognise their brokenness. They are, as Henri Nouwen once so eloquently argued "wounded healers." It is as fellow-sinners, on a shared Eucharistic journey toward the parousia, that Priests will respond to their vocation to be ministers of the Eucharist. "I shall not drink again of this fruit of the vine until that day when I drink it new with you in my Father's kingdom" (Matt 26:29. See also Mark 14:25; Luke 22:16). Eucharist is not primarily a cultic ritual, but a way of life, breaking one's body and spilling one's blood, in memory of Jesus, until he comes again (see 1 Cor 11:26; *Sacrosanctum Concilium* 48).

Priests are called to recognise that their *primary* mission is to those most in need; those reaching out for God's goodness, love and forgiveness. This element in the Priest's vocation can often be hard to grasp, as just who the most poor and needy might be cannot always be determined with measurable social and economic criteria. The hunger for the transcendent is a genuine poverty that crosses all ages and all social, ethnic, religious and economic boundaries. It is this hunger that a Eucharistic ministry must serve, not only in ritual, but above all by the Priest's understanding what he does and imitating what he handles. At the end of the Rite for the Ordination of a Priest, the Bishop instructs the candidate: "Know what you are doing; and imitate the mystery you celebrate"

(*Agnoscite quod agitis; imitamini quod tractatis*).²⁶ The Eucharist is not a prayer wheel that we spin every morning, and more solemnly on Sundays. It is not only cult; but above all a way of life, the grammar of a Christian life.

This does not appear to be the view of some Priests today, and of some who aspire to be Priests. It is not always the fault of the individual, as there is an expectation among many of the faithful that the Priest be somehow "different" from them. The Priest is "better," and thus "superior" in the eyes of God. This is manifested in different forms of dressing, the use of special titles (Reverend, Most Reverend, Excellency, Eminence, Holiness), and privileged social recognition. In some cultures more than others, such clericalism is forced upon the Priest. Such a way of life generates a figure with an authority that betrays his vocation to love and service, as it is based on superiority and the exercise of power. Consequently, the Eucharistic nature of the Catholic Priesthood is betrayed. Such a betrayal leads to the shepherd not only abandoning his sheep but abusing them in his use and abuse of clerical power. Pope Francis has pointed to this view of the Priest as the root cause of our contemporary crisis. He urgently calls for its elimination so that we might once again be the Church of Jesus Christ.

> It is impossible to think of a conversion of our activity as a Church that does not include the active participation of all the members of God's people. Indeed, whenever we have tried to replace, or silence, or ignore, or reduce the People of God to small elites, we end up creating communities, projects, theological approaches, spiritualities, and structures without roots, without memory, without faces, without bodies and

---

26 For the English text, see International Commission on English in the Liturgy, *The Roman Pontifical. Revised by Decree of the Second Vatican Ecumenical Council and Published by Authority of Pope Paul VI* (Washington, DC: ICEL, 1978) 201. Similarly instructive are the words directed to a newly ordained Deacon: "Believe what you read, teach what you believe, and practise what you teach" (*Roman Pontifical*, 135).

ultimately, without lives. This is clearly seen in a peculiar way of understanding the Church's authority, one common in many communities where sexual abuse and the abuse of power and conscience have occurred. Such is the case with clericalism, an approach that not only nullifies the character of Christians, but also tends to diminish and undervalue the baptismal grace that the Holy Spirit has placed in the heart of our people. *Clericalism, whether fostered by priests themselves or by lay persons, leads to an excision in the ecclesial body that supports and helps to perpetuate many of the evils that we are condemning today. To say 'no' to abuse is to say an emphatic 'no' to all forms of clericalism* (Pope Francis, *Letter to the People of God*, Tuesday 21 August 2018. Stress mine).

Our New Testament reflection on the Priesthood should serve as a point of departure for all renewal of ministry in the church. No doubt other aspects of the New Testament's summons to holiness and mission could further enrich the above reflection. Developments in our Eucharistic theology and practice over the ages, in a Spirit-guided Church, must also play their part for an understanding of the Priesthood. However, where one starts a journey, and the road one takes, will shape all that follows. The Catholic Priesthood had its beginnings in the Eucharistic life of the Church. It should be nourished and renewed there.

5

The Book of Revelation: Hope in Dark Times

The Book of Revelation is no doubt the most challenging book in the New Testament. Most mainstream Christians do not read it, but many Christians have used the fierce and often threatening imagery as biblical judgment against individual people and institutions across the ages. This practice was passionately and widely used across all sides of the tragic and often violent divisions that shook the Christian church and European society in general in the sixteenth century.[1] It continues to guide many in their search to envision what will happen at the end of all time. Unfortunately, some fanatical groups (spectacularly, the mass suicides of members of the People's Temple at Jonesville in North Guyana in 1978, and the Siege of the Branch Davidian settlement at Waco, Texas, in 1993) have done great damage to themselves and to an understanding of Christianity through an incorrect reading of the Book of Revelation. It is not a book for religious fanatics, but over the centuries such Christians have kept it "in the news." It may seem odd to suggest that the message of this ambiguous and at times violent book may offer "hope in dark times."

Despite its challenging nature, the Christian Churches, especially in Western society, use the Book of Revelation in their liturgies. This is not so much the case in the East, where a long suspicion

---

[1] The art of Lucas Cranach the Elder (1472-1553) and Albrecht Dürer (1474-1528) are eloquent testimonies of that era. But they were not alone in graphically casting opposing Christian communities as the Antichrist, an expression that never appears in the Book of Revelation. See Eire, *Reformations*, 178-84.

of its helpfulness as a "Word of God" has existed.[2] In the Roman Catholic tradition, the so-called Office of Readings, part of its official *Prayer of the Church*, reads Revelation, in its entirety, from the Second to the Fifth Week of the Easter Season. At other places in the Church's liturgy, it appears regularly, especially as canticles and short readings in the *Prayer of the Church*, in the weekly readings or at the Sunday celebration of the Eucharist.[3]

From very early times, interpreters understood Revelation as the work an author named "John," writing to fellow-Christians from the island of Patmos, just off the coast of modern-day Western Turkey. Based on his words in Revelation 1:9: "I, John, your brother who share with you in Jesus the persecution and the kingdom and the patient endurance, was on the island called Patmos because of the word of God and the testimony of Jesus," John is understood to be suffering some form of isolation and imprisonment at the hands of Roman authorities for his witness to Christian faith.

A Christian Apocalypse?

Most contemporary commentators regard the text as directed to Asian Christians, identified in the seven letters found in 2:1-3:22, who are suffering persecution and martyrdom. The use of powerful images, clothed in highly symbolic and sometimes unimaginable language, tells of the mysterious but inevitable violent intervention of God at the end of time, conquering all evil powers. The classification of the Book of Revelation as a Christian

---

[2] See Koester, *Revelation*, 33-35. Koester shows the mixed reception the document received in the east down to 350 CE and concludes: "Ambivalence about Revelation would continue in the eastern churches" (p. 35).

[3] The heavy concentration upon texts from Revelation during the Easter Season, and on Sundays (that recall the Easter event) raises the question of the relevance of the dictum *lex orandi lex credendi* for the interpretation of the book. See Francis J. Moloney, *Reading Revelation at Easter Time* (Collegeville: Liturgical Press, 2020).

apocalypse determines this dominant interpretation. It exhorts Asian Christians to resist the many evils associated with the Roman imperial system, even in the face of persecution and death. In the end, Rome will be destroyed and God will reign supreme.[4]

Late in the first and into the second Christian century, Jews and Christians developed an abundant form of literature classified as "apocalyptic." Such literature had already appeared in the Old Testament, especially in the Book of Daniel that appeared in mid-160 CE, during a time of severe persecution in Israel under the Seleucids, ruled by Antiochus IV from 175-164 BCE. In general terms, apocalyptic literature addresses communities that are facing difficulties that no human endeavour can reverse. Apocalypses are at one-and-the-same time earthly, because they address a human situation; and other-worldly, because divine intervention into human suffering resolves the crisis. *In the end*, God will punish and destroy the wicked, while the persevering faithful and those slain for the faith will be victorious. I have accentuated *in the end* because this is an essential element of apocalyptic literature. In more technical terms, the conflict between the good and the wicked is resolved by God's *eschatological intervention*, a decisive "end of human history" event.[5]

---

4 Although they differ in detail, influential representatives of this widely held apocalyptic interpretative paradigm are: Adela Yarbro Collins, *The Apocalypse*, New Testament Message 22 (Wilmington, DE: Michael Glazier, 1979); David E. Aune, *Revelation*, 3 vols., Word Biblical Commentary 52A–C (Dallas: Word, 1979-98); G. K. Beale, *The Book of Revelation*, New International Greek Testament Commentary (Grand Rapids: Eerdmans, 1999); Heinz Giesen, *Die Offenbarung des Johannes*, Regensburger Neues Testament (Regensburg: Pustet, 1997); Pierre Prigent, *Commentary on the the Apocalypse of St. John*, trans. Wendy Pradels (Tübingen: Mohr Siebeck, 2001); Ian Boxall, *The Revelation of Saint John*, Black's New Testament Commentary (London: A. & C. Black, 2006); Edmondo F. Lupieri, *A Commentary on the Apocalypse of John*, trans. Maria Poggi Johnson and Adam Kamesar, Italian Texts and Studies on Religion and Society (Grand Rapids: Eerdmans, 2009); James L. Resseguie, *The Revelation of John: A Narrative Commentary* (Grand Rapids: Baker Academic, 2009).

5 These few sentences do not do justice to the complexity of the history and the nature of the Jewish apocalyptic movement and its literature. Among many, see the authoritative work of John J. Collins, *Apocalypse, Prophecy, and Pseudepigraphy. On Jewish Apocalyptic Literature* (Grand Rapids: Eerdmans,

The Book of Revelation certainly uses an apocalyptic literary form, but this form has been adapted by a Christian author who is convinced that Jesus, the slain Lamb (see 5:6; 13:8), has been raised. As the author, a man named "John" (see 1:1, 4, 9; 22:8), opens his book he exclaims: "To him who loves us and freed us from our sins by his blood, and made us to be a kingdom, priests serving his God and Father, to him be glory and dominion forever" (1:5b-6. See also 5:10). This is hardly the voice of a suffering figure, asking his audience to persevere until God makes a final intervention to destroy the destroyers (see 11:18). On the contrary, he believes that Christians are *already members of a royal priesthood* because of the death and resurrection of Jesus. It is hardly Christian to ask believers to wait, and perhaps suffer, across a period that will lead to God's final intervention. What follows will suggest that the Book of Revelation, despite the literary form that it borrows from Jewish and Christian apocalyptic literature, is a Christian book, not a traditional apocalypse, but rather an extraordinary instruction on "hope in dark times."

Date and Author

Even though we correctly read and interpret Revelation as a unified literary piece, its final form probably resulted from a long literary journey marked by years of epistolary communication, missionary preaching, prophetic utterance and even liturgical experiences. There appear to be hints of the first documented persecution of Christians by the Emperor Nero (64 CE), who ruled from 54-68 CE, and allusions to the late first century widespread sentiment that Nero was not dead but would return from the East

---

2015). His definition of an "apocalypse" is widely accepted: "A genre of revelatory literature within a narrative framework, in which a revelation is mediated by an otherworldly being to a human recipient, disclosing a transcendent reality with is both temporal, in so far as it envisions eschatological salvation, and spiritual, insofar as it involved another, supernatural world" (pp. 4-5).

(Parthia) to overthrow current Roman authority. This so-called *Nero-redivivus* expectation is generally (but not only) associated with such passages as the description of the beast rising out of the earth in 13:12: "It exercises all authority of the beast in its presence and makes all the inhabitants of the earth worship the first beast, whose mortal wound was healed," and the interpretation of the number 666 in 13:18 as "Nero."[6]

Since late in the second Christian century, especially under of the influence of Irenaeus' *Against Heresies* 5.30.3 (c. 180 CE), the Book of Revelation has been associated with the latter years of the Emperor Domitian (Emperor: 81-96 CE). It is possible that traditions coming from across fifty years, from the 60s till the end of the first century CE formed the Book of Revelation as we have it in our Bibles. Its final articulation, however, forms a carefully constructed literary, pastoral, and theological unit.[7] Justin Martyr (100-165 CE. See his *Dialogue with Trypho* 81.4) already regarded the book as part of early Christian literature. From the time of Irenaeus, the author has been identified with the Apostle, John the son of Zebedee, although some claimed that this could not be the case, given the obscurity and complexity of the book (Gaius: early third century CE; Dionysius of Alexandria: latter half of the third century). It differed too radically from the Johannine Gospel and Letters. The first Christian church historian, Eusebius, who reports the views of Gaius and Dionysius, also indicated his doubts

---

6 Giving numerical value to the letters of the Greek "Nerōn Caesar" produces 666. See especially Richard Bauckham, *The Climax of Prophecy. Studies in the Book of Revelation* Edinburgh: T. & T. Clark 84-407.

7 Earlier scholarship questioned this. See especially Robert H. Charles, *A Critical and Exegetical Commentary on the Revelation of St. John*, International Critical Commentary (Edinburgh: T. & T. Clark, 1920). The case for literary unity has been strongly argued by Leonard L. Thompson, *The Book of Revelation: Apocalypse and Empire* (New York: Oxford University Press, 1990) 37-42, and is nowadays generally taken for granted (see Corsini, Boring, Bauckham, *The Climax*, x; Boxall, Koester). However, Aune, *Revelation*, 1:cxviii-cxxxiv, has recently argued for identifiable "editions" in the canonical text.

about traditional Johannine authorship in his *Historia Ecclesiastica* (3.28; 7.25) early in the fourth century CE (c. 322-326 CE).

Nowadays, most would claim that it is not possible for us to identify the person and the role of the author with any precision. The author names himself "John," and this claim should be accepted. It was a widely used name, but there are no clear indications who this "John" might be. We simply do not have enough information from the world that produced Revelation, or from the document itself, to make a firm decision about the precise identity of the "John" of Revelation. David Aune, one of the most significant commentators on the Book of Revelation, satisfactorily identifies the author as follows:

> While the final author-editor of Revelation was named "John," it is not possible to identify him with any other early Christian figures of the same name, including John the son of Zebedee or the shadowy figure of John the Elder. The otherwise unknown author of Revelation in its final form was probably a Palestinian Jew who had emigrated to the Roman province of Asia. ... He regarded himself as a Christian prophet.[8]

The Jewishness of John is strikingly evident in his extraordinary use of the Sacred Scriptures of Israel, and his familiarity with the literary forms of Jewish apocalyptic. The text of the Book of Revelation is full of repeated allusions to the Scriptures, especially the Torah, Isaiah, Ezekiel, and Daniel. However, unlike other early Christian authors, John never cites his biblical sources. But his literary world is entirely Jewish.[9]

---

[8] Aune, *Revelation*, 1:lvi. I have modified Aune's description by eliminating his identification of the author as a Jew fleeing during the first Jewish revolt in 66-70 CE. This cannot be proven.

[9] On John's use of Israel's Sacred Scriptures, see Beale, *Revelation*, 76-99, and Steve Moyise, *The Old Testament and the Book of Revelation*, Journal for the Study of the New Testament supplement Series 115 (Sheffield: Sheffield Academic Press, 1995). Although they disagree on John's use of them, Beale and Moyise argue convincingly for Israel's Scriptures as the determining source for the Book of Revelation.

A Christian Prophecy?

The use of the letters to the seven churches (2:1-3:22) links Revelation to the genre of a letter, although those "letters" do not follow the traditional form of an early Christian letter. No doubt the document was written by a Christian to be communicated to fellow-Christians, and the use of letter-features indicates that such was the case. However, its major literary characteristics are apocalyptic and prophecy. The problem with labelling Revelation as a Christian version of traditional Jewish "apocalyptic" is that this label determines the interpretation. To use a well-worn image: the tail wags the dog. This approach does not do justice to the fact that the victory of the Lamb is portrayed as *already won* across the narrative.

After the epistolary salutation of 1:1-3, Jesus Christ is presented in the prologue to the document as part of a heavenly trinity, the first-born from among the dead, and the ruler of kings on earth (vv. 4-5). The audience participates in the letters to the seven churches, which may have a deeper meaning than seven letters of exhortation and warnings to seven churches in Asia, indicating the recipients of John's document (2:1-3:22). Behind the letters, the audience senses allusions to Israel's sacred history, from the primeval history of Genesis (2:4-5, 7) to Christ, standing at the door, knocking (3:20). The promises made to the victors across the letters (see 2:7, 11, 17, 26-28; 3:5, 12, 21) may be an appeal to the audience to be a truly Christian people and church, "a kingdom of priests, serving his God and Father" (1:6. See also 5:10).[10] The letters are followed by the vision of a solemn liturgy that takes place in heaven (4:1-5:15). The climax of that vision is the appearance of a Lamb, already victorious: slain yet standing (5:6). The heavenly court sings his praise, recognising that his death has ransomed all humankind

---

10 Many of the promises to the victors in the letters of 2:1-3:22 return in the description and the role of the New Jerusalem in 21:9-22:5. See Corsini, *Apocalisse*, 383-86; Boxall, *Revelation*, 312; Resseguie, *Narrative Commentary*, 258; Ugo Vanni, "Liturgical Dialogue as a Literary Form in the Book of Revelation," *New Testament Studies* 37 (1991) 348-64.

(5:9-14). *Because of this* he is "worthy to take the scroll and open its seals" (v. 9). The Lamb receives universal praise and worship (vv. 11-14). The "narrative" has only just begun, yet John has proclaimed that the slain yet standing Lamb is already victorious.

This victory is narrated *before* the sevens of the seals, the trumpets, and the bowls, and is told again as each seven comes to closure. It is repeated in the silence that greets the opening of the seventh Seal (8:1) marking the end of the period from creation to Jesus' death and resurrection (see 7:1-8), and the establishment of period of universal salvation enabled by that death and resurrection (7:9-17). It is promised in the blowing of the sixth trumpet that "in the days when the seventh angel is to blow his trumpet, the mystery of God will be fulfilled" (10:7). Consequently, the blowing of the seventh trumpet results in the opening of God's temple, as "the kingdom of the world has become the kingdom of the Lord and his Christ" (11:15-19).

After a three-fold preparation, addressing the ambiguity of the human condition (12:1-18), describing the action of Satan's agents in spreading evil (13:1-18), and God's initial intervention on behalf of the saints of Israel (14:1-20), the seven bowls are poured out in 15:1-16:21. Again prefaced by a heavenly encounter (15:1-8), the lines are drawn for battle (16:1-21). The battle of Harmagedon tells of the definitive conflict between good and evil at the cross of Jesus Christ.[11] The victory is once more announced: "It is done" (16:17). The three-fold consequences of this definitive victory are then spelt out in detail. Babylon is destroyed (17:1-19:10), all evil power is definitively eliminated by God's victory in the death and resurrection of Jesus (19:11-20:15), and the chosen ones are gathered into the messianic kingdom that may not be "other-worldly," but a God-given Christian community (21:9-22:5).

---

11 The transliteration of *harmagedōn* as "Harmagedon" respects the NRSV. In English commentary and in popular reference to an end-time battle, however, it is frequently rendered as "Armegaddon."

John's audience is not given a road map to God's other-worldly eschatological victory but is roundly and repeatedly instructed that life and light have been made available in the New Jerusalem, the Christian community as it should be (see 22:1-5). Revelation does not hold its audience in anxious tension, dominated by exhortation to "endure" persecution and suffering, or "resist" false claims to divinity, waiting for God's final saving intervention. These themes, especially the theme of "resistance," are certainly present, but they are not the key to its secrets. John repeatedly affirms that the victory has already been won by "the Lamb who was slain from the foundation of the world" (13:8 AT).[12]

Among others, Craig Koester has recognised this odd aspect of the document when read as a thoroughgoing example of an apocalyptic literary form. He points out, as I have, that "Revelation departs from the usual pattern" of apocalyptic literature. He states that "[t]he eschatological struggle had already begun with the Messiah's exaltation and would culminate at his return. Those events define the present time."[13] But this does not explain John's repeated claim that the victory has already been won; indeed, "It is done" (16:17). For John, it has not "already begun" with the Messiah's exaltation. It is not "in process," but has been realised

---

12 This is the obvious translation of the Greek of 13:8: *hou ou gegraptai to onoma autou en tōi bibliōi tēs zōēs tou arniou tou esphagmenou apo katabolēs kosmou*. The NRSV, however, translates: "and all the inhabitants of the earth will worship it, everyone whose name has not been written from the foundation of the world in the book of life of the lamb that was slaughtered." The translators could not accept that the Lamb was slaughtered from the foundation of the world. They place the better translation in a note to the text. Aune, *Revelation*, 2:747, agrees with the NRSV translators, commenting that "it is logically and theologically impossible to make sense of the statement that 'the Lamb was slaughtered before the foundation of the world'." Koester, *Revelation*, 575, agrees. Rejecting what is clearly stated by the Greek, they fail to see the unique theological contribution John makes to developing Christian thought, with its own logic, as they work with a linear time that John transcends.

13 Koester, *Revelation*, 107.

in the perennially available saving action of God in the death and resurrection of Jesus. It is available in the New Jerusalem, the Christian church.

No doubt the recipients of John's Book of Revelation faced difficulties. Many of these difficulties were created by the widespread influence of the Greco-Roman religious practices within the powerful and universal political presence of the Roman Empire. Some of them, if we are to judge by what is said to the seven churches (see 2:4, 14-16, 20-23; 3:1-3, 15-16), arise from the fragility of their own commitment. But John's primary concern is not to exhort them to wait in faith and hope for God's final eschatological victory. The document is studded, from beginning to end, with proclamations of the victory of God from all time in and through the slain and risen Lamb (see 5:6, 9-14, 7:12-8:1; 11:15-19; 16:17-21; 18:20-24; 19:1-8, 17-21; 20:11-15; 21:1-22:5). There must be a tension, as in all Christian literature, between what God has already achieved in and through Jesus Christ, and his final return. But the decisive victory has been won. God's saving history, revealed throughout Israel's story and in the Christian church, rejoices in what God has done for humankind across history through the saving event of the death and resurrection of Jesus Christ, from before the foundation of the world. Although not a solitary voice in the New Testament (see Rom 16:25-26; Col 1:17-20; Eph 1:1-7; 2 Tim 1:9-10), John makes a singular contribution to emerging Christian thought by associating the saving power of Jesus Christ's death and resurrection with the entire course of human history (see 5:6; 13:8).[14]

---

14 The widespread Eastern Christian iconographic theme of the *Anastasis* portrays the risen Jesus' *descensio ad inferos* (descent into hell), leading Adam and Eve into life by taking their hands. The Old Testament kings and prophets look on. (See the rightly famous *Anastasis* fresco in the Eleventh-century Church of Holy Saviour in Chora). Although the artistic tradition is associated with the *temporal*, indicating what happened in the silence of Holy Saturday (see 8:1), it can also be interpreted as an indication of the *transtemporal* saving effects of Jesus' death and resurrection "from the foundation of the world" (13:8).

The recipients of Revelation were certainly made aware of what God has *already* achieved. They are nevertheless exhorted to call out: "Come, Lord Jesus!" (22:20). The use of the category "realised eschatology" does not indicate that all expectations of God's final intervention in the return of Jesus Christ as judge have been eliminated from John's understanding of sacred history.[15] The recipients of Revelation are exhorted to live confidently in the glitter of a Greco-Roman world, aware of the saving effects of the death and resurrection of Jesus. But they must still face the challenges of a world marked by the ambiguous presence of grace and sin: "Let the evildoer still do evil, and the filthy still be filthy, and the righteous still do right, and the holy still be holy" (22:11. See also vv. 14–15).[16] Such ambiguity will be finally resolved only when the Lord Jesus comes (22:20).

John regards his work as prophecy (1:3; 19:10; 22:7, 10, 18, 19). He has been given a commission to prophesy (10:11). A link with traditional biblical prophecy is certainly a feature of John's practice of interlacing his narrative with allusions to the biblical prophets, especially Isaiah, Ezekiel, and Daniel. The Hebrew Bible, and not the speculations of Jewish or Jewish-Christian apocalyptic, forms the essential literary backbone to Revelation, even though it is never directly cited.[17] There was another understanding of the expression "prophet" in early Christianity, a prolongation of the spirit of traditional prophecy that makes a link with both the Hebrew Bible and the message of Jesus. Contemporary Gospel studies show that many of the so-called "words of Jesus" are in

---

15 In this, the Seer of Revelation matches the strong presence of a realised eschatology that does not ignore the importance of a traditional end-time eschatology of the Fourth Gospel. See *New Testament Matters I* pp. 179–203: "God, Eschatology, and 'This World': Ethics in the Gospel of John."
16 Although highlighted in the epilogue of Revelation (see 22:11, 14-15), the theme of the ongoing presence of evil and lack of repentance, despite God's action in the death and resurrection of Jesus Christ, is regularly stated (see 2:1-3:22; 16:8-9, 10-11, 21; 18:4; 21:8, 27; 22:3).
17 See above, n. 9.

fact "words of early Christian prophets." As M. Eugene Boring puts it: "Christian prophets were thus those who spoke the message of the risen Lord directly to the Christian community."[18] John's prophetic utterances address Christians at the end of the first century with the message of the saving effects of the death and resurrection of Jesus.

Genre Bending

In his 2001 Presidential address to the Society of Biblical Literature, Harold W. Attridge suggested that the author of the Fourth Gospel regularly used traditional genres that lead an audience to expect usual outcomes. But he "bends" them, thus taking an audience into unexpected and unexplored possibilities.[19] He describes the practice as follows:

> In many cases where it is possible to identify significant generic parallels, and therefore presume that the form in question generates regular expectations, the reader encounters something quite odd about the way in which the generic conventions seem to work.[20]

John's marriage of letter-prophetic-apocalyptic literary forms, with the dominant form being apocalyptic, "bends" expectations. The expectation is that an author's use of apocalyptic envisions an eschatological salvation.[21] While the message of God's intervention in the descent of the heavenly Jerusalem remains in place, for John the victory has already been won, and the gift of the heavenly Jerusalem refers to the earthly reality of the Christian church. The key to the genre bending in Revelation is the death and resurrection

---

18 Boring, *Revelation*, 25.
19 Harold W. Attridge, "Genre Bending in the Fourth Gospel," *Journal of Biblical Literature* 121 (2002) 1-21.
20 Attridge, "Genre Bending," 11.
21 See above, n. 5, for John J. Collins' widely accepted description of apocalyptic, where God's eschatological intervention is an essential part of the genre.

of Jesus of Nazareth, a consequence of the incarnation, an event that took place once-and-for-all within a human story. For John, this event transformed human history, from the beginning of time till the present age. It is the center-point of God's perennial saving presence, giving meaning to the whole of human history.[22]

Further Questions

There is no evidence that Patmos was a penal settlement for persecuted Christians. The only piece of evidence is Revelation 1:9. Perhaps John's self-introduction may be more about his preparedness to undergo trials because of his missionary and prophetic role: "because of the word of God and the witness to Jesus" (AT of *dia ton logon tou theou kai tēn martyrion Iēsou*) than his endurance as a persecuted Christian. As Craig Koester admits: "John is the only person known to be sent there."[23] Too much has been constructed upon this "decidedly unimaginative" (Boxall) biographical interpretation of 1:9.

Despite Eusebius' claim that he was a violent persecutor of Christians (*Historia Ecclesiastica* 3.17-20), there is little or no

---

22 The remainder of this essay, starting from some contemporary questioning of traditional interpretation of the Book of Revelation, depends upon the author's study, *The Apocalypse of John*. Documentation for discussions surrounding the case made below appears in that study. It is inspired by two works of Eugenio Corsini, *Apocalisse prima e dopo* (Turin: Società Editrice Internazionale, 1980) (English translation: *The Apocalypse. The Perennial Revelation of Jesus Christ*)), and *Apocalisse di Gesù secondo Giovanni*.

23 Koester, *Revelation*, 239. Despite this, Koester (239-43) accepts that he is in Patmos as the result of a lenient sentence from provincial authority. For a survey of the interpretation of Patmos since 1900, see Ian Boxall, *Patmos in the Reception History of the Apocalypse*, Oxford Theology and Religion Monographs (Oxford: Oxford University Press, 2013), 230-31. He regards the dominant interpretation of Patmos as a penal settlement as "decidedly unimaginative" (p. 5). On the missionary interpretation, see Leonard K. Thompson, *The Book of Revelation. Apocalypse and Empire* (New York: Oxford University Press, 2014), 172-73; Corsini, *Apocalisse*, 81

evidence that Christians suffered a systematic persecution under Domitian.[24] This is nowadays widely acknowledged. Most have recourse to the suggestion that he imposed the Emperor cult on the Empire, and that Revelation is a response to his false claim to divine authority. Evidence for the practice of the Emperor cult in Asia is widespread,[25] but evidence for the persecution of the Asian Christians for lack of observance of the cults is hard to find. Such practices certainly became prevalent later in the second Christian century but drawing them back into the last decade of the first century is widely regarded as anachronistic.[26] As Ramsey MacMullen puts it: "Had the church been wiped off the face of the earth at the end of the first century, its disappearance would have caused no dislocation in the empire, just as its presence was hardly noticed at the time. ... Simply, it did not count."[27]

Almost all interpreters read 1:10-11, 19-20, and 2:1-3:22 as an indication that seven Asian churches were the recipients of this apocalyptic circular letter. For many, John wrote Revelation to address the trials and temptations of the seven churches, suffering under Domitian, tempted by or forced into the Emperor cult. Interpreters strain to identify people and problems explicitly

---

24 Thompson, *The Book of Revelation*, 107-115.
25 See Steven J. Friesen, *Imperial Cults and the Apocalypse of John. Reading Revelation in the Ruins* (New York: Oxford University Press, 2001).
26 See Thompson, *The Book of Revelation*, 104-107; Friesen, *Imperial Cults*, 25-131; Hans-Josef Klauck, *The Religious Context of Early Christianity. A Guide to Greco-Roman Religions*, trans. Brian McNeil (Minneapolis: Fortress, 2003), 250-330; Wes Howard-Brook and Anthony Gwyther, *Unveiling Empire. Reading Revelation Then and Now*, Foreword by Elizabeth McAlister (Maryknoll, NY: Orbis, 1999), 115-19; Jeffrey Brodd and Jonathan Reed, eds., *Rome and Religion. A Cross-Disciplinary Dialogue on the Imperial Cult*, Writings from the Greco-Roman World Supplement Series 5 (Atlanta, GA: SBL Press, 2011), especially the essays (which generated and concluded the discussion) of the Roman historian, Karl Galinski, "The Cult of the Roman Emperor: Uniter or Divider?" (pp. 1-21), and "In the Shadow (or Not) of the Imperial Cult: A Cooperative Agenda" (pp. 215-25).
27 Ramsey MacMullen, *Christianizing the Roman Empire (A.D. 100-400)* (New Haven: Yale University Press, 1984), viii.

mentioned in the letters (e.g. Nicolaitans, Antipas, Jezebel, Balaam, Balak, and the synagogue of Satan). It is equally difficult to identify why John credits certain strengths and failures to some communities, and not to others. As Koester remarks: "in almost every instance the images used for one city would fit the others just as well."[28] The focus upon the named Asian churches and their failures in the face of Roman persecution and the imposition of the Emperor cult as the dominant motivation for the writing of Revelation is running out of support in contemporary scholarship.

Why did John choose these "seven" churches? There were other (more important?) cities in the region where Christian communities were located that are not mentioned (e.g. Colossae). Across the Book of Revelation, the number "seven" is an indication of completeness. Perhaps the "seven" churches are a symbol of the whole church, and not only the names of churches to which Revelation was sent.[29] Interpreters regularly find parallels between the letters to the seven churches in 2:1-3:22 and the description of the New Jerusalem in 21:9-22:5. John challenges a fragile church, struggling in the midst of the allure of Greco-Roman society and its *mores*, as he opens his document (2:1-3:22). He closes it with a description of the church as God's gift (21:9-22:5).

As we have seen, the identification of the beast whose name is 666 as Nero (13:18), necessarily identifies the corrupting presence of evil (see 13:1-18) with the Roman Empire. The association of the prostituted woman with the "seven mountains on which the woman is seated" (17:9) is widely accepted as an endorsement of this identification. Although aware of the symbolic importance of the number "seven" in Revelation, almost all interpreters regard this as an allusion to Rome. In the first place, 17:1-14 relies heavily

---

28 Koester, *Revelation*, 233. See also Beale, *Revelation*, 227: "[A]ll the letters deal generally with the issue of witnessing for Christ in the midst of pagan culture."

29 Among many, see Richard Bauckham, *The Theology of the Book of Revelation*, New Testament Theology (Cambridge: Cambridge University Press, 1993) 114-17. The number "seven" does not indicate "perfection," but "completion."

on the use of "seven" to indicate "completeness" (see 17:1 [twice], 7, 9 [twice], 11). The woman is intimately associated with universal and ongoing corrupt use of power. Rome certainly is part of the current problem. However, the seven mountains represent the presence of corrupt power across Israel's history, from Babylon to Rome. Interestingly, Rome has always been associated with seven "hills" (Greek: *lophos*), never with "mountains" (Greek: *oros*, as in 17:9). Werner Foerster objects to the association of *oros* with Rome: "that the hills are the hills of Rome does not fit too well." He associates himself with the importance of the use of "seven" as he suggests that they indicate "a power that spans the centuries."[30]

"Babylon the Great" (18:2) is traditionally identified with Rome. A case can be made for the identification of "Babylon the Great" with the now destroyed former Jerusalem, unfaithful Israel, "drunk with the blood of the saints and the blood of the witnesses to Jesus" (17:6). Perhaps these "saints" are not Christian martyrs but are the holy ones of Israel. The New Jerusalem, understood by John as the Christian church, replaces the former Jerusalem, too easily corrupted and "drunk with the blood of the saints."

If Patmos is not a penal colony, John was not there enduring a suffering imposed by Roman authority. If there was no systematic persecution under Domitian, nor widespread imposition of the Emperor cult in the Asian churches at the end of the first century, a critical question emerges. Who are those who have suffered and even died because of their adherence to the Word of God and their testimony to Jesus in 1:2, 9; 6:9; 12:17; 18:24; 19:10; 20:4?

Who are the Saints?

Those who have suffered and even died at the hands of Satan and his beastly agents are regularly called "the saints" (8:3-4; 11:18; 13:7, 10; 14:12; 16:6; 17:6; 18:20, 24; 19:8; 20:6, 9). Who are they? Most interpreters take it for granted that they are Christian martyrs. In the light of the questions asked above, this claim should

---

30 Werner Foerster, *"oros," Theological Dictionary of the New Testament* 5 (1968): 487. In *1 Enoch* 24:3-4, Jerusalem is described as "seven mountains."

be queried. It is more likely that John looks back to the recent past, during the persecution of Antiochus IV, to the Saints of the Most High, those holy ones in Israel who were loyal to the commandments of God, and placed their hopes in the messianic promises of the prophets (see Dan 7:21, 25, 27; 9:5-6a, 10). John's biblical allusions draw from across many pages of the Hebrew Scriptures, especially (but not only) the Torah, Isaiah, Ezekiel, and Daniel. His regular references to those who suffer and are slain for the word of God and the messianic promises of the prophets (see 1:2, 9; 6:9; 12:17; 18:24; 19:10; 20:4) look back to the era *before* the historical events of the death and resurrection of Jesus Christ. The experiences and vindication of the suffering and slain "saints" come to him from Israel's recent experience of persecution under Antiochus IV of Syria, and the writing that emerged from that experience: the Book of Daniel.

The literary character of the prophet Daniel played admirably into John's argument. On the one hand, the literary fiction created by Daniel set the tales across the four empires of the Babylonians (Dan 1-5), the Medes (6:1), the Persians (10:1), and the Greeks (10:20). The earlier chapters (Dan 1-6) do not necessarily refer to the period of Antiochus IV. They convey a message of persecution of Jewish saints across the entirety of its history under political and religious tyranny. Across Daniel 7-12, allusions to the period of Antiochus IV and the Maccabean revolt are clear. The book appeared in its current state between 167-164 BCE. By the time John wrote the Apocalypse, Daniel was exercising considerable influence in Jewish literature. Even in the pre-Christian period, in both the early Greek translations and Qumran, Jewish interpreters recognised that Daniel addressed the period of Antiochus IV. The Jewish historian Josephus regarded Daniel as "one of the greatest prophets" (*Jewish Antiquities* 10.10-11 §266).[31]

---

31 For surveys of the reception of Daniel, see Maurice Casey, *Son of Man. The Interpretation and Influence of Daniel 7* (London: SPCK, 1979), 51-141; John Goldingay, *Daniel*, Word Biblical Commentary 30 (Nashville: Thomas

Sharply aware of the recent persecution and executions under Antiochus IV, John can address his audience by looking back to the prophet Daniel, claiming that the "saints" of Israel already participated in the life-giving fruits of the death and resurrection of Jesus. Daniel indicates why this happened: they observed the commandments and listened to the prophets (see Dan 9:5-6, 10. See also Bar 1:14-2:5; 3:1-8). As Steve Moyise puts it: "Whether they were facing actual persecution or not, it seems clear that John wishes them to see their situation in the light of the life and death struggle of Daniel and his friends."[32] We cannot be sure, but John's continual recourse to Daniel may well have been the reason for the choice of the apocalyptic genre for his document, however much he has "bent" the genre because of his focus upon the death and resurrection of Jesus.

For John, Israel's "saints" (see especially Dan 7:15-27) anticipated eternal redemption provided by the blood of the crucified and risen Lamb, slain before the foundation of the world (Rev 5:6; 13:8). At the heart of John's message lies the perennial presence of the reality of Jesus' death and resurrection, and its saving effects. Corrupt political and religious tyranny led to the life-giving participation of the saints across the whole of the Israel's regularly corrupted religious and political history, from Babylon to Rome. The presence of the satanic did not begin or end with Rome, however much the Roman Empire and the Imperial Cult may have impacted on John's audience. The history of corruption, rejection of God, and persecution has marked the whole span of Israel's sacred history, and it has always been marked by the presence of its "saints."

Nelson, 1989), xxvi-xxxviii; John J. Collins, *Daniel*, Hermeneia (Minneapolis: Fortress, 1993), 72-89.

32 Moyise, *The Old Testament*, 58.

A Proposed Literary Design

The following literary design of Revelation 1:1-22:21, read as a single utterance, no doubt the result of a long literary history, depends upon three criteria. One of them is theological and the other two are literary.

1. The central message of the Book of Revelation is that the death and resurrection of Jesus reveal the meaning of the history of God's intervention into the affairs of humankind, recorded in the period of Israel and the period of the Christian community, a sacred history that runs from the foundation of the world to the time of the church.

2. This message is repeated multiple times, making known (i.e. revelation: *apokalypsis*), the full meaning of the perennial presence of God's saving action in and through Jesus Christ.

3. The "sevens" determine the literary shape of the whole utterance. Each "seven" is introduced by a description of heavenly encounters (1:9-20; 4:1-5:14; 8:2-6; 15:1-8). The pouring out of the seven bowls, the climactic announcement of Jesus' victory through death and resurrection, receives the most extensive treatment (12:1-22:5).

There are surprises at every turn. Even though John is moved to communicate with his audience within the political, religious and social presence of the Roman Empire, he does not limit his criticism to Rome. Inspired by Daniel's critique of all who have brought corruption and evil into Israel's history, from Babylon to Rome, his concern is to indicate that the death and resurrection of Jesus is a victory over *all* evil powers, and *all* false gods. For example, the books of Genesis and Exodus provide the background for the account of the woman and the dragon in 12:1-18. Daniel is used to develop a critique of the beast that reaches beyond an attack on Roman authority and its vassals to *all* corrupting authorities and their agents in 13:1-18.

The figure of the woman (*hē gunē*) looms large. Despite her glorious first appearance (12:1), by the time the passage closes in vv. 17-18, she and her descendants are in an ambiguous situation, pursued by Satan, but protected by God. In 17:1-6, mounted on the beast, her ambiguity has disappeared. The woman has made her decision to enter an unholy union with evil. But that is not the end of her story. She returns at its end as the bride of the Lamb in 21:1-22:5. Such readings are possible because the battle of Armegeddon in 16:1-21 can be understood as the crucifixion of Jesus, fulfilling what was promised in 10:7: "In the days when the seventh angel is to blow his trumpet, the mystery of God will be fulfilled, as he announced to his servants the prophets." In the crucifixion of Jesus, the pouring out of the seventh bowl, "it is done" (16:17), a definitive victory over evil that has already been described in the opening of the seventh seal (8:1) and the blowing of the seventh trumpet (11:15-19).

Revelation is to be read as a steady statement and restatement of the saving effects of the death and resurrection of Jesus Christ, acting from before all time (5:6; 13:8), a call to live through challenge, conflict, suffering, and failure, in the light of the victory of the Lamb. The earliest extant Latin interpreter of the Book of Revelation, Victorinus of Pettau (c. 250-303), argued that the opening vision of the slain and standing Lamb as the only one with authority to open the seals of the scroll indicates that the meaning of the whole of Scripture is revealed through Christ's death and resurrection (*Commentary on the Apocalypse*, 1.4; 4.1-5.3).[33] As far as the internal order of the document is concerned, he suggests:

> We ought not pay too much attention to the order of what is said. For the sevenfold Holy Spirit, when he has passed in review the events to the last time, to the very end, returns again to the same times and supplements what he had said incompletely (*Commentary on the Apocalypse* 8.2).[34]

---

33 For the texts, see Weinrich, *Latin Commentaries on Revelation*, 2, 6-10.
34 Weinrich, *Ancient Christian Texts*, 12. Koester, *Revelation*, 33, explains: "People were not to look for a sequential outline of future events in revelation but were to ask about its underlying meaning. ... Revelation recapitulates the same meaning many times."

By means of ever-deepening statement and restatement, the book is a celebration of the significance of the death and resurrection of Jesus, the mystery of God perennially present across the whole of sacred history, from the beginning of creation down to the time of the Christian church.

I - 1:1-8: *Prologue*

II- 1:9-3:22: *The Seven Churches:*

1:9-20: Part One: *A two-staged encounter between the John and the heavenly*

2:1-3:22: Part Two: *The Seven churches: retelling Israel's story leading to the coming of the Son of Man, Messiah. The letters recapture Israel's sacred history to address the dangers of mediocrity in the Asian churches*

III – 4:1-8:1: *The Seven Seals*

4:1-5:14: Part One: *A heavenly liturgy prepares for the opening of the seals*

6:1-8:1: Part Two: *Opening the seals:*

6:1-8: *The opening of the first four seals: the human situation with steady allusions to Genesis*

6:9-8:1: *The opening of the final three seals: the divine response to the human situation*

IV – 8:2-11:19: *The Seven Trumpets*

8:2-6: Part One: *a heavenly liturgy prepares for the blowing of the trumpets*

8:7-11:19: Part Two: *Blowing of the trumpets:*

8:7-13: *The blowing of the first four trumpets with steady allusions to Exodus*

9:1-11:19: *The blowing of the final three trumpets and the woes upon humankind*

V – 12:1-22:5: The Seven Bowls

12:1-14:20: *The threefold* **preparation** *for the pouring out of the bowls:*

> 12:1-17: Part One: *The woman and the ancient serpent, the Devil and Satan*
>
> 13:1-18: Part Two: *The two beasts: collusion of corrupt religious and political authority*
>
> 14:1-20: Part Three: *The salvation of the faithful in Israel, an anticipated effect of the blood of the Lamb*

> **15:1-16:21: The pouring out of the seven bowls:**
>
>> 15:1-18: *A heavenly liturgy prepares for the opening of the seals*
>>
>> 16:1-9: *Pouring out of the first four bowls (allusions to the plagues in Egypt)*
>>
>> 16:10-21: *Pouring out of the last three bowls: leading to the Lamb's saving action*

17:1-22:5: *The threefold* **consequences** *of the death of Christ:*

> 17:1-19:10: First consequence: *the destruction of Babylon (Jerusalem)*
>
> 19:11-20:15: Second consequence: *the destruction of all evil power*
>
> 21:9-22:5: Third consequence: *the gathering of the chosen*

VI – 22:6-21: The Epilogue

22:6-9: *The words of the interpretation of this book: the angel, the prophet, Jesus, and the call to worship God*

22:10-17: *The words of the interpretation of this book: the angel, the prophet, Jesus, and the call to "come"*

22:18-21: *The words of the interpretation of this book: warning, promise, and response.*

Consequences

The use of "sevens" determines the narrative: the seven churches (1:9-3:22), the seven seals (4:1-8:1), the seven trumpets (8:2-11:19), and the seven bowls (12:1-22:5). They are framed by a Prologue (1:1-8) and an Epilogue (22:6-21). To place the churches, the seals, the trumpets, and the bowls at the centre of the book's argument, John uses other literary indicators. All four "sevens" have a "preparation" for their administration. A heavenly revelatory experience introduces the Letters (1:9-20), heavenly liturgies introduce the seals (4:1-5:14), the trumpets (8:2-6), and the bowls (15:1-8).

Given the climactic importance of the seven bowls (15:1-16:21), concluding and clarifying much of what has been said more enigmatically in the letters, the seals, and the trumpets, greater attention is given to the development of this section, linked by the appearance of three "signs" (*sēmeia*) in heaven (See 12:1, 3; 15:1). John provides the description of the pouring out of the bowls (15:1-16:21) with a three-part *preparation*, describing the ambiguity and the promise inherent in God's initial intervention (12:1-14:20). He follows the pouring out with a threefold description of the *consequences* of the pouring out of the bowls, indicating the destruction of all evil forces, and the conclusion and perfection of God's initial intervention in the death and resurrection of Jesus Christ. This event opens a new era marked by the presence of the Christian community (17:1-22:5).[35] Ambiguity remains, but God has conquered evil (17:1-20:15) and the grace of the Lord Jesus is available in the church (21:1-22:5).

---

35 The interpretation offered here indicates my response to the question I raised in n. 3. The traditional dictum *lex orandi lex credendi* applies. The Christian church's consistent use of Revelation at Easter time, and in celebrations that recall Easter, points to its being a book that should be understood in the light of the death and resurrection of Jesus, not a prophecy about the end of time. See Francis J. Moloney, *Reading Revelation at Easter Time* (Collegeville, MN: Liturgical Press, 2020).

John is not writing into a situation experiencing systematic persecution or being forced into Emperor worship. John's Christians are not told to "keep the faith," with the promise that, *in the end*, God will come in power and might to destroy the persecutors. Revelation is none-the-less directed to Christians facing a situation of great ambiguity, caught between belief in the saving effects of the death and resurrection of Jesus, and a subsequent lifestyle that belief requires, and the allure of the glittering Greco-Roman world within which they lived. It that respect, a "theology of resistance" is part of John's message but subordinated to the proclamation of the perennial saving presence of God in the death and resurrection of Jesus. In the meantime, "outside are the dogs and sorcerers and fornicators and murderers and idolaters, and everyone who loves and practises falsehood" (22:15) and "the righteous still do right, and the holy still be holy" (v. 11).

John exhorts Christians living in the Greco-Roman world of the late first century to shun the immoral and commercial glitter of that world, aware that they already enjoy the life given by God in and through the death and resurrection of his Son. John was neither a starry-eyed apocalyptic thinker, nor someone who thought that Christians already lived the glories of the risen life (see 1 Cor 15:20-58). Like all other early Christian writers, he faced the ambiguous reality of Christians called to live their lives in imitation of the crucified and risen one within a socio-political-religious context that radically opposed such a lifestyle.

All post-Christ believers live the in-between-time, negotiating its ambiguity. John exhorts his audience to look back upon the "endurance" of the saints in the face of devastating evil that was part of the Israel's sacred history, the result of the fall of humankind and the fall of Satan (see 14:12). Demonic disasters challenged humankind, and creation itself, a result of those "falls." But from the foundation of the world, redemption by the blood of the slaughtered lamb was available (5:6; 13:8). Those who observed the Law, and listened to the messianic prophecies, already in the period prior to the historical event of Jesus Christ, had been swept into that redemption. They share in the "first resurrection." "Over these the second death has no power, but they will be priests of God and Christ and they will reign with him a thousand years."[36] John encourages his early Christians to shun the false promises of the demonic world that still surround them, as they await God's final appearance. The world of false promises and its agents have not disappeared because of the death and resurrection of Jesus, as the ambiguity of Christian history itself indicates so eloquently.

Living the in-between-time, Christians cry out "Come, Lord Jesus!" (22:20). John wrote his book to instruct them that they had every reason for hope, courage, and confidence as they lived their Christian lives in the expectation of a final coming. John attempts to focus a Christian community, aware of the allusive possibilities of apocalyptic language, upon the vividly remembered treasure of the holy ones of Israel, especially as the Book of Daniel represents "the holy ones." "Christians lived quiet lives, not much different from other provincials. The economy, as always, had its ups and downs; and the government kept the peace and demanded taxes."[37] This situation, however, could easily lead to an uncritical accommodation of the traditions and mores of the Greco-Roman world.

Such a way of life was unacceptable in the Christian church, the perfection of God's promises, founded upon the death

---

[36] This interpretation of the "thousand years reign" as the period of Israel, prior to the unleashing of Satan for the final battle of Jesus' death and resurrection, challenges almost all interpretations of Rev 20:1-6. The thousand years do not indicate a precise chronological period that will mark the end of the Christian era, but the long period that elapsed between the original fall of Satan (see 9:1-2; 12:7-12) and his return only to be vanquished definitively by Jesus' death and resurrection (16:1-21). The passage has troubled interpreters from the beginnings of Christianity. To this day, many Christian traditions are determined by their interpretation of the nature and timing of the "thousand-year reign": amillenarian, premillenarian, postmillenarian, and dispensationalist. For a good survey, explaining these terms, see Koester, *Revelation*, 741-50.

[37] Thompson, *Book of Revelation*, 95. See also pp. 164-67.

and resurrection of Jesus. John writes to make them aware, to encourage them, and to instil hope in challenging times. He tells them that the faithfulness required of those who live in the blessedness of the post-Christ era had already been lived by people who were faithful unto death in the period between the original "fall" of Satan and humankind (see 9:1-2; 12:7-12) and the death and resurrection of Jesus (see 16:1-21; 20:1-6). The victory of the saints of Israel, already participating in the death and resurrection of Jesus, was the result of their obedience to the Law and their belief in the messianic promises of the prophets. They are already gathered in glory (see 6:9-11; 7:1-8; 14:1; 15:1; 20:1-6). John uses this message to address early Christians living the challenges of the in-between-time during which access to God is no longer through a temple in Jerusalem, but through the gift of the temple of the Lord God Almighty and the Lamb (21:22), the Christian community. For John, they have solid reasons for hope in dark times.

6

Tracing a Literary Structure in the Book of Revelation

> Revelation is not a book, not even narrowly a text,
> but an ever expanding and contracting multimedia constellation.
>
> Timothy Beal[1]

The reception of the Book of Revelation has been marked by one sensation after another. The use and abuse of the book raises serious questions about its value as a Christian document and as a literary piece. For some, it maintains its place within the Christian canon of Sacred Scripture as an inspired utterance from Christianity's earliest days.[2] For others, Revelation's ambiguity and violence is little short of dangerous. "Toxic poisons trickle from it. Consciousness-altering fumes waft out of it. Desperate hope and vindictive joy issue from it".[3] For some, it is the result of a series of disturbing editorial activities, parts of which may have had their beginnings in pre-Christian times.[4] For others, it is a unified literary

---

1 Timothy Beal, *The Book of Revelation. A Biography, Lives of Great Religious Books* (Princeton: Princeton University Press, 2018) 199.
2 See, for example, John and Gloria Ben-Daniel, *Saint John and the Book of Revelation. From Essenes to End-Times* (Jerusalem: Beit Yochanan, 2019).
3 Stephen D. Moore, *Untold Tales from the Book of Revelation: Sex and Gender, Empire and Ecology* (Atlanta, GA: SBL Press, 2014) 1. For a recent survey, see Beal, *The Book of Revelation*. Beal focuses upon Revelation's multitextual origins, its mixed early reception, Augustine, Hildegard of Bingen, Joachim di Fiore, Cranach's decoration of the Luther Bible, the use of Revelation to "other" alternative religious views, James Hampton's architectural version of Joachim's interpretation, now on display in the Smithsonian, Washington, DC, and Evangelical Rapture.
4 The most serious contemporary representative of this approach to Revelation is Aune, *Revelation*.

utterance.[5] Richard Bauckham describes rejection of the literary unity of the book as "a crass failure to appreciate the specific literary integrity of the work as it stands".[6]

Contemporary commentators who claim that the book must be read and interpreted as a literary whole, however, show little unanimity regarding the literary structure and logical sequence of the argument of John's book. There is widespread agreement that John's prophetic use of an apocalyptic literary form exhorts suffering Christians to endure suffering and persecution inflicted by Rome, looking forward confidently to God's eschatological victory in the second coming of Jesus Christ. But "[n]early every commentator produces a different schema that purports to reflect the development of the material".[7]

Most proposals for a literary structure of the Book of Revelation are determined by the instructions of the one like the Son of Man, given to John in 1:19: "Now write what you have seen, what is, and what is to take place after this".[8] Timothy Beal summarises with a "big picture" description.[9]

I. Introduction and opening vision of "one like the Son of Man" (Revelation 1:1–20)
II. Letters to seven churches in Asia (2:1–3.22)
III. The throne room of heaven (4:1–5:14)

---

[5] The bulk of contemporary commentary supports this view. See, for example, Thompson, *Book of Revelation*, 37–52; Koester, *Revelation*, 69–71.
[6] Bauckham, *The Climax of Prophecy*, x.
[7] Friesen, *Imperial Cults and the Apocalypse of John*, 170. For surveys, see Ugo Vanni, *La Struttura Letteraria dell'Apocalisse* (Aloisiana. Scritti publicati sotto la direzione della Pontificia Facoltà Teologica per l'Italia Meridionale sezione "San Luigi" 8; Rome: Herder, 1971) 19–99; Aune, *Revelation*, 1:xc–xcix; Beal, *The Book of Revelation*, 108–44.
[8] For a detailed presentation of Rev 1:19 as the "interpretative key" to the literary and theological structure of the whole document, see Beale, *Revelation*, 152–70. See also Ramsey Michaels, "Revelation 1:19 and the Narrative Voices of the Apocalypse," *New Testament Studies* 12 (1965–66) 89–105.
[9] Beal, *The Book of Revelation*, 11–12.

IV. Tribulations, ending with the fall of Babylon, personified as a woman (5:1–18:24)
V. The second coming and the thousand-year reign of Christ, and the Last Judgment (19:1–20:15)
VI. The new heaven, new earth, and new Jerusalem (21:1–22:21).

One senses the determining influence of what is seen, what is, and what is to come (1:19).

Criteria for Determining a Literary Structure

Many literary structures depend upon two criteria. One of them is "outside" the text: a reconstructed *Sitz im Leben der Kirche* that produced Revelation late in the first Christian century. The other is "inside" the text, in the reported words of one like the Son of Man to John in 1:19. The former depends upon the almost universal acceptance, until recent times, that John wrote his book to persecuted and suffering Asian Christians, pointing them through present suffering and death toward the eschatological victory of God.[10] Once this perspective is accepted, and it has a pedigree that reaches back to Justin Martyr, Papias (?), Irenaeus and Augustine,[11] literary structures can be developed that read

---

10 I claim that this paradigm has been dominant "until recent times" because a "new look" is emerging in Revelation studies. Basic to this recent approach were the works of Thompson, *Book of Revelation* (1990) and Friesen, *Imperial Cults* (2001). See Moloney, *The Apocalypse*, 33–38; Idem, "Hope in Dark Times" (see above, pp. 95–120); Sigve K. Tonstad, *Revelation*, Paideia Commentaries on the New Testament (Grand Rapids, MI: Baker Academic, 2019) 3–41. The dominant eschatological paradigm still plays an important role, exemplified by Craig Koester's recent outstanding commentary.

11 Major early voices questioned this pedigree. Chief among them were Origen and Eusebius of Caesarea. See Moloney, *The Apocalypse*, 2–5. In the middle of the second Century, Justin Martyr indicates to Trypho that his millennial interpretation of Revelation is not accepted by many contemporary "true Christians" (Dial. 80.2: πολλοὺς δ'αὖ καὶ τῶν τῆς καθαρᾶς καὶ εὐσεβοῦς ὄντων Χριστιανῶν γνώμης τοῦτο μὴ γνωρίζειν ἐσήμανά σοι. Text from P. Bobichon,

Revelation following the temporal indications of 1:19: what is seen, is now, and what will be.[12]

They begin with John's experience on Patmos and his evaluation of the *present* situation of seven churches in Asia. From there he uses the Hebrew Scriptures and Jewish apocalyptic traditions to portray the horrors of the Roman Empire and its cults.[13] This reflects *what is*. The attempts of Roman authority to impose its religions and cults upon the Asian churches must be resisted. *What is to come*? The Hebrew Bible and Jewish apocalyptic traditions again come into play to describe the definitive destruction of the evil powers, when only God and his Christ will be worshipped in the New Jerusalem (22:3-5). For some, the New Jerusalem is an earthly experience, the definitive establishment of

---

Justin Martyr, Dialogue avec Tryphon: édition critique, 2 vols. [Fribourg: Academic Press Fribourg, 2003] 1.404-5). My colleague, Dr Stephen Carlson, has pointed out that we are unsure about Papias. His witness is shrouded in mystery. He is an Asian Christian who knows some traditions of the book (if not the book itself). Nothing has survived of his view regarding the circumstances of the writing of the book, and which "John" is its author.

12 Many have traced structural elements within the narrative of Revelation. See, for example, Aune, *Revelation*, 1:c-cv. The work of Charles H. Giblin has been influential. See Charles H. Giblin, "Structural and Thematic Correlations in the Theology of Revelation 16-22," *Biblica* 55 (1974) 487-504; Idem, "Revelation 11:1-13: Its Form, Function, and Textual Integration," *New Testament Studies* 30 (1984) 433-59; Idem, "Recapitulation and the Literary Coherence of John's Apocalypse," *The Catholic Biblical Quarterly* 56 (1994) 81-95. See his synthesis in Idem, *The Book of Revelation: The Open Book of Prophecy*, Good News Studies 34 (Collegeville, MN: Liturgical Press, 1991) 12-18. For his influence, see J. J. Clabeaux, "Revelation," *The Paulist Biblical Commentary*, 1574-77. The temporal framework provided by 1:19 remains a determining criterion.

13 The Hebrew Bible and Jewish apocalyptic literature are the most important "intertextual" influences upon John's narrative. However, scholarship regularly looks beyond those sources. For extensive reference to a multitude of non-biblical and non-Jewish literatures, some quite late, see Aune, *Revelation*. Bruce J. Malina, *On the Genre and Message of Revelation: Star Visions and Sky Journeys* (Peabody, MA: Hendrickson, 1996) looks to Greco-Roman astral myths and reads them in the light of what he claims took place in Jesus Christ

the Kingdom, while for others it is an eschatological "other-worldly" experience that lies ahead of those currently suffering under Roman insult and persecution.

Attention needs to be devoted to elements within Revelation that may indicate an author's attempts to construct a literary artifice. The book opens with a Prologue that presents God, Jesus Christ, and the seven spirits. John has been given a task to communicate an authoritative word of God (v. 3: ἡ προφητεία) to recipients in seven churches in Asia who have been freed from their sins by blood of Jesus Christ, a kingdom of priests, serving his God and Father, the Alpha and the Omega, the lord of all history (1:1–8).[14] It is widely accepted that 22:6–21 serves as a conclusion to the book, restating themes that first appeared in the Prologue.[15]

The dominant textual marker across the remaining narrative (1:9–22:5) is the regular appearances of "sevens": seven letters to the churches (1:9–3:22), seven seals opened in a pattern of 4 + 3 (6:1–8:1), seven trumpets blown in a pattern of 4 + 3 (8:7–11:19), and seven bowls poured out in a pattern of 4 + 3 (16:1–21).[16] However, because of the awkward location of these "sevens," attempts to base a literary structure upon them have not been widely accepted. The letters, the seals, and the trumpets dominate 1:9–11:19, but the pouring out of the bowls is delayed

---

[14] The Greek ἡ προφητεία should not be simply rendered as "prophecy." The primary dictionary meaning of the word is the act or gift of interpreting the divine will or purpose. See Danker, *A Greek-English Dictionary*, 889, s.v. προφητεία (§§1–2).

[15] See, among many, Vanni, *La Struttura Letteraria*, 107–115; Aune, *Revelation*, 3:1148–49; Koester, *Revelation*, 847

[16] John's use of "seven" is important. The number indicates "completion", not necessarily "perfection." That is limited to the number "three." Not only does "seven" appear with the letters, the seals, the trumpets, and the bowls, but based on Dan 9, half of "seven", three and a half years, or one thousand two hundred and sixty days, are used for a time of trial. In my opinion, the solution to the 666 problem comes from a three-fold repetition of the number "six," one short of completion. The number is a human reality (13:18: ἀριθμὸς γὰρ ἀνθρώπου ἐστίν): forever frustratingly short of possible perfection. See Moloney, *The Apocalypse*, 209–11. See also Beale, Revelation, 721–77. See the helpful summary of John's use of numbers in Resseguie, *The Revelation of John*, 28–32.

until 16.:1–21. What does the interpreter make of 4:1–5:14, 8:2–6, 12:1–14:20, 15:1–8, and 17:1–22:5?

There is no consistent response to this question. The description of the heavenly court of 4:1–5:14 can be interpreted as an opening heavenly liturgy that indicates the primacy of God and the Lamb, and 17:1–22:5 describes the destruction that will come with the eschatological establishment of God and his Christ in the New Jerusalem. But the sequence of the woman clothed with the sun (12:1–18), the appearance of the two beasts (13:1–18), and the Lamb with the 144,000, the one like the Son of Man accompanied by six angels (14.1–20), generates difficulty. As Richard Bauckham has observed: "Most attempts to discover the structure of Revelation have found it particularly difficult to see how chapters 12–14 fit into the overall structure".[17] Faced with the challenge of tracing a logical and theological literary sequence across 12.1–14.20, Charles Brütsch resigns himself: "Mieux vaut donc renoncer à tracer un plan strict dans l'Apocalypse."[18]

Perhaps such desperate measures are not called for. Beginning with a working hypothesis that the "sevens" are the key to the book's literary structure, what is developed within and around those "sevens" may determine the shape of the remaining material. Accepting that 1:1–8 serves as a Prologue, matched by an Epilogue in 22:6–21, the following passages call for initial investigation: the relationship between 1:9–20 and the writing of the "seven" letters (2:1–3:22), the relationship between 4:1–5:14 and the opening of the "seven" seals (6:1–8:1), the relationship between 8:2–6 and the blowing of the "seven" trumpets (8:7–11:19), the relationship between 15:1–8 and the pouring out of the "seven" bowls (16:1–21). Once that has been investigated, some suggestions might emerge concerning the possibility of "three"

---

17 Bauckham, *Climax of Prophecy*, 15.
18 Charles Brütsch, *La Clarté de l'Apocalypse*, 5th ed. (Geneva: Labor et Fides, 1966) 191. See the perceptive remarks on why this is the case in Aune, *Revelation*, 1:xci.

scenes, each with its own literary unity, that *prepare* for the pouring out of the bowls: the woman and the dragon (12:1-18), the two beasts (13:1-18), and the Lamb, the Son of Man, and the first fruits (14:1-20). A parallel literary activity may also be traced in "three" scenes, each with its own narrative unity, that indicate *consequences* of the pouring out of the bowls (16:1-21): the destruction of the whore and Babylon (17:1-19:20), the definitive destruction of Satan (19:21-21:8), and the gift of the New Jerusalem (21:9-22:5).

Heavenly Encounters: Rev 1:9-20, 4:1-5:11, 8:2-6, and 15:1-8

John's report of his encounter with "a loud voice" (1:10-11) and his sight of the seven golden lampstands with one like a Son of Man in their midst (vv. 12-16) begins "on earth." He is on the island called Patmos, as a result of his missionary zeal for the churches (v. 9).[19] But subsequent encounters take place because of an experience that transfers him into another sphere: "I was in the spirit on the Lord's day (ἐγενόμην ἐν πνεύμα ἐν τῇ κυριακῇ ἡμέρᾳ)" (v. 10). This first encounter between John and the heavenly is not as explicit as those of 4:1-5:11, 8:2-6, and 15:1-8. They are located in the heavenly sphere. In 1:9-20, the heavenly location of John's auditory (v. 10: ἤκουσα) and visionary (v. 12: εἶδον) experiences must be inferred. His claim that he heard the loud voice like a trumpet and saw one like the Son of Man while in the spirit is repeated in his explicitly heavenly experience of 4:1-5:14 (see 4:2: ἐγενόμην ἐν πνεύμα). The golden lampstands (1:12), the gold sash (v. 13), the whiteness of the hair (v. 14) and the appearance of the one like the Son of Man (vv. 15-16), not to speak of the authoritative nature of the figure's actions and message (vv.

---

19 Reading the reason for John's presence at Patmos (διὰ τὸν λόγον τοῦ θεοῦ καὶ τὴν μαρτυρίαν αὐτοῦ) as a result of his missionary activity, not as an imprisonment. For this position, and the discussion surrounding it, see Moloney, *The Apocalypse*, 50-52.

17-20), make it clear that what is reported in 1:9-20 is no earthly encounter.

The heavenly nature of the encounters that preface the seals (4:1-5:14), the trumpets (8:2-6) and the pouring out of the bowls (15:1-8) need only be affirmed, as a location "in heaven" (ἐν τῷ οὐρανῷ) or "before God" (ἐνώπιον τοῦ θεοῦ) is explicitly stated. John reports visionary experiences through the regular use of the verb "to see" (εἶδον).

4.1: μετὰ ταῦτα εἶδον, καὶ ἰδοὺ θύρα ἠνεῳγμένη ἐν τῷ οὐρανῷ.
8.2: καὶ εἶδον τοὺς ἑπτὰ ἀγγέλους οἳ ἐνώπιον τοῦ θεοῦ ἑστήκασιν.
15.1: καὶ εἶδον ἄλλο σημεῖον ἐν τῷ οὐρανῷ.

A further significant feature unifies these passages: in each of them someone is commissioned to enable the "seven" that immediately follows.

- The command of the loud voice like a trumpet to "write in a book what you see and send it to the seven churches" (v. 11) leads to the appearance of one like the Son of Man. Once the sequence of the seven letters begins, John writes a message from one like the Son of Man to each of the churches (2:1, 8, 12, 18; 3:1, 7, 14). The function of 1:9-20 is to indicate the heavenly origins of the letters, the commissioning of John to write the messages of one like the Son of Man to Ephesus, Smyrna, Pergamum, Thyatira, Sardis, Philadelphia, and Laodicea.[20]

- The heavenly vision of God the creator of all things (4:1-11) and the slain and risen Lamb (5:1-14), concluding with the universal worship of both God and the Lamb (vv. 12-14),

---

20 The "seven churches" are a symbol of the church itself. The letters call the church's attention to its frailties in 2.1-3.22. The church as it should be is presented in the description of the New Jerusalem in 21.1-22.5. See Bauckham, *The Theology of the Book of Revelation*, 114-17; Corsini, *Apocalisse de Gesù Cristo*, 3836; Boxall, *Revelation*, 312; Resseguie, *Revelation*, 258.

provides the context for the commissioning of the Lamb to open the seals. The threefold use of the verb λαμβάνω in 5:7–9 creates different possibilities. The primary dictionary meaning of λαμβάνω is "to take," but it can also mean "to receive."[21] The syntax and the narrative sequence of vv. 5–9 suggest that the slain yet standing Lamb, located between the throne and the four living creatures "went and *received* (εἴληφεν) the scroll from the right hand of the one who is seated on the throne" (v. 7). No one is worthy to open the seven seals of the scroll (vv. 2–4), but the one seated on the throne (see 4:2–7) commissions the Lamb by using his authoritative right hand to pass it to him. Once the Lamb has "*received* the scroll (ὅτε ἔλαβεν τὸ βίβλιον)" (v. 8), the elders sing a new song: "You are worthy to *receive* (λάβειν) the scroll and to open its seals, for you were slaughtered and by your blood you ransomed for God saints from every tribe and language and people and nation" (v. 9). The death and resurrection of Jesus, the Lion of the tribe of Judah, the Root of David, transcends the limitations all in heaven on earth or under the earth (vv. 3–5). God commissions the crucified and risen Christ to open the seals.[22]

- The brevity of the description of the opening of the seventh seal and its consequences (8:1), lead many commentators to ignore the fact that in 8:2 the seven angels who stand before God are given seven trumpets. They associate v. 1 with vv. 2–5

---

21 See Danker, *A Greek-English Dictionary*, 583–85, for the wide range of possible meanings of λαμβάνω.
22 Support for the interpretation of the verb as "to receive" comes from the context. In response to the question of the mighty angel in 5.2, "Who is worthy (τίς ἄξιος) to open the scroll and break its seals?" the four living creatures and the twenty-four elders proclaim: "You are worthy to receive (ἄξιος εἶ λαβεῖν) the scroll and to open its seals" (v. 9). The Lamb's "worthiness" (because of his redemptive death and resurrection (v. 9)) is the likely motivation for the right-handed gift of the scroll to a worthy recipient (v. 7).

to generate a literary unit of 8.1–5.²³ This cannot be correct. In the first place, the opening of the seventh seal, completing the pattern of 4 + 3 found across all the "sevens," must not be separated from the opening of the first six seals.²⁴ Secondly, as the slaughtered but standing Lamb received the scroll from the right hand of the one on the throne in 5:7, so also in 8:2 the seven angels who stand before God were given the seven trumpets (ἐδόθησαν αὐτοῖς ἑπτὰ σάλπιγγες). Rightly has James Resseguie pointed out that the use of divine passive verb ἐδόθησαν is "a grammatical clue indicating who controls the universe."²⁵ As the loud voice in heaven commissioned John to write what the one like the Son of Man would dictate to the seven churches (1:10, 2:1, etc.), and as the one seated on the throne commissioned the slain yet living Lamb to open the seals (5:7–10), a heavenly authority commissions the seven angels to blow the seven trumpets (8:2. See v. 7). An

---

23 For example, Koester, *Revelation*, 442, regards the silence of 8.1 as creating a time of reverence for God and a context of prayer, allowing time for the prayers of the saints (8:3–5) to be offered at the altar. Only after that are the trumpets blown (v. 6). For various reasons, Yarbro Collins, *The Apocalypse*, 54–55; George R. Beasley-Murray, *The Book of Revelation*, rev ed., New Century Bible (London: Oliphants, 1978) 149–52, Prigent, *Commentary on the Apocalypse of St John*, 297–302; Beale, *Revelation*, 454–64; Clabeaux, "Revelation," 1588–89, read 8:1–5 as a literary unit. For Austin Farrer, *The Revelation of St. John the Divine. A Commentary on the English Text* (Oxford: Clarendon, 1964) 111–15, a literary unit of 8:1–12 embraces both the seventh seal and the first four trumpets.

24 Beyond the scope of this essay, a further feature unites the 'sevens": they all close with reference to the effects of death and resurrection of Jesus (3:20; 8:1; 11:15–19; 16:11–21). See Moloney, *The Apocalypse*, 81–83, 123-27, 162–66, 236–54. Despite his millenarian interpretation of Revelation, its earliest Latin commentator, Victorinus of Pettau, correctly intuited that "the sevenfold Holy Spirit ... returns again to the same times and supplements what he had said incompletely." For the translation, see William C. Weinrich, *Ancient Christian Texts: Latin Commentaries on Revelation* (Downers Grove: IVP Academic, 2011) 12.

25 Resseguie, *Revelation*, 142. See also Boxall, *Revelation*, 132.

inclusio indicates the literary unity of 8:2–11:19. The heavenly encounter closes with "peals of thunder, rumblings, flashes of lightning, and an earthquake" (8:5), as the blowing of the seventh trumpet closes with "flashes of lightning, rumblings, peals of thunder, an earthquake, and heavy hail" (16:19).[26]

- A considerable amount of John's narrative fills the textual space between the blowing of the seventh trumpet (11:15–19) and the pouring out of the seven bowls (16:1–21). Confusion exists regarding the structure and meaning of 15:1–8.[27] Critical to the understanding of 15:1–8 is the framing of the episode by indications of an "ending". In v. 1 and v. 8, the aorist passive and the aorist subjunctive passive of the verb τελέω appears (v. 1: ἐτελέσθε; v. 8: τελεσθῶσιν). This is a hint that John has arrived at the last of his "sevens." With the pouring out of the bowls, "the wrath of God is ended (ἐτελέσθε)" (v. 1). Seven angels with seven plagues are commissioned for this task by one of the four living creatures that stood by the throne in 4:6. One of them "gave (ἔδωκεν) the seven angels seven golden bowls full of the wrath of God" (15:7). The temple of God might be open, but

---

26 The phenomena described are not identical. They are so close that any audience is struck by them. See Bauckham, *Climax of Prophecy*, 203–204. This literary feature is missed by those who see 10.1–11.14 as an "interlude" during which the Christian martyrs give witness. See, for example, Boxall, *Revelation*, 130; Koester, *Revelation*, 436.

27 By way of example, Boxall, *Revelation*, 216–17, separates 15:1–4 from 15:5–16.21. The space between the end of the seven trumpets (11:19) and the beginning of the pouring out of the seven bowls (15:5) is filled with seven "visions," thus maintaining a steady rhythm of "seven." See also Resseguie, *Revelation*, 203–205; Beale, *Revelation*, 784–86. There is a crucial difference between the "sevens" that John numbers, and a "seven" uncovered by interpreters. Koester, *Revelation*, 631–36, regards 15.1–4 as the end of a fourth cycle of visions. The fifth cycle begins in 15:5 and runs till 19:10, although it contains a "pause" across 17:1–18:24 (an extended delay before God administers final justice). See his explanation on pp. 637, 681–82. On the literary unity of 15:1–16:21 (although the result of editorial work), see Aune, *Revelation*, 2:863–68.

it is empty, closed "until the seven plagues of the seven angels were ended (τελεσθῶσιν)" (v. 8). Both literary and narrative reasons indicate that 15:1–8 reports a heavenly encounter that serves to introduce the account of the pouring out of the seven bowls (16.1-21), commissioning the seven angels who will pour them out. The pouring out of the bowls presents the death of Jesus Christ, the final battle at Harmagedon (v. 16), bringing the dominance of evil to an end (see v. 17: γέγονεν).[28]

The first three "sevens" (letters, seals, and trumpets) are satisfactorily adjacent. The later location of the pouring out of the seven bowls (15:1-16:21) generates a challenge for any suggestion that the "sevens" play a determining role in the literary structure of Revelation. Are there indications *within Revelation* that throw light on the role of 12:1–14:20 and 17:1–22:5 in John's overall literary design?[29]

Preparing for Harmagedon: Rev 12:1–18, 13:1–18, and 14:1–20

There is general agreement that 12:1–14:20 is formed by three major visions: the woman and the dragon (12:1–18), the two beasts (13:1–18), and the Lamb, the Son of Man, and six angels (14:1–20).

First preparatory vision

The visions of the woman and of the dragon are described as a σημεῖον ... ἐν τῷ οὐρανῷ (12:1, 3). The same expression, described as *another* portent in heaven (ἄλλο σημεῖον ἐν τῷ οὐρανῷ)

---

28 For an extended exegesis of 15:1–16:21 in support of this claim, see Moloney, *The Apocalypse*, 229–54.
29 The stress indicates the aim of this study: to find hints *within the text* for a literary structure not determined by the reconstruction of a *Sitz im Leben der Kirche* that lies outside John's text.

appears in 15:2, opening the commissioning of the seven angels with seven plagues who will pour out the bowls (15:1–16:21). Thus, 12:1–14:20 opens with the vision of two portents in heaven (σημεῖον ἐν τῷ οὐρανῷ), and 15:1–16:21 begins with the vision of *another* σημεῖον ἐν τῷ οὐρανῷ. John's other uses of σημεῖον are negative (13:13, 14; 16:14; 19:20). Powers of evil may have access to miraculous portents, sourced by the beast (see 13:11–14). But they are not "in heaven."[30] The uses of σημεῖον ἐν τῷ οὐρανῷ in 12:1, 3 and 15:1 serve as textual markers to highlight the opening of two distinct narrative sections: 12:1–14:20 and 15:1–16:21.

The literary unity of 12:1–18 is not disputed. The narrative is made up of the description of the woman, the son, and the dragon (vv. 1–6), heavenly warfare (vv. 7–12), and a resumption of encounters between the woman, now bereft of her son, and the dragon (vv. 13–18). The meaning of the passage, as well as its sources, is hotly debated.[31] Despite mainstream interest in Greco-Roman background, the indication in v. 9 that the dragon is "that ancient serpent, who is called the Devil and Satan, the deceiver of the whole world" surely points to an imaginative development of Genesis 2–5.[32]

On the loss of the son eagerly sought by the dragon (v. 3) but snatched (ηρπάσθη) to God on his throne (v. 5), the woman flees into the wilderness (ἔρεμος) where she is protected and nourished. The heavenly potential of humankind (v. 1. See Gen 2:4b–24) is

---

30 It could be objected that the use of σημεῖον ἐν τῷ οὐρανῷ applied to the great red dragon in 12.3 is negative, but such in not the case for John. Both the woman and the dragon are ἐν τῷ οὐρανῷ (v. 1 and v. 3). The dragon is a powerful angelic figure (vv. 3–4), until defeated and cast down from heaven to the earth because "there was no longer any place for them ἐν τῷ οὐρανῷ" (v. 8).

31 The most favoured source-hypothesis is the pre-Christian Greco-Roman tradition of Leto, impregnated by Zeus and pursued by the dragon Python, and a parallel myth surrounding Isis and Typhon. See, for example, Koester, *Revelation*, 555–57.

32 For an extended exegesis of 12:1–18 in support of the following sketch, see Moloney, *The Apocalypse*, 167–88.

lost, but God has prepared a place of protection and nourishment (vv. 5–6. See Gen 3:1–24). The great red dragon is also "in heaven", along with its own potential (vv. 3–4), but war breaks out and "the devil and Satan, the deceiver of the whole world", like the woman, suffers a change of place (vv. 13–12). He and his cohort are thrown down to earth, as "there was no longer any place for them in heaven" (v. 8). Rejoicing follows, as the heavenly situation has changed, but the situation "on earth" has now also been tragically challenged (vv. 10–12)

"On earth," the dragon pursues the woman as she flees into the wilderness (εἰς τὸν ἔρημον) a second time (vv. 13–14). The two flights must be distinguished.[33] The woman's initial flight after her son has been snatched away from her (vv. 5-6) reflects humankind's loss of innocence and banishment from Eden (Gen 3:24). After the dragon's fall to earth, he pursues the woman, but she is protected by God through phenomena that recall Israel's Exodus experience: God's presence with Israel in the desert (v. 14a; see Exod 19:4; Deut 32:10–11), the gifts of the quail and the manna (v. 14b; see Exod 16:1–36), and the opening of the Reed Sea (v. 15; see Exod 14:21–29). Temptation and evil have been let loose "on earth". The woman is pursued by Satan but protected by God (vv. 13–16). Frustrated by this situation, the dragon went off "to make war on the rest of her children" (v. 17). John has addressed the never-ending tension that exists between humankind and the powers of evil.

Second preparatory vision

Satan takes up a position of authority between the land and the sea (v. 18).[34] From there he will commission his agents.[35] He sees

---

[33] Against majority opinion. See, for example, Beale, *Revelation*, 668; Prigent, *Apocalypse*, 38.

[34] On 12.18 as a "bridge verse," see Giesen, *Die Offenbarung*, 302

[35] For an extended exegesis of 13.1–18 in support of the following sketch, see Moloney, *The Apocalypse*, 189–211.

to the rising of the beast from the sea, corrupt political authority (13:1-10), and the beast from the land, corrupt religious authority (vv. 11-18).[36] Their collusion is aimed at the corruption of "all the inhabitants of the earth" (v. 18). The beast from the earth works that all might bear the mark of the beast from the sea the on the right hand or the forehead (vv. 16-17). But for the Christian audience of John's book, that mark only brings further unresolvable frustration: 666 (v. 18).[37] From the beginning of all time, Satan has pursued humankind through his agents. Some have resisted. Their names are "written in the book of life of the Lamb that was slaughtered from the foundation of the world".[38] They are not Christian martyrs, but the saints of Israel who lived according to God's word and accepted the messianic promises of the prophets "from the foundation of the world" (see Dan 7.15-27; 9.5-6, 10). Not only have the powers of evil been rampant from all time; the saving effects of the death and resurrection of Jesus Christ have also been present.[39]

---

36 The dragon gave his power to the beast from the sea (13.2: ἔδωκεν αὐτῷ ὁ δράκων τὴν δύναμιν αὐτοῦ) and the beast from the land exercises all the authority of the beast from the sea (v. 12: καὶ τὴν ἐχουσίαν τοῦ πρώτου θηρίου πᾶσαν ποιεῖ ἐνώπιον αὐτοῦ). Because of his fall (9:1-2; 12:7-9) Satan needs agents (see 20:1-6).

37 See above, note 16.

38 This is the obvious translation of the Greek οὗ οὐ γέγραπται τὸ ὄνομα αὐτοῦ ἐν τῷ βιβλίῳ τῆς ζωῆς τοῦ ἀρνίου τοῦ ἐσφραγμένου ἀπὸ καταβολῆς κόσμου. It appears in the margin of New Revised Standard Version. The NRSV text associates the beginning of the world with the book. Despite the Greek, majority opinion is expressed by Aune, *Revelation*, 2:747: "It is logically and theologically impossible to make sense of the statement that the Lamb was slaughtered before the foundation of the world." See also Koester, *Revelation*, 575. On the contrary, it is crucial for the interpretation of Revelation to capture John's understanding of the transtemporal saving effects of Jesus' death and resurrection, "from the foundation of the world". See the excursus on this question in Moloney, *The Apocalypse*, 199-204.

39 John is concerned about challenges to Christian communities, but the description of the suffering of the saints that appears regularly in his book (10:7; 11:6-13, 18; 16:5-6; 18:20, 24), under the influence of Daniel, refers to the holy ones

Third preparatory vision

The literary unit of 14:1-20 is formed by two major sections.[40] In 14:1-5, the Lamb is surrounded by the first fruits of his being slain yet standing: 144,000 from Israel who have been faithful to the Law and the Prophets. They are "the first fruits of the Lamb" (v. 4). A longer section is dedicated to a description of the victory of the one like the Son of Man (vv. 6-20). The figure of the Son of Man, with a golden crown on his head and a sharp sickle in his hand, is located at the centre of the passage (v. 14). Three angels introduce him, announcing that the hour for his victory has come (first angel: vv. 6-7), the fall of Babylon (second angel: v. 8), and the torment of those who have worshipped the beast, matched by the blessedness of those already saved in the time of Israel (third angel: vv. 9-13). The appearance of the one like the Son of Man (v. 14) is followed by three further angels. The condemnatory prophecy of Isaiah's vision of the winepress in Isaiah 63:6-7 has been re-imagined. The hour for the victory of the one like the Son of Man has come (first angel: vv. 6-7), an angel joins the harvesting, sickle in hand (second angel: v. 17), and the vintage is gathered "outside the city," producing blood that covers the earth (third angel: vv. 18-20).[41]

The saving effects of Jesus' death and resurrection have been perennially available (vv. 1-5; see 13.8). The historical event of Jesus' execution "outside the city" generated a universal saving flow of blood (vv. 6-20). As Eugenio Corsini puts it: "The death of Christ, therefore, appears as the judgment of God in its dual aspect: the gathering of the elect (reaping) and the condemnation and

---

of Israel who have observed the law and accepted the messianic promises of the prophets (see 6:9; 12:17; 14:12; 20:4). See the excursus on this question in Moloney, *The Apocalypse*, 53-55.

40 For an extended exegesis of 14:1-20 in support of the following sketch, see Moloney, *The Apocalypse*, 213-28.

41 On the blood that flowed from the winepress "trodden outside the city" as the blood of Christ, see Moloney, *The Apocalypse*, 224-27.

destruction of the evil forces (the vintage and the pressing of the grapes)."42

John returns of the literary feature of "seven" in 16:1-21. He indicates that this is the "final" such sequence (15:1, 8). It features a proclamation from the loud voice from the throne, "It is done," as the seventh bowl was poured out (v. 17: γέγονεν). The powers of evil assembled at Harmagedon (v. 16) have been defeated (vv. 18-21). It has been prefaced by three distinct narrative units: 12:1-18, 13:1-18, and 14:1-20.

The Consequences of Harmagedon: Rev 17:1–19:10, 19:11–21:8, and 21:9–22:5

Contemporary commentary regards some of the narratives found in 17.1–22.5 as "interludes."[43] These suggestions miss the striking literary parallel between 14:6-20 and 17:1-22:5. In 14:6-20, one like the Son of Man is at the centre of the passage (14:14), accompanied by three angels before (vv. 6, 8, 9) and three angels after (vv. 15, 17, 18) his majestic presence (v. 14). An identical pattern can be found in the macro-sequence of 17:1-22:5:

17:1-18: An angel who had one of the seven bowls shows John the judgment on the "great whore."

18:1—20: An angel announces the fall of Babylon.

18:21-19:10: An angel announces the humiliation of Babylon.

19:11-16: The Word on a white horse is victorious over the nations.

---

42 Corsini, *The Apocalypse*, 272.
43 These "interludes" are especially important for Koester, *Revelation*, 681-82, for whom 17.1-18 is a third "interlude." The others are 7.1-17 and 10.1-11.14. See also M. Eugene Boring, *Revelation, Interpretation* (Louisville, KY: John Knox, 1989), 178-79; Aune, *Revelation*, 3:915; Boxall, *Revelation*, 228-29; Prigent, *Apocalypse*, 478 n.1. The "interludes" provide pauses before God carries out his final act. The following macro-structure of 17:1–22:5 does not allow for such literary "interludes."

19:17-21: An angel announces the destruction of all wicked powers.

20:1-21:8: An angel binds Satan for a thousand years.

21:9-22:5: An angel who had one of the seven bowls invites John to witness the "bride of the Lamb" and the river of life.

As well as the literary parallel between 14:6-20, the macro-structure of 17:1-22:5 is self-contained, framed by the two-fold appearance of angels who had one of the seven bowls: the first (17:1) and the last (21:9) of the six angels, and the contrasting roles of a woman (17:1-6; 21:9-14). Within that macro-structure, John articulates three distinct themes. Three consequences of the victory of Harmagedon follow: Babylon, the locus of all evil is destroyed (17:1-19:10), all evil powers are destroyed or rendered powerless (19:11-21:8), and the chosen are gathered (21:9-22:5).

Vision of the first consequence

Not without its obscurities,[44] 17:1-19:10 describes the destruction of Babylon (17:1-18), the lament over its destruction (18:1-20), the rejoicing of heaven, and the marriage of the Lamb (19:1-10).[45] Despite long-held conviction that the beast with whom the woman shares abominable intimacy is Rome (see vv. 7-14), the message is more universal. The woman is a symbol of Jerusalem, "the great

---

44 The major challenge for interpreters is the identification of the seven heads, seven mountains, the seven kings, five who have fallen, those that remain, and an eighth that goes to destruction, the ten horns that are ten further kings, all of whom make war on the Lamb and are conquered in 17:8-14. Most relate the symbols to the city of Rome and the kings with its Emperors and their vassals. A serious problem for this interpretation is that Rome is responsible for the destruction of Rome in vv. 16-18. For an identification of the kings as symbols of a more universal ("seven") abuse of power and the city as Jerusalem, see Moloney, *The Apocalypse*, 261-67.

45 For an extended exegesis of 17:1-19:10 in support of the following sketch, see Moloney, *The Apocalypse*, 255-92. For some, 18:1-24 forms a distinct literary unit. See, for example, Aune, *Revelation*, 3:975-83; Prigent, *Apocalypse*, 499; Giesen, *Offenbarung*, 389-90; Koester, *Revelation*, 712.

city" (v. 18) whose long collusion with evil political and religious authorities led to the execution of Jesus. She is now destroyed, and the "words of God" are fulfilled (vv. 15-18).[46] All who have profited from the prostitution of the woman lament (18.1-24), while "the prophets and saints" of Israel whose blood has been shed in Jerusalem (v. 24) can rejoice as God has given judgment for them against that city (v. 20). Heaven rejoices, the marriage of the Lamb has come, and the bride of the Lamb makes herself ready. As this passage opened, the ambiguity of ἡ γύνη (12:13-18) was negatively resolved in 17:1-6 (v. 4: ἡ γύνη). It will be positively resolved in the marriage of the Lamb, announced (but not enacted) as the passage closes in 19:6-9 (v. 7: ἡ γύνη).

Vision of the second consequence

The second consequence of Harmagedon is the destruction of all wicked powers (19:11-21:8).[47] It opens with a description of the fierce rider on the white horse whose name is not known (19:11-12), but whose function is clear. He brings integrity (v. 11), makes God known (v. 13), and brings judgment (v. 15). Accompanied by a heavenly army, he exercises his messianic authority through the shedding of his blood (v. 13a, v. 15).[48] Through the cross, he is established as King of kings and Lord of lords (v. 16). John describes, separately, two aspects of the righteous war against all evil (19:17-21 and 20:7-10). Each aspect of the battle is followed by judgment (20:1-6 and 20:11-21:8).

In the first aspect of the battle, the destruction of the forces of evil begins (19:17-21). The beast from the sea and his false

---

46 For the original recipients of Revelation, the physical destruction of Jerusalem was well-known. On these issues, see Moloney, *The Apocalypse*, 268-70.
47 These are the most challenging pages in Revelation. For an extended exegesis of 19.11-21.8 in support of the following sketch, see Moloney, *The Apocalypse*, 293-324.
48 As with the blood of 14:20, so also the garment dipped in blood worn by the rider of the white horse in 19:13 refers to the blood of Christ. See Moloney, *The Apocalypse*, 298-99.

prophet (the beast from the land of 13:11–18) are "thrown down alive (ζῶντες) into the lake of fire that burns with sulfur" (19:20). All the rest (see vv. 17b-19) are destroyed by the rider on the horse (v. 21).

Judgment follows. Satan has fallen (see 9:1–12; 12:7–12). He must exercise his corrupting power through his agents (see 12:13–13:18). "That ancient serpent, who is the devil and Satan" (20:2; see 12:9) has long been rendered powerless, locked and sealed in the pit. The "thousand years" is the age that lasts from Satan's original fall until he is released (vv. 1–2). "After that he must be let out for a while" (v. 3). The thousand years mark the period of Israel, during which Satan's agents have spread pain, warfare, death, and wickedness. Those in Israel who have been slain because of their observance of the Law and the acceptance of the promises of the prophets will "reign with Christ" (vv. 4–5). They belong to "the first resurrection" and will not face "the second death" (v. 6). All others who die must wait for Christ's victory to come to life (v. 5).[49]

The second aspect of the battle is reported in 20:7–10. The Christian era, continuing God's sacred history, begins with the release of Satan (v. 7: λυθήσεται ὁ σατανᾶς) for the definitive battle at the end of the thousand years. Recalling the description of Harmagedon (see 16:12-21), the battle becomes universal. The nations, Gog and Magog, and innumerable forces gather for the kill, but they are destroyed by fire (vv. 8–9). Thrown down, the devil joins the beast and the false prophet in the lake of fire and

---

49 This interpretation of the "thousand-year reign" as the period of Israel prior to the unleashing of Satan for the final battle of Jesus' death and resurrection, inspired by Corsini, *Apocalypse*, 372–79, challenges most interpretations of Rev 20:1–6. Many Christian traditions are determined by their interpretation of the nature and timing of the "thousand-year reign". For a survey, see Koester, *Revelation*, 741–50. Like almost all interpreters Koester regards "the souls of those beheaded for their testimony to Jesus and for the Word of God" (20:4) as Christian martyrs, not the saints of Israel who lived by the Law and believed in the prophetic witness to Jesus Christ, as above.

sulfur. They are not destroyed, but tormented day and night forever and ever (v. 10).[50]

Judgment, resulting in both destruction and blessing, follows (20:11-22:8). Everyone is summoned before the one seated on the great white throne (vv. 11-14; see Dan 7:9-10). At the "second death", those whose names are not written in the book of life are cast into the lake of fire (v. 15). Those who conquer sin and evil will dwell in the New Jerusalem, a heavenly holy city like a bride adorned for her husband. God will dwell with mortals; death and suffering will be no more (21:3-4). But the place of the wicked will be in the burning lake (v. 8).

Vision of the third consequence

The vision of the final consequence of the victory at Harmagedon (21:9) recalls the vision of the first consequence (17:1):

> Then one of the seven angels who had the seven bowls came and said to me, "Come, I will show you the judgment of the great whore who is seated on many waters" (17:1).
> Then one of the seven angels who had the seven bowls full of the seven last plagues came and said to me, "Come, I will show you the bride, the wife of the Lamb" (21.9).

Simple yet subtle literary techniques indicate the end of the cycle of three consequences, and by recalling the seven angels who had the bowls of the seven last plagues, John also links these three consequences with Harmagedon, the result of the angelic pouring out of the seven bowls (15:1-16:21). After the violent judgment

---

[50] In both aspects of the battle, most evil forces are destroyed (see 19:21; 20:8-9), but the beast and the false prophet are "alive" (19:21: ζῶντες). Satan joins them in endless torment (20:10). This detail explains the ongoing existence of evil, even in the New Jerusalem (see 21:27; 22:11, 15). As Collins remarks: "The repeated rebellions of Satan impress upon the reader the irrepressible character of the forces of evil and chaos. ... The definitive defeat of Satan implies that even though chaos is irrepressible, it is less powerful, less real than creative order" (*Apocalypse*, 141).

that dominated the first two consequences, the third reports the gift of the New Jerusalem (21:9–22:5).[51]

The angel shows John the bride of the Lamb, his wife (21:9: τὴν νύμφην τὴν γυναῖκα τοῦ ἀρνίου). The bride is the heavenly Jerusalem, coming down from heaven (v. 10), whose description is highlighted by a structure based upon the number twelve and light-filled embellishment (vv. 11–21). The ambiguous situation of the woman in 12:13–18 was negatively resolved by the whore mounted on and destroyed by the beast (17:1–6, 15–18). But a third possibility now emerges: the woman (ἡ γύνη) united in marriage as the bride of the Lamb.[52] All whose names are written in the Lamb's book of life will dwell in the city where its temple is the Lord God and the Lamb, where "the glory of God is its light, and its lamp is the Lamb" (vv. 22–23). All nations will stream to it, but those who practise abomination or falsehood are excluded (vv. 24–27). The passage closes with a final intervention of an angel from the pouring out of the bowls.[53] He shows the life-giving water and tree of life. The nations will be healed, the servants of the Lamb, marked by his sign will worship, and there will be no more night. "The Lord God will be their light, and they will reign forever and ever".

---

51 For an extended exegesis of 21.9–22.5 in support of the following sketch, see Moloney, *The Apocalypse*, 325–44. Commentators differ on the role of 22:6–9. Does it precede the Epilogue, or form part of it? For the discussion, concluding that vv. 6–9 "should be read as a bridge passage," see Moloney, *The Apocalypse*, 345–46.

52 Although not a structural element in the narrative, John's recourse to the figure of ἡ γύνη in 12:1–18; 17:1–6, 15–18, and 21:9 (see 21:2) is a deliberate use of the symbol of "the woman" to address humankind's potential. See the recent reflections of Edmondo F. Lupieri, "L'Apocalisse dopo Corsini: un eredità in evoluzione", *Apocalisse ieri oggi e domani. Atti della giornata di studio in memoria di Eugenio Corsini. Torino, 2 ottobre, 2018*, ed. C. Lombardi and L. Silvano (Alessandria: Edizione dell'Orso, 2018) 19–28.

53 The angel is not explicitly mentioned in 22:1, but the verb καὶ ἐδειξέν μοι ποταμόν requires a subject: who showed John the river of life? The antecedent must be the angel of 21.9. See Prigent, *Apocalypse*, 624; Koester, *Revelation*, 817.

Consequences

Timothy Beal insists that Revelation's birth, a stitching together of "various bits and pieces of Jewish scriptures and other mythologies," was "monstrous." His overview of a variety of receptions of the book suggests that "this hideous progeny" will "continue to go forth and prosper."[54] He also suggests that a way around this problem might be "to go back and read some more Bible, to reread the texts that form the scriptural core of these delusions."[55] But are they delusions?

The Book of Revelation will continue to generate "monstrous" interpretations, but we need to "go back and read some more Bible", beginning with a careful reading of Revelation itself. Despite its tragic impact upon Christian history and Christian lives, the book's long-standing role in the Christian canon asks that we focus upon the text itself. This study suggests that it was shaped as follows:

I   **The Prologue (1:1–8)**

II   **Seven letters (1:9–3:22).** A heavenly encounter that commissions John to write what the one like the Son of Man says to the churches (1:9–20), and the letters to the seven churches (2:1–3:22).

III   **Seven seals (4:1–8:1).** A heavenly encounter that commissions the slain but standing Lamb as worthy to open the seals (4:1–5:14), and the opening of the seven seals in a sequence of 4 + 3 (6:1–8:1).

IV   **Seven trumpets (8:2–11:19).** A heavenly encounter that commissions seven angels with trumpets (8:2–6), and the blowing of the seven trumpets in a sequence of 4 + 3 (8:7–11:19).

V   **Seven Bowls (12:1–22:5)**

---

54 All citations are from Beal, *The Book of Revelation*, 208.
55 Beal, *The Book of Revelation*, 206.

12:1–14:20: The threefold preparations for the pouring out of the bowls:

    12:1–17: First preparatory vision: *The woman, the son, and the ancient serpent.*

    13:1–18: Second preparatory vision: *The two beasts: the collusion of corrupt religious and political authority.*

    14:1–20: Third preparatory vision: *The salvation of the faithful in Israel, an anticipated effect of the blood of the Lamb.*

15:1–16:21: The pouring out of the seven bowls:

    15:1–8: *A heavenly liturgy prepares for the opening of the seals.*

    16:1–9: *Pouring out of the first four bowls.*

    16:10–21: *Pouring out of the last three bowls: leading to the Lamb's saving action.*

17:1–22:5: The threefold consequences of the death and resurrection of Christ:

    17:1–19:10: Vision of the first consequence: *the destruction of Babylon.*

    19:11–21:8: Vision of the second consequence: *the destruction of all evil power.*

    21:9–22:5: Vision of the third consequence: *the gathering of the chosen*

VI   The Epilogue (22:6–21)

This study attempts to discern indications within the text of Revelation to establish literary patterns and the shape of the whole narrative.[56] It presupposes that the focus of the Book of Revelation is not the end of time, although that is an element in its message

---

56 It draws upon the ground-breaking work of Corsini, *Apocalypse* (1983; original Italian: 1980), and his *Apocalisse* (2002).

(see 22:20). Its structure and meaning are determined by John's conviction that the saving effects of the death and resurrection of Jesus Christ have been available "from the foundation of the world" (13:8).

7

The Jews, Israel, and Jerusalem in the Book of Revelation

The "John" named as the author of the Book of Revelation (Rev 1:1, 4, 9; 22:8) is almost universally recognised by interpreters as a Jew.[1] There are several reasons for scholarly unanimity on the Jewishness of John the prophetic visionary. He is very familiar with the Sacred Scriptures of Israel. More than any other work in the New Testament, his book is dominated by direct citations and obvious allusions to Israel's Scriptures: especially Daniel, the Torah, and the prophets, with a keen focus upon Ezekiel and Isaiah.[2] Despite his abundant use of these Scriptures, he never mentions which book he is citing. John is so familiar with these texts that he takes it for granted that his audience will know he is referring to their shared sacred Scriptures. Secondly, he wrote in a highly original Greek, often developing his own grammar and syntax, and sometimes using words and expressions unique to his work. Greek was not his native language. He is entirely familiar with the literary form of Jewish apocalyptic literature (found, for example, in the almost contemporary Jewish books known to us as 1 Enoch [200–100's BCE] and 4 Ezra [200's CE]). His entire literary world was Jewish.[3]

---

1 For thorough surveys, see Aune, *Revelation*, 1:xlvii–lvi; Beale, *Revelation*, 34–36; Koester, *Revelation*, 65–69; Moloney, *The Apocalypse*, 4-6.
2 Among many, see Moyise, *The Old Testament in the Book of Revelation*. Gregory K. Beale, *John's Use of the Old Testament in Revelation*, Library of New Testament Studies 166 (London: Bloomsbury, 1999), suggests that certain passages in Revelation are almost midrash upon Daniel. Moyise argues that John adapts Daniel creatively.
3 As Koester, *Revelation*, 141, comments: "Some unusual aspects of the grammar may reflect Greek translations of the OT or forms of vulgar Greek that were used in Asia Minor, but at points the writer deliberately flouts the accepted

Although less certain, as we have no evidence from the text of the Book of Revelation, it appears that he had fled to Asia Minor from Palestine after the disaster of the Jewish Revolt of 65–70 CE.[4] His awareness of the situations and the experiences of the young Christian communities in the cities of Ephesus, Smyrna, Pergamum, Thyatira, Sardis, and Laodicea (2:1–3:22), all located in south-western Asia Minor (today's Turkey), toward the end of the first Century shows that he was familiar with that part of the world. He writes to those cities from the nearby island of Patmos, about sixty kilometres from the city of Miletus on the south-western coast of Asia Minor. He tells his audience that he finds himself there because of his zeal and preparedness to undergo sacrifice and suffering in his mission to them (1:9).[5]

Despite his obvious Jewishness, John's literary dependence upon Israel's sacred Scriptures, and its more apocalyptic writings, the narrative of Revelation has sometimes been interpreted as "anti-Jewish." How valid is this accusation, levelled against a book that is part of Christianity's sacred Scriptures? Our reflections upon this critical question, especially as we read Revelation in our multicultural and multi-faith third millennium, must begin with a description of what has been called "the parting of the ways" between first Century Judaism and earliest Christianity.

---

forms of grammar, which fits the idea that neither the writer nor the God to whom he bears witness is held captive by social convention."

[4] See Aune, *Revelation*, 1:lvi; Elaine Pagels, *Revelations: Visions, Prophecy, and Politics in the Book of Revelation* (New York: Viking, 2012) 7–8.

[5] Most interpreters regard the reason John gives in Rev 1:9 for his being on the island of Patmos (διὰ τόν λόγον τοῦ θεοῦ καὶ τὴν μαρτυρίαν τοῦ Ἰησοῦ) as forced imprisonment. The expression can equally well be rendered as a missionary motivation for his presence in Asia Minor: on account of the Word of God and to render witness to Jesus. See Thompson, *The Book of Revelation*, 172–73; Corsini, *Apocalisse*, 81.

The Parting of the Ways

Jesus was a Jew, as were his parents, the Twelve, his first disciples, and the first groups of people (most likely gathering in Jerusalem and Antioch) who accepted that the crucified Jesus of Nazareth was the long-awaited Christ. Although we cannot be certain, most authors who produced early Christian writings (Paul, the authors of the Gospels and the Acts of the Apostles ["Luke" may not have been Jewish],[6] the Letter to the Hebrews, the so-called Catholic Epistles, and Revelation) were Jews. They celebrated a unique ritual meal "in memory" of Jesus' death and resurrection (see 1 Cor 11:23–26; Luke 22:14–20), but they continued their adhesion to the God of Israel, and took part in Israel's ritual traditions (see, for example, Acts 3:1). That ritual meal, however innovative the summons to "remember" may have been, was celebrated according to Jewish traditions.[7] The very early conflict between Christians on the necessity to circumcise Gentile males who became Christians, evidenced most importantly in the Letters to the Galatians (see 5:1–12), to the Philippians (3:2–11), and in the Acts of the Apostles (see 15:1–35), is significant testimony to the pain that separation from Jewish origins generated for the earliest Christians.

The claim of the Christians that the crucified Jesus of Nazareth was the expected Messiah did not lessen their belief in the God of Israel, nor remove them from trust in the promises made to Israel. Nevertheless, as Paul eloquently pointed out about 52 CE, belief that a crucified criminal was the Christ necessarily created tension between them and their fellow-Jews: "We proclaim Christ crucified, a stumbling block to Jews" (1 Cor 1:23. See also Gal 3:13).[8]

---

6 François Bovon, *Luke*, trans. Christine M. Thomas, 3 vols., Hermeneia (Minneapolis: Fortress, 2002–2012) 1:8–10, helpfully identifies the author of Luke-Acts as a "god-fearer."

7 See the classical discussion of this question by Joachim Jeremias, *The Eucharistic Words of Jesus*, trans. Norman Perrin (London: SCM, 1966) 16–41.

8 See Konrad Schmid and Jens Schröter, *The Making of the Bible. From the First Fragments to Sacred Scripture*, trans. Peter Lewis (Cambridge, MA: Harvard University Press 2021) 182-221. Although the Acts of the Apostles was written much later (toward the end of the first Century), always focusing upon a

Prior to the Jewish War, several Jewish sects understood, lived, and celebrated their Jewishness differently. We know of the Pharisees, the Sadducees, the Essenes, the Zealots, and there may have been others. The earliest Christians formed another Jewish sect. According to the author of the Acts of the Apostles, they were recognised as such by Rabbi Gamaliel. After describing various other sects that had come and gone, he warns the Sanhedrin: "Keep away from these men and let them alone; because if this plan and this undertaking is of human origin, it will fail; but if it is of God, you will not be able to overthrow them" (Acts 5:38–39). The situation changed dramatically after the Jewish War of 65–70 CE.

After 70 CE, the city of Jerusalem and its temple had been destroyed. The land of Israel was entirely under the control of Roman authority. Only the Pharisees, a mobile and dynamic pastoral form of Judaism, were long-term survivors. They did not need the land, the city, and the temple with its priests and sacrifices. Wherever Jewish people gathered, in geographical Israel and beyond, the Pharisees went with the Torah, and reconstituted post-War Judaism from the devastating results of the War. Synagogues, a place where Jewish people "come together," emerged across the Mediterranean world reaching into Asia, Egypt, and Europe. Over the centuries, the Pharisaic Torah-based form of Judaism built a wonderful religious system that continues in today's Jewish life and practice.[9]

Christians also survived. Both Pharisaic Judaism and Christianity withstood the disasters of 70 CE. In many ways, both Christians and Jews were communities in search of an identity. This was especially clear for post-War Judaism that forged a new identity through its pastoral care and the interpretation and living of Torah, with its manifold possibilities. Christianity's identity was

---

positive outcome to suffering, its early chapters record these tensions (see Acts 4:1–22; 5:17–42; 6:8-15; 8:1–3).

9 See Martin Goodman, *A History of Judaism* (Milton Keynes: Penguin Random House, 2017) 229-88.

intimately associated with Judaism, its sacred Scripture, its beliefs, and traditions. However, the Christian belief that the God of Israel had entered human history in the person of Jesus of Nazareth, understood as the fulfilment of the messianic prophecies and the saviour of humankind, necessarily clashed with post-War Judaism. Gradually a "parting of the ways" marked the relationship between Judaism, now without land, city, temple, priesthood, and sacrifices, and Christianity, moving further and further into a hostile relationship with its parent, Judaism, as they claimed that God's Messiah had come in Jesus of Nazareth. As post-War Judaism focused more intensely upon Torah and its interpretation for its lifeblood, Christians focused more intensely on what they believed God had done for humankind in and through the life, teaching, death, and resurrection of Jesus Christ. Lines between Jews and Christians were not clear cut, and "the parting of the ways" took many forms, advancing at different speeds in different geographical locations across the closing decades of the first Century and into the second.[10] But the die had been cast.

---

10 See Stephen G. Wilson, *Related Strangers. Jews and Christians 70–170 C. E.* (Minneapolis: Fortress, 1995); Judith M. Lieu, *Image and Reality: The Jews in the World of Christians in the Second Century* (Edinburgh: T. & T. Clark, 1996). It is difficult to date the addition of the Twelfth Benediction (the so-called Birkat ha-Minim) to the Synagogue prayer of the Eighteen Benedictions (the Shemoneh Esrei). It is equally difficult to assess its implementation. It is safer to regard it as symptomatic of the parting of the ways, not its cause. See Schmid and Schröter, *The Making of the Bible*, 222-28. For a good summary of the debate, see Pieter Van Der Horst, "The Birkat ha-minim in Recent Research," *The Expository Times* 105 (1994) 363-68. See also the provocative contrasting studies of Joel Marcus, "Birkat Ha-Minim Revisited," *New Testament Studies* 55 (2009) 523-51, and Adele Reinhartz, *Cast out of the Covenant. Jesus and Anti-Judaism in the Gospel of John* (Lanham, MD: Lexington Books/Fortress Academic, 2018).

The Inevitable Polemic

Claim and counter claim across the gradually widening divide between Jews and Christians provide one of the essential elements for a sound understanding of the formative background of the emerging first Century Christian literature, known to us as the New Testament. There can be no avoiding the truth that historically conditioned anger lies behind some of that literature. Even though the earliest Gospel of Mark (c. 70 CE) is not as confrontational as Matthew (late 80s CE), Luke (late 80s CE), or John (c. 100 CE), the author has no difficulty in reading Israel's Scriptures as fulfilled in the life, teaching, death, and resurrection of Jesus Christ. Jesus' coming fulfils the prophecies of Isaiah and Malachi (Mark 1:2-3); he is the historically identifiable Son of Man of the prophet Daniel, the Suffering Servant from Isaiah (see, for example, Mark 10:45),[11] and his suffering and death fulfils Psalm 22 (see Mark 15:29, 32, 34). Israel's Scriptures were interpreted through Christian eyes.

The Gospel of Matthew, most likely written in the late 80's of the first Century, is marked by a growing tension (Matt 11:2–16:12) and a sustained hostility against the leaders of Israel, especially the Pharisees (see especially Matt 23:1-36). Only in Matthew do we find the terrible cry from the Jerusalem crowd during Jesus' Roman trial: "His blood be on us and on our children" (27:25). Such words were most likely never uttered, but the Gospel of Matthew developed them in a hostile situation of claim and counter claim. This anger shaped the way Matthew reacts to what he regarded as a false Jewish narrative. For example, he reports what he regards as a lie concocted by Jewish leadership about Jesus' disciples stealing Jesus' crucified body (28:11-15), concluding: "This story is still told among the Jews to this day" (28:16. See 27:57–28:20).[12] Matthew outstrips Mark in

---

11 See Moloney, *Mark*, 212-14.
12 This passage indicates an anti-Christian polemic among post-War Jews. However, there is little evidence of such polemic. The pillars of Rabbinic Judaism (the Mishnah and the Talmudim of Jerusalem and Babylon) largely ignore Christianity and its claims. See Trude Weiss-Rosmarin, ed., *Jewish*

understanding Jesus as the fulfilment of Israel's Scriptures (see 1:22-23; 2:5-6, 15, 17-18, 23; 3:2, 4:14-16; 8:17, etc.).

For Matthew, Jesus and his teaching "perfects" the Law and the prophets (see 5:17-20). As his story closes, the risen Jesus commissions his disciples for a mission that flies in the face of central beliefs and practices of post-War Judaism. Jesus is the Lord of creation, and all authority has been given to him. Subsequently, the disciples are to take the Gospel to all nations (not just the Chosen People), baptise them in the name of the Father, Son, and Holy Spirit (abandoning circumcision as an initiation rite), teaching them to observe all that Jesus has taught (and not Torah) (28:16-20).

The two volumes of Luke-Acts are more subtle, but the same mindset continues.[13] The author of Luke-Acts is especially heavy-handed in the speeches of Peter, Stephen, and Paul reported in the Acts of the Apostles. They lay the blame for the execution of Jesus upon the Jews (see, for example, Acts 2:36; 4:11-12, 25-27; 7:51-53; 10:39-43, etc.). Consequently, for this early Christian author (who composed these speeches late in the first Century), the Jews systematically reject the preaching of the good news about Jesus. "The apostles" turn away from them to "bring salvation to all the earth" (13:47. See 13:46-52). The Gospel of John notoriously and consistently uses the expression "the Jews" to describe the characters in his story who reject Jesus, and his disciples. The only credible explanation of this phenomenon lies in the apparent decision on the part of Israel's leadership to expel from the Synagogue anyone who believed and confessed that Jesus was the Christ (John 9:22; 12:42; 16:2). We cannot be sure of when and how that happened, but the animosity between Jesus, his followers, and "the Jews" in the Fourth Gospel is perhaps the most severe form of anti-Jewish rhetoric in the New Testament (see especially

---

Expressions on Jesus. An Anthology (New York: Ktav, 1977). See especially pp. 1-98: Jacob Z. Lauterbach, "Jesus in the Talmud."

13 See Jack T. Sanders, *The Jews in Luke-Acts* (London: SCM, 1987).

8:44, where Jesus says to "the Jews": "You are from your father the devil"). Jesus accuses them to have lost sight of the manifestation of the glory of God in the person of Jesus because they were too concerned with the superficiality of their own importance (12:43).[14]

Perhaps the best summary of the early Church's self-understanding as transcending its Jewish origins is stated as a Christian author from late in the first Century begins what we call the Letter to the Hebrews:

> Long ago God spoke to our ancestors in many and various ways by the prophets, but in these last days he has spoken to us by a Son whom he appointed heir of all things, through whom he also created the worlds (1:1)

Overwhelmed by their belief in the centrality of the person, teaching, death, and resurrection of Jesus of Nazareth, it was inevitable that early Christians would arrive at this point.

They arrived there in a time of religious and social conflict with their parent, Israel. Two major witnesses manifest their unhappiness with this situation. At the end of his story of Jesus' ministry, the evangelist John wonders why "the Jews" had not accepted Jesus as the one who makes God known. But he has no adequate response (John 12:37–43).[15] Even more poignantly, Paul asks how God's chosen people came to reject Jesus, and he – in great personal anguish (see 9:1-5) – insists that they retain their unique place in God's saving history (Rom 9-11). Like John, but more eloquently, he closes his reflections by leaving this mystery with God: "O the depth of the riches of the wisdom and knowledge of God! How unsearchable are his judgments and how inscrutable his ways!" (11:33).[16]

---

14 On the issue of "the Jews" in the Gospel of John, see Moloney, "Israel, the People, and the Jews in the Fourth Gospel," in *Johannine Studies* 1975–2017, 93-115.
15 See Moloney, *John*, 363–69 for this assessment of John 12:37-43.
16 See Brendan Byrne, *Romans*, Sacra Pagina 6 (Collegeville, MN: Liturgical Press, 1996) 358-62.

And there we must leave it, recognising our obligation to step out of the conflict that must remain within the time-warp of the late first Century. Judaism is the parent of Christianity, and Jews are our brothers and sisters. John Ashton helpfully pointed us in the right direction as he summarised the situation late in the first Century: [One must] "recognise in these hot-tempered exchanges the type of family row in which the participants face one another across the room of a house which all have shared and all call home."[17]

Writing of the Johannine presentation of "the Jews," David Rensberger articulates a serious warning that applies to much early Christian literature, including the New Testament: it "serves as a very sobering reminder that words once written leave their writer's control, and that no one can expect to utter violent words without facing a violent consequence."[18] Despite the tragedies of Christian treatment of our Jewish brothers and sisters in the past, especially (but not only) the recent past, Jews and Christians come from the same home; we are all children of Abraham, called to an unconditional love of the one true God of Israel (see Deut 6:1-4).[19]

The Polemic in John's Revelation

Like all early Christian witnesses, John regards the death and resurrection Jesus Christ as crucial to an understanding of God's

---

17 John Ashton, *Understanding the Fourth Gospel* (Oxford: Clarendon, 1991) 151.
18 David Rensberger, "Anti-Judaism and the Gospel of John," in *Antijudaism and the Gospel*, ed. William R. Farmer (Harrisburg, PA: Trinity Press International, 1999) 152. See a parallel Jewish reflection by Jules Isaac, especially in the light of the Christian reception of Matt 27:25: "The Crime of Deicide. Proposition 16," in Weiss-Rosmarin, *Jewish Expressions of Jesus*, 253–83.
19 Dedicated to the characterisation of the leaders of Israel in the Gospel of Matthew, *mutatis mutandis* the urgent pastoral need to understand this fundamental truth has been well articulated by Byrne, *Lifting the Burden*, 1–8.

way with humankind. This view necessarily renders his own Jewishness different from that of the established Jewish communities in Asia. However, he has a distinctive view of the role and effects of Jesus Christ's death and resurrection that separates him from the early Christian authors described above. Two associated issues determine John's unique presentation of Israel, the Jews, and Jerusalem. They are both intimately linked with his understanding of God's sacred history, and the sequence of events that determine that history.

Most interpreters and translators of Revelation refuse to render accurately the Greek of Revelation 13:8. John is describing those who give allegiance to the beast from the sea (see 13:1). A literal translation of the original states that their "name has not been written <u>in the book of the life of the Lamb that was slaughtered from the foundation of the world</u>" (οὗ γέγραπται τὸ ὄνομα αὐτοῦ <u>ἐν τῷ βιβλίῳ τῆς ζωῆς τοῦ ἀρνίου τοῦ ἐσφαγμένου ἀπὸ καταβολῆς κόσμου</u>) (v. 8). Most critics claim that it is illogical and historically irresponsible to suggest that the Lamb was slain "from the foundation of the world."[20] They thus translate the expression as a description of the absence of the names of the sinful "from the foundation of the world in the book of life." This is a misunderstanding of one of John's major contributions to emerging Christian thought.

Secondly, John regularly refers to "the saints" who have suffered and died, sometimes associating them with those who have kept the word of God and listened to the prophets (see 5:8–10; 6:10; 8:3–4; 11:18; 13:7, 10; 14:12; 16:5–6; 17:6; 18:20, 24; 20:9). The expression "the saints" came to John from the Book of Daniel. The author of Daniel uses it for those in Israel who withstood the Seleucid persecution of Antiochus IV and maintained their adhesion to the God of Israel, cost what it may. They are victorious

---

20 See Aune, *Revelation*, 2:747; Koester, *Revelation*, 575. See also NRSV. The translation of the Greek endorsed above is provided in the margin of the NRSV.

over the forces of evil (see especially Dan 7:18, 22, 27). John does not use the expression to refer to Christians who have suffered under Diocletian, as is widely assumed. There was no systematic persecution of Christians or forced emperor-worship at the end of the first Century.[21] As Ramsay McMullen puts it: "Had the church been wiped off the face of the earth at the end of the first century, its disappearance would have caused no dislocation in the empire, just as its presence was hardly noticed at the time. ... Simply, it did not count."[22] In his search for models that will serve him in his instruction of the Asian churches, John looks back across Israel's history, singling out the "holy ones" who have persevered, lived by the word of God, and listened to the messianic prophecies.

For John, Israel's entire history has been marked by saints who have lived by the law and the prophets. No matter "when" they have lived and died, they have been saved by the death and resurrection of Jesus. The saving effects of the death and resurrection of Jesus must not be tied to the chronological time in history when it took place (e.g. 33 CE). They have been perennially present. However strange it may appear to a modern mind, *from all time* the holy ones in Israel have been swept up into the saving effects of the Lamb "slain before the foundation of the world" (13:8).[23] Various moments of God's saving history must not be separated: the story of Israel with its Law and Prophets, and the story of the Christian church. form one sacred story. The death and resurrection of Jesus Christ is the swivel around which they move, and it makes sense of both! Jews and Christians are not enemies.

---

21 This is almost universally accepted by historians. See the summary in Thompson, *The Book of Revelation*, 95–115.
22 McMullen, *Christianizing the Roman Empire* (AD 100-400), viii.
23 The notion of the perennial presence of the saving effects of Jesus' death and resurrection "from the foundation of the world" is central to John's thought, but it is also present in other New Testament witnesses. On this, see Moloney, *The Apocalypse*, 199–204. Beyond the texts considered there, see also Matt 13:35; 25:34.

As the Church experiences ambiguity in the Greco-Roman world of the late first Century (see 2:1–3:22), John uses apocalyptic language to point to the perennial struggles that have always gone on between good and evil. The saints from the period of the Seleucid persecutions kept the word of God and listened to the prophets. They serve as models for the Asian churches. The suffering of the saints did not begin with the Christian Church. As the Book of Daniel regularly points out, it has marked the whole of Israel's history: Assyria, Babylon, the Medes, Persia, and Rome (see especially Dan 7:1–8).

When the Lamb opened the fifth seal, John saw "the souls of those who had been slaughtered for the word of God and for the testimony they had given" (6:9). They are to wait until their number is "complete" (v. 11: ἕως πληρωθῶσιν). The opening of the sixth seal presents one hundred and forty-four thousand "sealed out of every tribe of Israel" (7:4–8). They are joined by "a great multitude that no one could count" (v. 9) who have access to the throne because of the blood of the Lamb (vv. 13–15). For *both* groups "the Lamb at the center of the throne will be their shepherd, he will guide them to springs of the water of life, and God will wipe away every tear from their eyes" (v. 17). The same double-staged access to life through the perennial saving effects of the death and resurrection explains the temple and the witnesses in 11:1-13. John's understanding of Israel and Christianity as part of a continuous story, determined by the perennial saving effects of the Lamb slain before the foundation of the world (13:8) is fundamental to his argument. As such, it throws light upon his explicit references to the Jews, Israel, and Jerusalem.

The Jews

In the letters to Smyrna (2:8–11) and to Philadelphia (3:7–13), John identifies what was most likely a regular experience for Christians in those cities: opposition from the Jewish community. Given John's understanding of the Jewish people as an integral part in a long saving history, on both occasions he accuses these opponents of not really being Jews. If they had been, they would courageously live by God's word, and accept the promise of the messianic prophecies. In John's judgment, they have not done so. On the contrary, they adhere to God's archenemy: Satan, "the deceiver of the whole world" (see 12:9; 20:2, 7). From John's perspective, authentic Jews were "saints" who hold to the word of God and listen to the messianic prophecies. In Smyrna (2:9) and Philadelphia (3:9), this has not happened. Some ethnic Jews have transferred their allegiance from the word of God and the messianic prophecies to collude with the powers of evil (Satan). John can thus claim that they are not Jews like the saints who went before them, whatever their ethnicity. They belong to the Synagogue of Satan. These are the only times in Revelation that "the Jews" are mentioned.

Israel

The nation Israel is presented in the same positive light. The letter to Pergamum (2:12-17), uses the background story of God's presence to his people during their period of wandering in the desert. Names are applied to two figures, Balaam and Balak, who cannot be identified in any first Century time and place, least of all in Pergamum. John uses those names to recall the episode in the desert where the Lord overcame collusion between them "to put a stumbling block before the people of Israel" (v. 14). They seek to deceive the Israelites into eating food sacrificed to idols and thus to practise fornication, a temptation that is overcome (Num 22:1-24:25). We have already seen that the first fruits of the saving effects of the death and resurrection of Jesus Christ are "one hundred forty-four thousand, sealed out of every tribe of the people of Israel" (7:4). The walls of the New Jerusalem are penetrated by twelve gates, inscribed "with the names of the twelve tribes of the Israelites" (21:12), and built on twelve foundations bearing the names of the twelve apostles (v. 14). John's sparse use of the name of the nation "Israel" demonstrates the continuity that exists between Israel and the Church, the New Jerusalem, determined by the death and resurrection of Jesus Christ.

Jerusalem

At first sight, John could be seen as critical of the historical Jerusalem. He regards it not only as the place where Jesus was executed (11:8), but as the seat of corrupt political and religious authorities that colluded with another corrupt political and religious authority to promote that execution. This affirmation depends upon the identification of "Babylon" with the political and religious leadership in Jerusalem (14:8; 16:19; 17:5; 18:2, 10, 21). John develops a narrative that portrays two beasts, one from the sea and the other from the land (13:1-18), as the corrupt political and religious agents of Satan. It is with these agents that corrupt political and religious agents in Jerusalem collude to execute Jesus Christ. This collusion is developed in 17:1-18. For John, the wicked collusion between Rome and the evil leaders of Jerusalem, dramatically portrayed as a whore mounted on the beast, led to the destruction of the whore in a way that recalls the destruction of Jerusalem in 70 CE: "They will make her desolate and naked; they will devour her flesh and burn her up with fire" (v. 16). It leads to the fall and disappearance of Babylon (18:1-24). At the end of the first Century, only of a corrupt and sinful Jerusalem can it be said: "And in you was found the blood of the prophets and of saints" (v. 24. See Mark 12:1-12; Matt 22:1-14).[24]

Rome destroyed her corrupt ally in 70 CE. The beast (Rome) destroys the whore (Babylon/Jerusalem). John's understanding of

---

[24] Anachronistic reference to the later Roman practice of Christian martyrdom (third and early fourth Century) must be avoided. See W. H. C. Frend, "Persecutions: Genesis and Legacy," in *The Cambridge History of Christianity. Volume 1: Origins to Constantine*, eds. Margaret M. Mitchell and Frances M. Young (Cambridge: Cambridge University Press, 2006) 503-23.

Jerusalem as a whore comes to him from Ezekiel (see Ezek 16), a regular source for his imagery. It is tempting (and traditional) to read 17:18, "The woman you saw is the great city that rules over the kings of the earth," as Rome. But, as has already been made clear in 16:19-20, another allusion to Ezekiel (see Ezek 5:1-4), the whore is the corrupted city of Jerusalem: "The great city was split into three parts and the cities of the nations fell. God remembered great Babylon and gave her the wine-cup of the fury of his wrath and every island fled away, and no mountains were to be found."[25] For John, the Jew, Rome's destruction of corrupted Jerusalem, the whore of Rome (the scarlet beast of 17:3), is a tragic end of the now corrupt "great city" (v. 18).

But this destruction was not the end of God's holy city, sacred to the Jews as God's dwelling place. For John, the political and religious authorities in Jerusalem who colluded with such Roman authorities were the sinful face of Jerusalem. Like the Jews who are no longer Jews but a Synagogue of Satan (2:9; 3:9), corrupt Jerusalem leadership should not be recognised as the city of "Jerusalem." That is why John calls the city, its leaders, and all the sinful people and practices that dwell there "Babylon" (see 18:1-24). The death of Jesus brings that "Babylon" to an end (15:1-16:21) and leads to Rome's destruction of the city (17:1-18:24). Judgment follows (19:1-20:15); a New Heaven, a New Earth, and a New Jerusalem emerge (21:1-22:5).

The narrative of Revelation matches the Gospel accounts of the collusion between Roman and Jewish leadership that led to the death of Jesus (see Mark 3:6; 15:1-20; Matt 12:14; 27:1-31; Luke 6:11; 23:13-25; John 11:45-53; 18:28-19:16). Jewish leadership (Babylon, the whore) sold out to the powers of evil. But John never condemns the city of Jerusalem. The death and resurrection of Jesus sees to the continuation of Jerusalem in the New Jerusalem.

---

25 On 16:19-20 as a reference to Jerusalem, dependent upon Ezekiel's shaving and weighing his hair in three parts in Ezek 5:1-4, see Moloney, *The Apocalypse*, 251-53.

As there was once "Jerusalem," there is now a "New Jerusalem." Because of the death and resurrection of Jesus, the New Jerusalem has no temple, but God dwells in the New Jerusalem, "for its temple is the Lord God the Almighty and the Lamb" (21:22).

John makes it clear, however, that the New Jerusalem is not an other-worldly reality. Despite the hyperbolic descriptions of the city, its walls, its gates and its interior, all the promises made to the seven churches in 2:1–3:22 are fulfilled in the New Jerusalem which is a gift from heaven ("the holy city of Jerusalem coming down from heaven and God" [21:10]). The "ideal" described in the promises to the stumbling churches of Asia (2:7; 2:17; 3:21) becomes "real" in the New Jerusalem, the Christian Church (22:2; 21:18–21; 22:1–2).[26] But there can be no escaping the ambiguity of the human condition and human communities. Those who dwell in the New Jerusalem continue to live in an ambiguous situation: "Let the evil doer still do evil, and the filthy still be filthy, and the righteous still do right, and the holy still be holy" (22:11. See also v. 15).

Conclusion

As with his allusions to the Jews (2:9; 3:9), to the nation Israel (2:14; 7:4; 21:12), so also with his stunning transformation of Jerusalem into the New Jerusalem (17:1–22:5) John does not replicate the antagonism between Jews and Christians found elsewhere in the New Testament. For John, the perennial saving effects of the death and resurrection of Jesus Christ have generated a God-designed continuity between Israel's sacred history and the life and practice of the Christian Church.

These reflections opened with a recognition of John's deep association with – even embodiment of – the sacred Scriptures of Israel (see 19:10; 22:9). In the epilogue to his book (22:6–21), he

---

26 For more detail, see Moloney, *The Apocalypse*, 343-44.

issues a warning that has long troubled interpreters. He threatens dire punishment for anyone who "adds to" the prophecy of this book (v. 18), or "takes away from the words of the book of this prophecy" (v. 19). Can John be so arrogant that he regards his own book as an untouchable word of God? If so, he is the only author in the New Testament to make such a claim.

It all depends upon what John means when he refers to "this book." He is not writing of his own book, but the sacred Scriptures of Israel that must never be altered in any way.[27] They tell the story of God's care for humankind with God's Law, and they are filled with the messianic promises of the prophets. John's book only makes sense because of the unchangeable truths that have come to him from his Jewish life and practice, enlightened by the unchangeable and perennial truths announced in Israel's sacred Scriptures. John's book makes sense because of "this book." For him, only the word of God articulated in Israel's Scriptures stands forever (see Isaiah 40:8; 1 Peter 1:23-25).

---

27 See Moloney, *The Apocalypse*, 358–62.

8

Postscript:
A Review of Christopher Rowland, *By an Immediate Revelation: Studies in Apocalypticism. Its Origins and Effects*[1]

Christopher Rowland was the Dean Ireland's Professor of the Exegesis of Holy Scripture at the University of Oxford from 1991 till 2014. His doctoral dissertation at the University of Cambridge (1975) focused upon the influence the vision of the first chapters of the Prophet Ezekiel had upon Judaism and early Christianity. It resulted in his influential book *The Open Heaven: A Study of Apocalyptic in Judaism and Early Christianity*.[2] This large collection continues to reflect upon and develop these themes. Rowland shares his conviction and experience that apocalypticism continues to exercise a transforming power in an unjust society.

An opening essay sets the theme and describes the genesis and ongoing importance of Rowland's views on apocalypticism ("rationale and retrospect"). He divides the studies into: Section 1, "The Nature of Apocalypticism" (9 essays), Section 2, "Apocalyptic, Eschatological and Related Themes in the New Testament" (19 essays), Section 3, "The Reception of Apocalypticism and Its Significance" (8 essays), Section 4, "William Blake: Apocalyptic Poet and Painter" (6 essays), and Section 5, "Coda" (2 essays). All but two essays have been previously published. The unpublished essays were written to honour his colleagues at the University of

---

1 Wissenschaftliche Untersuchungen zum Neuen Testament 473. Tübingen: Mohr Siebeck, 2022.
2 London: SPCK, 1982.

Cambridge, Andrew Chester, and the recently deceased Nicholas Lash.

It is not possible to survey all forty-four essays in a single review. However, Rowland's critical and innovative contributions emerge regularly across the book. The expression "apocalyptic" is an adjective in English. It is often used (based on the German *Apokalyptik*) as a noun with a dazzling number of possible applications. Rowland has long avoided this conundrum by using the clumsy but nominal "apocalypticism." His studies of the impact of Ezekiel 1, Isaiah 6, and Daniel 7 on Jewish and Christian literature led him to the conviction that apocalyptic literature is not determined by a literary form. Apocalyptic is a "revelation" (see Rev 1:1) to human beings of the mysteries of the divine world. It does not refer to revelations of what is to occur at some stage in the future (eschatological apocalypticism), but to the revelation of the divine in present experiences. Rowland insists that apocalypticism and eschatology do not always work in tandem.

An historical mystical experience is generated by a "visionary appropriation of Scripture in which the words offer the opportunity to 'see again' what had appeared to prophets and seers in the past or to become a means of prompting new visions whereby there can be a discernment of higher spiritual realities" (p. 401). The utterances of the visionary are not "invented" in imitation of parallel forms of literature. Nor are they subjective musings. They are the result of personal experience. The title of Rowland's collection comes from the words of a New England visionary, Anne Hutchinson, banished from the Massachusetts Bay area for questioning Puritan teachings in 1637. During her public trial, she claimed that what she argued came to her "by an immediate revelation."

The bulk of the essays (Section 2) is devoted to the role of such immediate revelations across the New Testament. Rowland is naturally interested in Paul's claim to have had such an experience in 2 Corinthians 12:1–10, but he regards the Pauline intervention as based upon an authoritative wisdom "secret and hidden, which God decreed before the ages for our glory" (1

Postscript: A Review

Cor 2:7). Paul's balance between the observance of the Law, and freedom from the Law is determined and authorised by his access to this "immediate revelation." Among the Gospels, Rowland is particularly interested in Matthew's singling out the "least of these" (Matt 25:40, 45) as the socially deprived (rejecting the interpretation of the expression as reference to the Christian community), and the Gospel of John. Continuing a direction taken by his Oxford colleague, John Ashton, he suggests that the Fourth Gospel is apocalyptic upside down. Given Johannine Christology, the "immediate revelation" does not come from above, but can be seen in the person of Jesus, below. He interprets John 1:51 as a movement of the angels from heaven to earth to gaze upon a vision of the divine in the Son of Man on earth (pp. 204-214).

His several reflections upon the Book of Revelation depend upon a setting of suffering and marginalisation toward the end of the Neronian period (54–68 CE). Revelation from above (heavily dependent upon the visionary's relived experience of Ezek 1 and Dan 7) addressed that situation in the light of what God had done in and through the slain and risen Lamb, adopting the contemporaneous apocalyptic literature's road map for the end of time. Rich essays reflect upon the reception of the Book of Revelation, especially by Ticonius (fourth century), Joachim de Fiore (twelfth century), and the poetic and artistic creations of William Blake (1757-1827).

This is a valuable book that raises important and creative questions around apocalyptic thought and writing. As well as the many technical studies, Rowland's concern for the marginalised, whose concerns are authoritatively raised by an apocalyptic "immediate revelation" is a timely reminder of the social obligations of those who live and preach Christianity. His essays to honour his Cambridge colleagues are fine examples of how this can be done. As all essays are published in the form in which they originally appeared, there is much repetition of Rowland's major concerns. He begs pardon of the reader, indicating that Mozart did the same thing in the alternative finale of his Fifth Piano Concerto (KV 82). I am not sure the comparison fits.

The sharp separation between apocalyptic and eschatology has not convinced everyone. Brendan Byrne has recently argued that the post-Reformation tension between grace and works in Paul can only be adequately addressed on the basis that the apostle's theology is both thoroughly apocalyptic and at the same time operates within an eschatological "overlap" period that modifies the Jewish messianic expectation of the time.[3]

The setting of the Book of Revelation remains a problem. Now widely accepted that there was no systematic persecution or enforced Emperor-worship in the final decade of the first century,[4] some *Sitz im Leben der Kirche* must be found for a message that asks suffering Christians to persevere as they await the imminent end. The association of Nero with an earlier persecution of Christians in Rome is now questioned.[5] Patmos was never a prison settlement: "John is the only person known to have been sent there."[6] Perhaps "the Saints" are not persecuted Christians, but those who have listened to the Word of God and accepted the prophetic witness to the Messiah, of whatever era (1:9; 6:9; 12:17; 18:24; 19:10; 20:4). "From the foundation of the world" (13:8) they participate in a kingdom, freed from their sins by the blood of Jesus, "priests serving his God and Father" (Rev 1:5–6; see 5:9–10).[7]

---

[3] Byrne, *Paul and the Economy of Salvation*.

[4] See especially the collection of essays in Brodd and Reed, eds., *Rome and Religion*.

[5] See especially Brent D. Shaw, "The Myth of the Neronian Persecution," *Journal of Roman Studies* 105 (2015) 1–28.

[6] Koester, *Revelation*, 243. For Koester's excellent survey of the evidence, see pp. 239–43.

[7] Moloney, *The Apocalypse*. My own intuition, yet to be developed, is that a setting in Asia Minor that parallels the situation addressed by 1 Peter best matches John's situation. Paul J. Achtemeier puts it well: "The persecutions faced by the readers of 1 Peter were in the nature of the case due more to

Postscript: A Review

The wide availability of this collection from a leading authority on the origins and effects of apocalypticism is a significant contribution to our understanding of early Christianity, and a reminder to all who preach the Gospel to listen to its call for the suffering and marginalised.

---

unofficial harassment than to official policy, more local than regional, and more at the initiation of the general populace as a result of a reaction of the lifestyle of Christians" (1 Peter, 35–36). Among other parallels, both authors call upon believers to recognise their priestly role: "priests, serving his God and father" (Rev 1:6; see 5:10; 20:6), "you are a chosen race, a royal priesthood (1 Peter 2:9; see 2:5) and both broach the possibility of the perennial saving effects of the death and resurrection of Jesus (Rev 13:8; 1 Peter 3:18–22). Interestingly, both Colossians (1:15–20) and Ephesians (1:3–14) expand upon this theme and are traditionally associated with early Christian communities in Asia Minor.

Bibliography

The following comprehensive Bibliography, located at the end of *New Testament Matters - Two* provides a full list of all studies and books referred to across both volumes of *New Testament Matters - One and Two*.

★★★

Abrahams, Israel. *Studies in Pharisaism and the Gospels.* First Series. Cambridge: Cambridge University Press, 1917.

Abrams, M. H. *A Glossary of Literary Terms.* 5th ed. New York: Holt, Reinhart & Winston, 1985.

Achtemeier, Paul. *1 Peter. A Commentary on First Peter.* Hermeneia. Minneapolis, MN: Fortress, 1996.

Aguilar Chiu, Joseé Enrique, Clifford, Richard J., Dempsey, Carol J., Schuler, Eileen M., Stegman, Thomas D., and Witherup, Ronald D., eds. *The Paulist Biblical Commentary.* New York: Paulist, 2018.

Aland, Kurt, and Barbara. *The Text of the New Testament. An Introduction to the Critical Editions and to the Theory and Practice of Modern Textual Criticism.* Translated by E. F. Rhodes. Grand Rapids, MI: Eerdmans, 1987.

Allison, Dale C. Jr. *Constructing Jesus. Memory, Imagination, and History.* Grand Rapids, MI: Baker Academic, 2010.

―――――. "Divorce, Celibacy and Joseph (Matthew 1.18–25 and 19.1-12)." *Journal for the Study of the New Testament* 49 (1993) 3–10.

―――――. *Studies in Matthew. Interpretation Past and Present.* Grand Rapids, MI: Baker Academic, 2005.

Anderson, Hugh. *The Gospel of Mark*. New Century Bible. London: Oliphants, 1976.

Ashton, John. *Understanding the Fourth Gospel*. Oxford: Clarendon, 1991.

Attridge, Harold. "Genre Bending in the Fourth Gospel." *Journal of Biblical Literature* 121 (2002) 1–21.

───────. "How Priestly is the 'High Priestly Prayer' of John 17?" *The Catholic Biblical Quarterly* 73 (2013) 1–14.

Aune, David E. *Revelation*. 3 vols. Word Biblical Commentary. Dallas: Word: 1997–1998

Back, Frances. *Gott als Vater der Jünger im Johannesevangelium*. Wissenschaftliche Untersuchungen zum Neuen Testament 2.336. Tübingen: Mohr Siebeck, 2012.

Barrett, Charles Kingsley. "Christocentric or Theocentric? Observations on the Theological Method of the Fourth Gospel." Pages 1–18 in *Essays on John*. London: SPCK, 1982.

───────. "The House of Prayer and the Den of Thieves." Pages 13–20 in *Jesus und Paulus. Festschrift für Werner Georg Kümmel zum 70. Geburtstag*. Edited by Earle Ellis and Eric Grässer. Göttingen: Vandenhoeck & Ruprecht, 1975.

Barton, John. *A History of the Bible. The Book and Its Faiths*. Milton Keynes: Allen Lane, 2019.

Bauckham, Richard. *The Climax of Prophecy. Studies in the Book of Revelation*. Edinburgh: T. & T. Clark, 1993.

───────. *The Theology of the Book of Revelation*. New Testament Theology. Cambridge: Cambridge University Press, 1993.

Bauer, David R. *The Structure of Matthew's Gospel*. Journal for the Study of the New Testament Supplement Series 31. Sheffield: Sheffield Academic Press/Almond Press, 1988.

---------. *The Word. On the Translation of the Bible*. Milton Keynes: Allen Lane, 2022.

Beal, Timothy. *The Book of Revelation. A Biography*. Lives of Great Religious Books. Princeton: Princeton University Press, 2018.

Beale, Gregory K. *John's Use of the Old Testament in Revelation*. Library of New Testament Studies 166. London: Bloomsbury, 1999.

---------. *The Book of Revelation: A Commentary on the Greek Text*. New International Greek Testament Commentary. Grand Rapids, MI: Eerdmans, 1999.

Beale, Gregory K, and Carson, Donald A. *Commentary on the New Testament Use of the Old Testament*. Grand Rapids, MI: Baker Academic, 2007.

Beare, Frederick W. *The Gospel According to Matthew*. Oxford: Blackwell, 1981.

Beasley-Murray, George R. *The Book of Revelation*. Revised Edition. New Century Bible. London: Oliphants, 1978.

Becker, J. Christiaan, *Paul the Apostle: The Triumph of God in Life and Thought*. Minneapolis, MN: Fortress, 1980.

ben Daniel, John and Gloria. *Saint John and the Book of Revelation. From Essenes to End-Times*. Jerusalem: Beit Yochanan, 2019.

Bennema, Cornelis. "A Comprehensive Approach to Understanding Character in the Gospel of John." Pages 36–58 in *Characters and Characterization*. Edited by Skinner.

---------. "A Theory of Character in the Fourth Gospel with Reference to Ancient and Modern Literature." *Biblical Interpretation* 17 (2009) 375–421.

---------. *Encountering Jesus. Character Studies in the Gospel of John*. Milton Keynes, Paternoster, 2009.

———. *Encountering Jesus: Character Studies in the Gospel of John*. 2nd ed. Minneapolis, MN: Fortress, 2014.

Benoit, Pierre. "Christian Marriage according to Saint Paul." *The Clergy Review* 65 (1980) 309–21.

Bieringer, Raimund, Didier Pollefeyt, and Frederique Vandercasteele-Vaneuville, eds. *Anti Judaism and the Fourth Gospel: Papers of the Leuven Colloquium 2000*. Assen: Van Gorcum, 2001.

Black, C. Clifton. Mark. *Images of an Apostolic Interpreter*. Studies on Personalities of the New Testament. Minneapolis, MN: Fortress, 2001.

———. *Mark's Gospel. History, Theology, Interpretation*. Grand Rapids, MI: Eerdmans, 2023.

———. *The Disciples according to Mark: Markan Redaction in Current Debate*. Journal for the Study of the New Testament Supplement Series 27. Sheffield: Sheffield Academic Press, 1989.

Blainey, Geoffrey. *Before I Forget: An Early Memoir*. Melbourne: Hamish Hamilton, 2019.

Blass, Frederik A., Debrunner, Albert, and Funk, Robert W. *A Greek Grammar of the New Testament and Other Early Christian Literature*. Chicago: Chicago University Press, 1961.

Bobichon, Philippe. *Justin Martyr. Dialogue avec Tryphon: édition critique*. 2 vols. Fribourg : Academic Press Fribourg, 2003.

Bode, E. L. *The First Easter Morning: The Gospel Accounts of the Women's Visit to the Tomb of Jesus*. Analecta Biblica 45. Rome: Biblical Institute Press, 1970.

Bolt, Peter G. *Jesus' Defeat of Death. Persuading Mark's Early Readers*. Society for New Testament Studies Monograph Series 125. Cambridge: Cambridge University Press, 2003.

Boomershine, Thomas. "Mark 16:8 and the Apostolic Commission." *Journal of Biblical Literature* 100 (1981) 225–39.

Borg, Marcus. *Jesus: A New Vision*. San Francisco: Harper & Row: 1988.

Boring, M. Eugene. *Revelation. Interpretation*. Louisville, KY: John Knox, 1989.

Bovon, François. *Luke*. Translated by Christine M. Thomas. 3 vols. Hermeneia. Minneapolis, MN: Fortress, 2002–2012.

―――――. *Luke the Theologian. Fifty-five Years of Research (1950–2005)*. Waco, TX: Baylor University Press, 2006.

Boxall, Ian. *Patmos in the Reception History of the Apocalypse*. Oxford Theology and Religion Monographs. Oxford: Oxford University Press, 2013.

―――――. *The Revelation of Saint John*. Black's New Testament Commentary. London: A. & C. Black, 2006.

Brodd, Jeffrey, and Jonathan Reed, eds. *Rome and Religion. A Cross-Disciplinary Dialogue on the Imperial Cult*. Writings from the Greco-Roman World Supplement Series 5. Atlanta, GA. SBL Press, 2011.

Brown, Peter. *Journeys of the Mind. A Life in History*. Princeton, NJ: Princeton University Press, 2023.

Brown, Raymond E. *An Introduction to the New Testament*. Anchor Bible Reference Library. New York: Doubleday, 1996.

―――――. *Priest and Bishop. Biblical Reflections*. Eugene, OR: Wipf & Stock, 1999.

―――――. *The Birth of the Messiah. A Commentary on the Infancy Narratives of Matthew and Luke*. New York: Doubleday, 1977.

―――――. *The Epistles of John*. Anchor Bible 30. New York: Doubleday, 1982.

---------. *The Gospel According to John*. 2 vols. Anchor Bible 29–29A. Garden City, NY: Doubleday, 1966-68.

Brown, Sherri. *Gift Upon Gift. Covenant Through Word in the Gospel of John*. Pittsburgh Theological Monograph Series. Eugene, OR: Wipf & Stock, 2010.

---------. "The Challenge of 2 Peter and the Call to Theiosis." *Expository Times* 128 (2017) 583–92.

Brown, Sherri and Moloney, Francis J. *Interpreting the New Testament: An Introduction*. Grand Rapids, MI: Eerdmans, 2019.

Brütsch, Charles. *La Clarté de l'Apocalypse*. 5th ed. Geneva: Labor et Fides, 1966.

Buchanan, George W. "Mark 11:15–19: Brigands in the Temple." *Hebrew Union College Annual* 30 (1959) 169–77.

Bultmann, Rudolf. *History of the Synoptic Tradition*. Translated by John Marsh. Oxford: Basil Blackwell, 1968.

---------. "New Testament and Mythology." Pages 1–44 in *Kerygma and Myth by Rudolf Bultmann and Five Critics*. Edited by Hans Werner Bartsch. Translated by Reginald H. Fuller. New York: Harper and Row, 1961.

---------. *Theology of the New Testament*. Translated by Kendrick Grobel. 2 vols. London: SCM Press, 1955.

Burridge, Richard A. *Imitating Jesus. An Inclusive Approach to New Testament Ethics*. Grand Rapids, MI: Eerdmans, 2007.

Byrne, Brendan. *A Costly Freedom. A Theological Reading of Mark's Gospel*. Collegeville, MN: Liturgical Press, 2008.

---------. *Life Abounding: A Reading of John's Gospel*. Collegeville, MN: Liturgical Press, 2014.

---------. *Lifting the Burden. Reading Matthew's Gospel in the Church Today*. Collegeville, MN: Liturgical Press, 2004.

---------. "Living Out the Righteousness of God: The Contribution of Romans 6:1–8:13 to an Understanding of Paul's Ethical Presuppositions." *The Catholic Biblical Quarterly* 43 (1981) 557–81.

―――――. *Paul and the Economy of Salvation: Reading from the Perspective of the Last Judgment*. Grand Rapids, MI: Baker Academic, 2021.

―――――. *Romans*. Sacra Pagina 6. Collegeville, MN: Liturgical Press, 1996.

―――――. *'Sons of God' – 'Seed of Abraham.' A Study of the Idea of the Sonship of God of All Christians in Paul against the Jewish Background*. Analecta Biblical 83. Rome: Biblical Institute Press, 1979.

―――――. "The Faith of the Disciple whom Jesus loved and the Community in John 20." *Journal for the Study of the New Testament* 23 (1985) 83–97.

Campbell, Anthony F. and O'Brien, Mark. *Sources of the Pentateuch. Text, Introduction, Annotation*. Minneapolis, MN: Fortress, 1993.

Casey, Maurice. *Son of Man. The Interpretation and Influence of Daniel 12*. London: SPCK, 1979.

Cassem, N. H. "A Grammatical and Conceptual Inventory of the Use of κόσμος in the Johannine Corpus with Some Implications for a Johannine Cosmic Theology. *New Testament Studies* 19 (1972–73) 81–91.

Caragounis, Chrys. "'Abide in Me': The New Mode of Relationship between Jesus and His Followers as a Basis for Christian Ethics." Pages 250–63 in *Rethinking the Ethics of John*.

Carroll, John T. *Luke. A Commentary*. New Testament Library. Louisville, KY: Westminster John Knox, 2012.

Carter, Warren. "Kernels and Narrative Blocks: The Structure of Matthew's Gospel." *The Catholic Biblical Quarterly* 54 (1992) 463–81.

──────. *Matthew and the Margins. A Sociopolitical and Religious Reading*. Maryknoll, NY: Orbis Books, 2000.

Chatman, Seymour. *Story and Discourse. Narrative Structures in Fiction and Film*. Ithaca, NY: Cornell University Press, 1978.

Chennattu, Rekha M. and Mary L. Coloe, eds. *Transcending Boundaries. Contemporary Readings of the New Testament. Essays in Honor of Francis J. Moloney*. Biblioteca di Scienze Religiose 187. Rome: LAS, 2005.

Clabeaux, John J. "Revelation." Pages 1571–1611 in *The Paulist Biblical Commentary*.

Clark, Manning. *The Quest for Grace*. Ringwood, Vic.: Viking, 1990.

Charles, Robert H. *A Critical and Exegetical Commentary on the Revelation of St. John*. International Critical Commentary. Edinburgh: T. & T. Clark, 1920.

Collins, Adela Yarbro. *Mark*. Hermeneia. Minneapolis, MN: Fortress, 2007.

──────. "Narrative, History and Gospel." *Semeia* 43 (1988) 145–53.

──────. *The Apocalypse*. New Testament Message 22. Wilmington, DE: Michael Glazier, 1979.

──────. *The Beginning of the Gospel. Probings of Mark in Context*. Minneapolis, MN: Fortress, 1992.

Collins, John J. *Apocalypse, Apocrypha, and Pseudepigraphy. On Jewish Apocalyptic Literature*. Grand Rapids, MI: Eerdmans, 2015.

──────. *Daniel*. Hermeneia. Minneapolis, MN: Fortress, 1993.

──────. *The Sceptre and the Star: The Messiahs of the Dead Sea Scrolls and Other Ancient Literature*. Anchor Bible Reference Library. New York: Doubleday, 1995.

Collins, John J., Hens-Piazza, Gina, Reid, Barbara, and Senior, Donald, eds., *The Jerome Biblical Commentary for the Twenty-First Century*. London: T. & T. Clark, 2022.

Collins, Raymond F. "'Blessed are those who have not Seen': John 20:29." Pages 173–90 in *Transcending Boundaries*. Edited by Chennattu and Coloe.

————. *Divorce in the New Testament*. Good News Studies. Wilmington, DE: Michael Glazier, 2002.

————. *First Corinthians*. Sacra Pagina 7. Collegeville, MN: The Liturgical Press, 1999.

————. "The Representative Figures of the Fourth Gospel." *The Downside Review* 94 (1976) 26–46; 118–32.

Congar, Yves. *My Journal of the Council*. Translated by Dennis Minns and Others. Adelaide: ATF Theology, 2012.

Connolly, Sean. *On Every Tide. The Making and Remaking of the Irish World*. London: Little, Brown, 2022.

Conzelmann, Hans. *The Theology of St. Luke*. Translated by G. Buswell. London: Faber & Faber, 1961.

Corsini, Eugenio. *Apocalisse di Gesù Cristo secondo Giovanni*. Sestante. Turin : Società Editrice Internazionale, 2003.

————. *The Apocalypse: The Perennial Revelation of Jesus Christ*. Translated by Francis J. Moloney. Eugene, OR: Wipf & Stock, 2019.

Cranfield, C. E. B. *The Gospel according to St Mark*. Cambridge Greek Testament Commentary. Cambridge: Cambridge University Press, 1959.

Crossan. John Dominic. *Cliffs of Fall: paradox and polyvalence in the parables of Jesus*. New York: Seabury, 1980.

————. "Mark and the Relatives of Jesus." *Novum Testamentum* 15 (1973) 81–113.

————. *The Historical Jesus: The Life of a Mediterranean Jewish Peasant*. San Francisco: HarperSanFrancisco, 1988.

Culpepper, R. Alan. *Anatomy of the Fourth Gospel*. Philadelphia, PA: Fortress, 1983.

───────. "Matthew and John.: Reflections on Early Christianity in Relation to Judaism." Pages 148–76 in *Designs for the Church in the Gospel of John. Collected Essays 1980–2020*. Wissenschaftliche Untersuchungen zum Neuen Testament 465. Tübingen: Mohr Siebeck, 2021.

───────. "The Johannine hypodeigma: A Reading of John 13:1-38." *Semeia* 53 (1981) 133–52.

───────. "The Relationship Between the Gospel and 1 John." Pages 95–120 in *Communities in Dispute*. Edited by Culpepper and Anderson.

───────. "The Weave of Tapestry: Character and Theme in John." Pages 18–35 in *Characters and Characterization*. Edited by Skinner.

Culpepper, R. Alan, and Paul N. Anderson, eds. *Communities in Dispute: Current Scholarship on the Johannine Epistles*. Early Christianity and Its Literature 13. Atlanta: SBL Press, 2014.

───────. *John and Judaism. A Contested Relationship in Context*. Resources for Biblical Study 87. Atlanta, GA: SBL Press, 2017.

Culpepper, R. Alan, and C. Clifton Black. *Exploring the Gospel of John. In Honor of D. Moody Smith*. Louisville, KY: Westminster John Knox, 1996.

Davies, William D. *The Gospel and the Land. Early Christianity and Jewish Territorial Doctrine*. Berkeley, CA: University of California Press, 1974.

Davies, William D. and Dale C. Allison, Jr. *The Gospel According to Saint Matthew*. 3 vols. International Critical Commentary. Edinburgh: T. & T. Clark, 1988–1997.

Bibliography

Dalton, William J. *Christ's Proclamation to the Spirits. A Study of 1 Peter 3:18–4:6.* 2nd ed. Analecta Biblical 23. Rome: Biblical Institute Press.

Daly-Denton, Margaret. *The Johannine Reception of the Psalms.* Arbeiten zur Geschichte des Spätjudentums und Urchristentums 47. Leiden: Brill, 2000.

Danker, Frederick W. *A Greek-English Dictionary of the New Testament and other Early Christian Literature.* 3d ed. Chicago: University of Chicago Press, 2000.

de la Potterie, Ignace. "Consécration ou sanctification du Chrétien d'après Jean 17 ? Pages 339–49 in *Le Sacré : Études et Recherches. Actes du Colloque organisé par le Centre International d'Études Humanistes et par l'Institut d'Études Philosophiques de Rome.* Edited by E. Castelli. Paris : Aubier-Montaigne, 1974.

_____. *The Hour of Jesus: The Passion and Resurrection of Jesus according to John. Text and Spirit.* Slough, UK: St Paul Publications, 1989.

Dewey, Joanna. "Mark as Interwoven Tapestry: Forecasts and Echoes for a Listening Audience." *The Catholic Biblical Quarterly* 53 (1991) 225–36.

Dinkler, Michael Beth. *Literary Theory and the New Testament.* Anchor Yale Bible Reference Library. New Haven, CT: Yale University Press, 2019.

Dix, Gregory. *The Apostolic Tradition of Hippolytus of Rome.* London: SPCK, 1937.

Dodd, Charles H. *The Interpretation of the Fourth Gospel.* Cambridge: Cambridge University Press, 1953.

Dowd, Sharon E. *Prayer, Power and the Problem of Suffering. Mark 11:22–25 in the Context of Markan Theology.* Society for Biblical Literature Dissertation Series 105. Atlanta, GA: Scholars Press, 1988.

Duffy, Eamon. *Ten Popes who Shook the World*. New Haven, CT: Yale University Press, 2011.

Duhm, Bernard. *Das Buch Jesaja, übersetzt und erklärt*. Göttingen: Vandenhoeck und Ruprecht, 1892.

Dunn, James D. G. *Jesus and the Spirit. A Study of the Religious and Charismatic Experience of Jesus and the First Christians as Reflected in the First Testament*. London: SCM, 1975.

_____. *The Theology of the Apostle Paul*. Grand Rapids, MI: Eerdmans, 1998.

Edsall, Benjamin A. *Paul's Witness to Formative Early Christian Instruction*. Wissenschaftliche Untersuchungen zum Neuen Testament 2.365. Tübingen: Mohr Siebeck, 2014.

Eire, Carlos M. N. *Reformations. The Early Modern World, 1450–1650*. New Haven, CT: Yale University Press, 2016.

Ernst, Joseph. *Das Evangelium nach Markus*. Regensburger Neues Testament. Regensburg: Pustet-Verlag, 1981.

Eshell, Esther. "Jeremiah, Book of." Volume 1. Pages 397–400 in *Encyclopedia of the Dead Sea Scrolls*. Edited by Lawrence Schiffman and James C. VanderKam. 2 vols. New York: Oxford University Press, 2000.

Evans, Craig A. "Jesus' Action in the Temple: Cleansing or portent or destruction?" *The Catholic Biblical Quarterly* 51 (1989) 237–70.

Falls, Thomas B. *Saint Justin Martyr. The First Apology. The Second Apology, Dialogue with Trypho, Exhortation to the Greeks, Discourse to the Greeks, The Monarchy or the Rule of God*. The Fathers of the Church. Washington, DC: The Catholic University of America Press, 1948.

Farrer, Austin. *The Revelation of St. John the Divine. A Commentary on the English Text*. Oxford: Clarendon, 1964.

Feuillet, André. *The Priesthood of Christ and His Ministers.* Translated by Matthew J. O'Connell. Garden City, NY: Doubleday, 1975.

Finnegan, J. *Encountering New Testament Manuscripts. A Working Introduction to Textual Criticism.* London: SPCK, 1975.

Fish, Stanley. *Is There a Text in This Class? The Authority of Interpretative Communities.* Cambridge, MA: Harvard University Press, 1980.

Fitzmyer, Joseph A. "A Recent Roman Scriptural Controversy." *Theological Studies* 22 (1961) 426–44.

——————. *First Corinthians.* The Anchor Yale Bible 32. New Haven, CT: Yale University Press, 2008.

——————. "Marriage and Divorce." Volume 2, pages 511–15 in *Encyclopedia of the Dead Sea Scrolls.* Edited by Lawrence H. Schiffman and James C. VanderKam. 2 vols. Oxford/New York: Oxford University Press, 2000.

——————. *The Acts of the Apostles.* The Anchor Bible 31. New York: Doubleday, 1998.

——————. "The Ascension of Christ and Pentecost." *Theological Studies* 45 (1984) 409–440.

Flannery, Austin, ed. *The Basic Sixteen Documents. Vatican Council II. Constitutions Decrees Declarations. A Completely Revised Translation in Inclusive Language.* Northport, NY: Costello Publishing Company, 1996.

Fledderman, H. "The Flight of a Naked Young Man." *The Catholic Biblical Quarterly* 41 (1979) 412–18.

Foester, Werner. *"oros."* Volume 5. Pages 475–87 in *Theological Dictionary of the New Testament.* Edited by Gerhard Kittel and Gerhard Friedrich. Translated by Geoffrey W. Bromiley. 10 vols. Grand Rapids, MI: Eerdmans, 1964–1976.

Ford, Norman M. *The Prenatal Person. Ethics from Conception to Birth*. Oxford: Blackwell, 2002.

———. *When Did I Begin? Conception of the Individual in History, Philosophy and Science*. Cambridge: Cambridge University Press, 1991.

France, Richard T. *The Gospel of Matthew*. New International Commentary on the New Testament. Grand Rapids, MI: Eerdmans, 2007.

Francis, Pope. *Apostolic Letter* Scripturae Sacrae Affectus *of the Holy Father Francis on the Sixteenth Hundred Anniversary of the Death of Saint Jerome*. Vatican City: Editrice Vaticana, 2022. An electronic version of an English translation of the text is available at: vatican.va/content/Francesco/ed/apost_letters/documents/papa-francesco-lettera-ap_20200_scripturae-sacrae-affectus.html.

———. *Evangelii Gaudium. The Joy of the Gospel. Apostolic Exhortation on the Proclamation of the Gospel in Today's World*. Vatican City: Libreria Editrice Vaticana, 2013.

Frankemölle, Hubert. "Pharisaismus im Judentum und Kirche." Pages 123–89 in *Gottesverächter und Menschenfeinder?* Edited by Horst Goldstein. Dusseldorf: Patmos, 1979.

Fredriksen, Paula. *From Jesus to Christ*. New Haven, CT: Yale University Press, 1988.

———. *Jesus of Nazareth, King of the Jews*. New York: Vintage Books, 2000.

———. "The Historical Jesus, the Scene in the Temple, and the Gospel of John." Pages 249–76 in *John, Jesus, and History. Volume 1: Critical Appraisals of Critical Views*. Edited by Paul N. Anderson, Felix Just, and Tom Thatcher. Society of Biblical Literature Symposium Series 44. Atlanta, GA: SBL Press, 2007.

Frend, W. H. C. "Persecutions: Genesis and Legacy." Pages 502–23 in *The Cambridge History of Christianity. Volume 1: Origins to Constantine*. Edited by Margaret M.

Mitchell and Frances M. Young. Cambridge: Cambridge University Press, 2006.

Friesen, Steven J. *Imperial Cults and the Apocalypse of John*. New York: Oxford University Press, 2001.

Frey, Jörg. *Die Johanneische Eschatologie*. 3 vols. Wissenschaftliche Untersuchungen zum Neuen Testament 96, 110, 117. Tubingen: Mohr Siebeck, 1997–2000.

Galinski, Karl. "In the Shadow (or Not) of the Imperial Cult: A Cooperative Agenda." Pages 215–225 in *Rome and Religion*. Edited by Brodd and Reed.

⸻⸻. "The Cult of the Roman Emperor: Uniter or Divider?" Pages 1–21 in *Rome and Religion*. Edited by Brodd and Reed.

Gaventa, Beverley R. *Acts*. Abingdon New Testament Commentaries. Nashville, TN: Abingdon, 2003.

Genette, Gerard. *Narrative Discourse. An Essay in Method*. Translated by Jonathan Culler. Ithaca, NY: Cornell University Press, 1980.

Giblin, Charles H. "Recapitulation and the Literary Coherence of John's Apocalypse." *The Catholic Biblical Quarterly* 56 (1994) 81–95.

⸻⸻. "Revelation 11.1–13: Its Form, Function, and Textual Integration. *New Testament Studies* 30 (1984) 433–59.

⸻⸻. "Structural and Thematic Correlations in the Theology of Revelation 16–22." *Biblica* 55 (1974) 487–504.

⸻⸻. *The Book of Revelation: The Open Book of Prophecy*. Good News Studies 34. Collegeville, MN: Liturgical Press, 1991.

Giesen, Heinz. *Die Offenbarung des Johannes*. Regensburger Neues Testament. Regensburg: Pustet, 1997.

Gnilka, Joachim. *Das Evangelium des Markus*. 5th ed. 2 vols. Evangelisch-Katholischer Kommentar zum Neuen Testament II/1-2. Zürich/Neukirchen-Vluyn: Benziger Verlag/Neukirchener Verlag, 1998.

Goldingay, John. *Daniel*. Word Biblical Commentary 30. Nashville, TN: Thomas Nelson, 1989.

Goodacre, Mark. *The Synoptic Problem: A Way through the Maze. Understanding the Bible and Its World*. London: T. & T. Clark, 2004.

Goodfriend, Elaine A. "Adultery." Volume 1, pages 82–86 in David N. Freedman, ed., 6 vols. *The Anchor Bible Dictionary*. New York: Doubleday, 1992.

Goodman, Martin. *A History of Judaism*. Milton Keynes: Penguin Random House, 2017.

Grundmann, Walter, *Das Evangelium nach Markus*. 6th ed. Theologische Handkommentar zum Neuen Testament 2. Berlin: Evangelische Verlagsanstalt, 1973.

Gundry, Robert H. *Matthew: A Commentary on his Literary and Theological Art*. Grand Rapids, MI: Eerdmans, 1982.

Halliwell, Stephen. Ed. and trans. *Aristotle Poetics*. Loeb Classical Library 199. Cambridge, MA: Harvard University Press, 1995.

Hansen, Anthony T. *The Prophetic Gospel. A Study of John and the Old Testament*. Edinburgh: T. & T. Clark, 1991.

Harvey, A. E. *Jesus and the Constraints of History*. London: Duckworth, 1982.

Harris, Horton. *The Tübingen School*. Oxford: Clarendon Press, 1975.

Havener, Ivan. *Q: The Sayings of Jesus*. Good News Studies 19. Wilmington, DE: Michael Glazier, 1987.

Hays, Richard B. *The Moral Vision of the New Testament. A Contemporary Introduction to New Testament Ethics*. San Francisco: HarperSanFrancisco, 1996.

Hengel, Martin. *Studies in the Gospel of Mark.* Translated by John Bowden. London: SPCK, 1985.

_____. *Was Jesus a Revolutionist?* Philadelphia, PA: Fortress, 1971.

_____. *The Charismatic Leader and His Followers.* Translated by James C. G. Grieg. Studies of the New Testament and Its World. Edinburgh: T. & T. Clark, 1981.

_____. *The Zealots. Investigations into the Jewish Freedom Movement in the Period from Herod I to 70 AD.* Edinburgh: T. & T. Clark, 1989.

Hoffman, Marella. Crow Glen. *The Spiritual Universe of an Irish Village.* Cambridge: Cambridge Editions, 2020.

Holloway, Paul A. *Philippians.* Hermeneia. Minneapolis, MN: Fortress, 2017.

Holmes, Michael W. *The Apostolic Fathers. Greek Texts and English Translations.* 3rd ed. Grand Rapids, MI

Holzmann, Heinrich J. *Die synoptischen Evangelien: Ihr Ursprung und geschichtlicher Charakter.* Leipzig: Wilhelm Engelman, 1863.

Hooker, Morna D. *Jesus and the Servant. The Influence of the Servant Concept of Deutero-Isaiah in the New Testament.* London: SPCK, 1959.

_____. *The Son of Man in Mark: a Study of the background of the term "the Son of Man" and its use in St. Mark's Gospel.* London: SPCK, 1973.

_____. "Traditions about the Temple in the Sayings of Jesus." *Bulletin of the John Rylands Library* 70 (1988) 7–19.

Howard-Brook, Wes, and Anthony Gwyther. *Unveiling Empire. Reading Revelation Then and Now.* Foreword by Elizabeth McAlister. Maryknoll, NY: Orbis, 1999.

Horrell, David G. *An Introduction to the Study of Paul*. 3rd ed. London: T. & T. Clark, 2006.

Horsley, Richard A. *1 Corinthians*. Abingdon New Testament Commentaries. Nashville, TN: Abingdon, 1998.

International Commission on English in the Liturgy. *The Roman Pontifical. Revised by Decree of the Second Vatican Ecumenical Council and Published by Authority of Pope Paul VI*. Washington DC: ICEL, 1978.

Instone-Brewer, David. *Divorce and Remarriage in the Bible*. Grand Rapids, MI: Eerdmans, 2002.

Isaac, Jules. "The Crime of Deicide. Proposition 16." Pages 253–83 in *Jewish Expressions of Jesus: An Anthology*. Edited by Trudy Weiss-Rosmarin.

Iser, William. *The Implied Reader: Patterns of Communication in Prose Fiction from Bunyan to Beckett*. Baltimore: Johns Hopkins University Press, 1978.

Iverson, Kelly R. "A Further Word on the Final Γάρ." *The Catholic Biblical Quarterly* 68 (2006) 79–94.

―――――. *Gentiles in the Gospel of Mark*. Library of New Testament Studies 339. London: T. & T/ Clark, 2007.

―――――. *Performing Early Christian Literature. Audience Experience and Interpretation of the Gospels*. Cambridge: Cambridge University Press, 2021.

―――――. *Reading Mark*. Cascade Companions. Eugene, OR: Wipf & Stock, 2023.

Jacobson, Rolf A. and Chan, Michael. *Introducing the Old Testament. A Historical, Literary, and Theological Survey*. Grand Rapids: Baker Academic, 2023.

Jastrow, Marcus. *A Dictionary of the Targumim, the Talmud Babli and Yerushalmi, and the Midrashic Literature*. 2 vols. New York: Pardes, 1953.

Jefford, Clayton N. *Reading the Apostolic Fathers. An Introduction*. Peabody, MA: Hendrickson, 1996.

Jeremias, Joachim. *The Eucharistic Words of Jesus*. Translated by Norman Perrin. London: SCM, 1966

Johnson, Brian D. "The Jewish Feasts and Questions of Historicity in John 5–12." Pages 117–29 in *John, Jesus, and History, Volume 2. Aspects of Historicity in the Fourth Gospel*. Edited by Paul N. Anderson, Felix Just, and Tom Thatcher. Early Christian Literature 2. Atlanta, GA: SBL Press, 2009.

Johnson, Luke Timothy. *The Acts of the Apostles*. Sacra Pagina 5. Collegeville, MN: Liturgical Press, 2006.

———. *The Letter of James*. Anchor Bible 37A. New York: Doubleday, 1995.

———. *The Mind in Another Place. My Life as a Scholar*. Grand Rapids, MI: Eerdmans, 2022.

Käsemann, Ernst. *The Testament of Jesus. A Study of the Gospel of John in the Light of Chapter 17*. Translated by Gerhard Krodel. London: SCM Press, 1968.

Kashow, Robert. "Traces of Ecclesiastes in the Gospel of John." *Neotestamentica* 46 (2012) 229–43.

Keenan, Marie. *Child Sexual Abuse and the Catholic Church. Gender, Power, and Organizational Culture*. New York: Oxford University Press, 2001.

Keener, Craig S. *A Commentary on the Gospel of Matthew*. Grand Rapids, MI: Eerdmans, 1999.

———. *The Gospel of John. A Commentary*. 2 vols. Peabody, MA: Hendrickson, 2003.

Keith, Chris. *Jesus' Literacy. Literacy, Scribal Culture, and the Teacher from Galilee*. Library of New Testament Studies 413. London: Bloomsbury, 2011.

Kelber, Werner. *Mark's Story of Jesus*. Philadelphia, PA: Fortress, 1979.

———. *The Kingdom in Mark. A New Place and a New Time*. Philadelphia, PA: Fortress, 1974.

———. *The Oral and Written Gospel. The Hermeneutics of Speech and Writing in the Synoptic Tradition, Mark, Paul and Q*. Philadelphia, PA: Fortress, 1983.

Kelle, Brad A. and Straw, Brent E. *The Oxford Handbook of the Historical Books of the Bible*. New York: Oxford University Press, 2021.

Kermode, Frank. *The Genesis of Secrecy: On the Interpretation of Narrative*. Cambridge, MA: Harvard University Press, 1969.

Kingsbury, Jack D. *Matthew: Structure, Christology, Kingdom*. Philadelphia, PA: Fortress, 1975.

———. *The Christology of Mark's Gospel*. Philadelphia, PA: Fortress, 1983.

———. *The Parables of Jesus in Matthew 13. A Study in Redaction Criticism*. Richmond, VA: John Knox, 1969.

Kitzberger, Ingrid Rosa, *Interfigural Readings of the Gospel of John*. Early Christianity and Its Literature 26. Atlanta: SBL Press, 2019.

———. ed. *The Personal Voice in Biblical Interpretation*. London: Routledge, 1999.

Klauck, Hans-Joseph. "Geschrieben, erfüllt, vollendet: Die Schriftzitate in der Johannespassion. Pages 140–57 in *Israel und Seine Heilstradition*. Edited by Labahn, Scholtissek, and Strottman.

———. *The Religious Context of Early Christianity. A Guide to Greco-Roman Religions*. Translated by Brian McNeil. Minneapolis, MN: Fortress, 2003.

Klawans, Jonathan. *Purity, Sacrifice, and Temple. Symbolism and Supersessionism in the Study of Ancient Judaism*. New York: Oxford University Press, 2006.

Kloppenborg, John S. *Q, The Earliest Gospel: An Introduction to the Earliest Stories and Sayings of Jesus*. Louisville, KY: Westminster John Knox, 2008.

Koester, Craig. "Hearing, Seeing, and Believing in the Gospel of John." *Biblica* 70 (1989) 327-48.

———. *Symbolism in the Fourth Gospel: Meaning, Mystery, Community*. 2nd ed. Minneapolis, MN: Fortress, 2003.

Knust, Jennifer and Wasserman, Tommy. *To Cast the First Stone. The Transmission of a Gospel Story*. Princeton: Princeton University Press, 2019.

Koester, Craig R. *Revelation*. Anchor Yale Bible 38A. New Haven, CT: Yale University Press, 2014.

Kurz, William. *Farewell Addresses in the New Testament*. Zacchaeus Studies : New Testament. Wilmington, DE: Michael Glazier, 1990.

Labahn, Michael. "'It's Only Love' – Is That All? Limits and Potentials of Johannine 'Ethic.' Pages 3-43 in *Rethinking the Ethics of John*. Edited by van der Watt and Zimmermann.

———. "Jesus und die Autorität der Schrift im Johannesevangelium: Überlegungen zu einem spannungsreichen Verhältnis." Pages 185-206 in *Israel und seine Heilstradition im Johannesevangelium. Festschrift für Johannes Beutler SJ zum 70. Geburtstag*. Edited by Michael Labahn, Klaus Scholtissek, and Angelika Strottman. Paderborn: Schöning, 2004.

Lagrange, Marie-Joseph. *Évangile selon Saint Marc*. Études Bibliques. Paris: Gabalda, 1920.

———. *Évangile selon Saint Matthieu*. Études Bibliques. Paris : Gabalda, 1927.

Lambrecht, Jan. "The Relatives of Jesus in Mark." *Novum Testamentum* 16 (1974) 241-58.

———. *The Sermon on the Mount. Proclamation and Exhortation*. Good News Studies 14. Wilmington, DE: Michael Glazier, 1985.

Lane, William L. *Commentary on the Gospel of Mark*. The New International Commentary on the New Testament. Grand Rapids, MI: Eerdmans, 1974.

Larsson, Tord. *God in the Fourth Gospel. A Hermeneutical Discussion of the History of Interpretation*. Coniectanea Biblica: New Testament Series 35. Lund: Almqvist, 2001.

Lauterbach, Jacob Z. "Jesus in the Talmud." Pages 1–98 in *Jewish Expressions on Jesus*. Edited by Trude Weis-Rosmarin.

LaVerdiere, Eugene. *The Beginning of the Gospel. Introducing the Gospel According to Mark*. 2 vols. Collegeville, MN: Liturgical Press, 1999.

Law, Michael. *When God Spoke Greek. The Septuagint and the Making of the Christian Bible*. New York: Oxford University Press, 2013.

Lazure, Noël. *Les Valeurs Morales de la Théologie Johannique (Évangile et Épitres)*. Études Bibliques. Paris : Gabalda, 1965.

Lee, Dorothy. *Flesh and Glory: Symbolism, Gender and Theology in the Gospel of John*. New York: Crossroad, 2002.

Levie, Jean. *The Bible, Word of God in Words of Men*. Translated by S. H. Treman. London: Geoffrey Chapman, 1961.

Lieu, Judith M. *Image and Reality. The Jews in the World of Christians in the Second Century*. Edinburgh: T. & T. Clark, 1996.

Lightfoot, R. H. *The Gospel Message of St Mark*. Oxford: Clarendon Press, 1950.

Lincoln, Andrew T. *The Gospel according to Saint John*. Black's New Testament Commentary. New York: Crossroad, 2005.

Lindars, Barnabas. *The Gospel of John*. New Century Bible. London: Oliphants, 1972.

Linnemann, E. "Der (wiedergerfundene) Markusschlus." *Zeitschrift für Theologie und Kirche* 66 (1969) 255–87.

Bibliography

Loader, William R. G. "Did Adultery Mandate Divorce? A Reassessment of Jesus' Divorce Logia. *New Testament Studies* 61 (2015) 67–78.

_____. "From Fundamentalism to Fundamentals." Pages 1–17 in *Faith at the Interface of Cultures. Law and Gospel, Johannine Studies, and Hebrews*. Edited by Edwin K. Broadhead, Paul Foster, and Wolfgang Kraus. Biblische Zeitschrift Supplements 14. Paderborn: Brill/Schönung, 2024.

_____. *Jesus in John's Gospel: Structure and Issues*. Grand Rapids, MI: Eerdmans, 2017.

_____. *Jesus Left Loose Ends. Collected Essays*. Adelaide: ATF Theology, 2021.

_____. *Sexuality and Gender: Collected Essays*. Wissenshaftliche Untersuchungen zum Neuen Testament 458. Tübingen: Mohr Siebeck, 2021.

_____. "Matthew's Theological Location." Pages 237–64 in *Jesus Left Loose Ends*.

_____. *Sexuality in the New Testament. Understanding the Key Texts*. Louisville, KY: John Knox Westminster, 2011.

_____. *The New Testament on Sexuality*. Grand Rapids, MI: Eerdmans, 2012.

_____. "The Central Structure of Johannine Christology." *New Testament Studies* 30 (1984) 188–216.

_____. *The Christology of the Fourth Gospel: Structure and Issues*. 2nd ed. Beiträge zur Biblischen Exegese und Theologie. Frankfurt: Peter Lang, 1992.

_____. *The Dead Sea Scrolls on Sexuality and Related Literature at Qumran*. Grand Rapids, MI: Eerdmans, 2009.

_____. *The New Testament on Sexuality*. Grand Rapids, MI: Eerdmans, 2012.

Lohfink, Gerhard. *Jesus of Nazareth. What He Wanted. Who He Was*. Translated by Linda M. Maloney. Collegeville, MN: The Liturgical Press, 2012.

Löhr, Hermut. "Ἔργον as an Element of Moral Language in John." Pages 228–49 in *Rethinking the Ethics of John*.

Lohmeyer, Ernst. *Das Evangelium des Markus übersetzt und erklärt*. 17th ed. Meyer Kommentar. Göttingen: Vandenhoeck & Ruprecht, 1967.

Lührmann, Dieter. *Das Markusevangelium*. Handkommentar zum Neuen Testament 3. Tübingen: Mohr Siebeck, 1987.

Lupieri, Edmondo F. *A Commentary on the Apocalypse of John*. Translated by Maria Poggi Johnson and Adam Kamasar. Italian Texts and Studies on Religion and Society. Grand Rapids, MI: Eerdmans, 2009.

_____. "L'Apocalisse dopo Corsini : una eredità in evoluzione." Pages 19–28 in *Apocalisse ieri oggi e domani. Atto della giornata di studio in memoria di Eugenio Corsini. Torino, 2 Ottobre, 2018*. Edited by C. Lombardi and L. Silvano. Alessandria: Edizione dell'Orso, 2018.

Luz, Ulrich. *Matthew. A Commentary*. Translated by James E. Crouch. 3 vols. Hermeneia. Minneapolis, MN: Fortress, 2001–2007.

Lyonnet, Stanislas. *Études sur l'Epître aux Romains*. Analecta Biblica 120. Rome : Biblical Institute Press, 1989.

McMullen, Ramsey. *Chistianizing the Roman Empire (AD 100–400)*. New Haven, CT: Tale University Press, 1984.

Maier, Johann. Art. "Temple." Vol. 2. Pages 921–27 in *Encyclopedia of the Dead Sea Scrolls*. Edited by Lawrence H. Schiffmann and James C. VanderKam. 2 vols. New York: Oxford University Press, 2000 .

Malbon, Elizabeth S. "Echoes and Foreshadowings in Mark 4–8: Reading and ReReading". *Journal of Biblical Literature* 112 (1993) 211–30.

Malina, Bruce L. *On the Genre and Message of Revelation: Star Visions and Sky Journeys.* Peabody, MA: Hendrickson, 1996.

———. *In the Company of Jesus. Characters in Mark's Gospel.* Louisville, KY: Westminster John Knox, 2000.

Marcus, Joel. "Birkat ha-Minim Revisited." *New Testament Studies* 55 (2009) 523–51.

———. *Mark.* The Anchor Yale Bible 27–27A. 2 vols. New York/New Haven, CT: Yale University Press, 2000–2009.

———. "Mark – Interpreter of Paul." *New Testament Studies* 46 (2000) 473–87.

———. "The Jewish War and the Sitz im Leben of Mark." *Journal of Biblical Literature* 103 (1992) 441–62.

Marshall, Christopher D. *Faith as a Theme in Mark's Narrative.* Society for New Testament Studies Monograph Series 64. Cambridge: Cambridge University Press, 1989.

Marxsen, Willi. *Mark the Evangelist. Studies in Redaction Criticism.* Translated by James Boyce and Others. Nashville, TN: Abingdon Press, 1969.

Matera, Frank J. *New Testament Ethics. The Legacies of Jesus and Paul.* Louisville, KY: Westminster John Knox, 1996.

———. *The Kingship of Jesus. Composition and Theology in Mark 15.* Society of Biblical Literature Dissertation Series 66. Chico, CA: Scholars Press, 1982.

———. "The Plot of Matthew's Gospel." *The Catholic Biblical Quarterly* 49 (1987) 233–53.

———. *The Sermon on the Mount: The Perfect Measure of the Christian Life.* Collegeville, MN: Liturgical Press, 2013.

Meeks, Wayne. "The Ethics of the Fourth Gospel." Pages 317–26 in *Exploring the Gospel of John. In Honor of D. Moody Smith.*

Meier, John P. *A Marginal Jew. Rethinking the Historical Jesus.* 5 vols. Anchor Yale Biblical Reference Library. New

York: Doubleday; New Haven, CT: Yale University Press, 1991–2016.

_____. "The Present State of the 'Third Quest' for the Historical Jesus: Loss and Gain." *Biblica* 80 (1999) 459–87.

Menken, Martin J. J. *Old Testament Quotations in the Fourth Gospel. Studies in Textual Form*. Contributions to Biblical Exegesis and Theology 15. Kampen: Kok Pharos, 1996.

Metzger, Bruce M. *A Textual Commentary on the Greek New Testament*. Stuttgart: Deutsche Bibelgesellshaft, 1994.

Michaels, Ramsey. "Revelation 1.19 and the Narrative Voices of the Apocalypse." *New Testament Studies* 12 (1965-66) 89–105.

Miller, Susan. *Women in Mark's Gospel*. Journal for the Study of the New Testament Supplement Series 266. London: T. & T. Clark, 2004.

Mlakhuzhyil, George. *The Christocentric Literary Structure of the Fourth Gospel*. 2nd ed. Analecta Biblica 117. Rome: Gregorian and Biblical Press, 2011.

Moloney, Francis J. *A Body Broken for a Broken People. Divorce, Remarriage, and the Eucharist*. Mulgrave, Vic.: Garratt Publishing, 2015.

_____. *A Friendly Guide to the Book of Revelation*. Mulgrave, Vic.: Garratt Publications, 2020.

_____. *"A Hard Saying." The Gospel and Culture*. Collegeville, MN: Liturgical 2001.

_____. *A Life of Promise: Poverty–Chastity–Obedience* (Wilmington DE: Michael Glazier, 1984.

_____. "An Adventure with Nicodemus." Pages 97–110 in Kitzberger, ed., *The Personal Voice*.

_____. "A Response: Where from and Where to." Pages 281–90 in Kitzberger, *Interfigural Readings*.

_____. *Belief in the Word. Reading John 1–4*. Minneapolis, MN: Fortress, 1993.

_____. "Before I Forget. Fifty Years with the New Testament." *The Australasian Catholic Record* 97 (2020) 397–410.

_____. *Beginning the Good News. A narrative approach*. Collegeville, MN: Liturgical Press, 1992.

_____. "Can Everyone be Wrong? A Reading of John 11:1–12:8." *New Testament Studies* 49 (2003) 505–27.

_____. "Closure: A Study of John 20:1–21:25." Pages 539–52 in *Johannine Studies*.

_____. "Die Offenbarung des Johannes: Hoffnung in dunklen Zeiten." *Zeitschrift für Katholische Theologie* 141 (2019) 495–516.

_____. *Die Offenbarung des Johannes und ihre Botschaft heute. Tageslesungen zur Osterzeit*. Translated by Ingrid Rosa Kitzberger. Sankt Ottilien: EOS Editions, 2022.

_____. *Disciples and Prophets. A Biblical Model for the Religious Life*. London: Darton, Longman & Todd, 1980.

_____. *Don Bosco in Australia and the Pacific 1923–2023*. Mulgrave, Vic.: Garratt Publishing, 2022.

_____. "Education of the Heart." Pages 99–117 in *Remembering a Dream. Studies for the Bicentenary of Don Bosco's Dream of 1824*. Manila: Don Bosco School of Theology, 2024.

_____. "For as Yet They Did not Know the Scriptures." Pages 505–19 in *Johannine Studies 1975-2017*.

_____. "From History, into Narrative, and Beyond." Pages 3–14 in Moloney, *Johannine Studies*.

_____. *Gebrochenes Brot für gebrochene Menschen. Eucharistie im Neuen Testament*. Translated by Ingrid Rosa Kitzberger. Freiburg: Herder, 2018.

_____. *Glory not Dishonor: Reading John 13–21*. Minneapolis, MN: Fortress, 1998.

_____. *Gospel Interpretation and Christian Life*. Scholars Collection 3. Adelaide: ATF Press, 2017.

_____. "'He Loved Them to the End.' Eucharist in the Gospel of John." Pages 11–29 in *The 51st International Eucharistic Congress. Lectures and Catecheses*. Cebu: University of San Carlos Press, 2017.

_____. "Israel, the People, and the Jews in the Fourth Gospel. Pages 93–115 in *Johannine Studies 1975-2017*.

_____. "Jesus of Nazareth. A Biographical Sketch." Pages 64–90 in *Reading the New Testament in the Church*.

_____. "John 21 and the Johannine Story." Pages 237–51 in *Anatomies of Narrative Criticism. The Past, Present, and Futures of the Fourth Gospel as Literature*. Edited by Tom Thatcher and Stephen D. Moore. Resources for Biblical Study 55. Atlanta, GA: SBL Press, 2008.

_____. *Johannine Studies 1975–2017*. Wissenschaftliche Untersuchungen zum Neuen Testament 372. Tübingen: Mohr Siebeck, 2017.

_____. *Letters to the Johannine Circle: 1–3 John*. Biblical Studies from the Catholic Biblical Association of America 2. New York: Paulist, 2020.

_____. "Literary Strategies in the Markan Passion Narrative (Mark 14,1–15,47). *Studien zum Neuen Testament und Seiner Umwelt* 28 (2003) 5–25.

_____. *Love in the Gospel of John. An Exegetical, Theological, and Literary Study*. Grand Rapids, MI: Baker Academic, 2013.

_____. "Mark 6:6b–30: Mission, the Baptist, and Failure." *The Catholic Biblical Quarterly* 63 (2001) 663–79.

_____. *Mary: Woman and Mother*. Homebush, NSW: St Paul Publications, 1988.

———. "Matthew 19,3–12 and Celibacy: A Redactional and Form Critical Study." *Journal for the Study of the New Testament* 2 (1979) 42–60.

———. "Mission in the Acts of the Apostles: The Protagonist is the Holy Spirit." *The Australasian Catholic Record* 96 (2019) 400–410.

———. "Narrative Criticism of the Gospels." *Pacifica* 4 (1991) 181–201.

———. "Pope Francis and the Word of God in the Catholic Tradition." Pages 53–64 in *Broken for You: Jesus Christ, the Catholic Priesthood & the Word of God*. Bayswater, Vic.: Coventry Press, 2018.

———. "Reading John 2:13–22: The Purification of the Temple." Pages 343–61 in *Johannine Studies*.

———. *Reading the New Testament in the Church. A Primer for Pastors, Religious Educators, and Believers*. Grand Rapids, MI: Baker Academic, 2015.

———. *Reading Revelation at Easter Time*. Collegeville, MN: Liturgical Press, 2020.

———. "Reform: Spirituality and the Person of Jesus: Christian Holiness and Deification (theosis)." *Pacifica* 30 (2017) 56–71.

———. "Revisiting the Temple: Mark 11:15–16 and 13:2." Pages 61–75 in *The Figure of Jesus in History and Theology*.

———. "Sacred Scripture at Vatican II." *Toronto Journal of Theology* 32 (2016) 183–200.

———. *Signs and Shadows. Reading John 5–12*. Minneapolis, MN: Fortress, 1996.

———. "Telling God's Story: The Fourth Gospel." Pages 107–22 in *The Forgotten God. Perspectives in Biblical Theology. Essays in Honor of Paul J. Achtemeier on Occasion on Occasion of His Seventy-Fifth Birthday*. Edited by Andrew Das and Frank J. Matera. Louisville, KY: Westminster John Knox, 2002.

———. *The Apocalypse of John. A Commentary*. Grand Rapids, MI: Baker Academic, 2020.

———. "'The Jews' in the Fourth Gospel. Another Perspective." Pages 20–44 in *The Gospel of John. Text and Context*.

———. "The Gospel of John as Scripture." Pages 333–47 in *The Gospel of John. Text and Context*.

———. *The Resurrection of the Messiah. A Narrative Commentary on the Resurrection Accounts in the Four Gospels*. New York: Paulist, 2013.

———. "The Fourth Gospel: A Tale of Two Paracletes." Pages 241–59 in *The Gospel of John: Text and Context*.

———. *The Shape of Matthew's Story*. Biblical Studies from the Catholic Biblical Association of America 9. New York: Paulist, 2023.

———. "Teaching the Most Difficult Text in the Gospel of Mark: Mark 9:42–50." Pages 129–50 in *Communication, Pedagogy, and the Gospel of Mark*. Edited by Elizabeth E. Shively and Geert van Oyen. Resources for Biblical Studies 83. Atlanta: SBL Press, 2016.

———. "The Book of Revelation: Hope in Dark Times." *Religions* 10 (2019) 1–15.

———. "The Centrality of the Cross: Literary and Theological Reflections on Mark 15:20b–25." *Pacifica* 21 (2008) 245–56.

———. "The Fourth Gospel and the Jesus of History." Pages 57–63 in *The Gospel of John. Text and Context*.

———. "The Fourth Gospel's Presentation of Jesus as 'the Christ' and J. A. T. Robinson's Redating". Pages 169–83 in *Johannine Studies 1975–2017*.

———. *The Gospel of John*. Sacra Pagina 4. Collegeville: Liturgical, 1998.

———. *The Gospel of John. Text and Context*. Biblical Interpretation 72. Boston: Brill, 2005.

———. "The Gospel of John as Scripture." Pages 333–47 in *The Gospel of John. Text and Context*.

———. *The Gospel of Mark. A Commentary*. Grand Rapids, MI: Baker Academic, 2002.

———. *The Johannine Son of Man*. 2d ed. Wipf & Stock, 2007.

———. "The Letters of John." Pages 1831–1849 in *The Jerome Biblical Commentary for the Twenty-First Century*. Edited by John J. Collins, Gina Hens-Piazza, Barbara Reid, and Donald Senior. London: T. & T. Clark, 2022.

———. *The Living Voice of the Gospel. The Gospels Today*. 2nd ed. Mulgrave, Vic.: Garratt Publishing, 2006.

———. "The Reinterpretation of Psalm VIII and the Son of Man Debate." *New Testament Studies* 27 (1981) 656–72.

———. *The Shape of Matthew's Gospel*. Biblical Studies from the Catholic Biblical Association of America 9. New York: Paulist, 2023.

———. "The Targum on Psalm 8 and the New Testament." *Salesianum* 37 (1975) 326–36.

———. *This is the Gospel of the Lord. Year C*. Homebush, NSW: Society of St Paul, 1991.

———. *This is the Gospel of the Lord. Year A*. Homebush, NSW: Society of St Paul, 1992.

———. *This is the Gospel of the Lord. Year B*. Homebush, NSW: Society of St Paul, 1993.

———. "Tracing a Literary Structure in the Book of Revelation." *The Catholic Biblical Quarterly* 84 (2022) 642–59.

———. "Whither Catholic Biblical Studies?" *The Australasian Catholic Record* 65 (1988) 83–93.

———. "Who is 'the Reader' in/of the Fourth Gospel?" Pages 219–33 in *The Interpretation of John*, ed. John Ashton. 2nd edition. Edinburgh: T. & T. Clark, 1997.

Moody Smith, Dwight. "When Did the Gospels Become Scripture?" *Journal for Biblical Literature* 119 (2000) 3–20.

Moore, Stephen D. *Untold Tales from the Book of Revelation: Sex and Gender, Empire and Ecology*. Atlanta, GA: SBL Press, 2014.

Morrison, Gregg S. *The Turning Point in the Gospel of Mark: A Study in Markan Christology*. Eugene, OR: Wipf & Stock, 2014.

Moyise, Steve. *The Old Testament and the Book of Revelation*. Journal for the Study of the New Testament Supplement Series 115. Sheffield: Sheffield Academic Press, 1995.

Murphy-O'Connor, Jerome. *Paul: His Story*. Oxford: Oxford University Press, 2004.

———. *St. Paul's Corinth. Texts and Archaeology*. Good News Studies 6. Wilmington, DE: Michael Glazier, 1983.

———. "The Structure of Matthew XIV–XVII." *Revue Biblique* 82 (1975) 360–84.

Myers, Ched. *Binding the Strong Man: A Political Reading of Mark's Story of Jesus*. Maryknoll: Orbis Books, 1986.

Niederwimmer, Kurt. *Die Didache*. 2nd edition. Kommentar zu den Apostolischen Vätern 1. Göttingen: Vandenhoeck & Ruprecht, 1993.

Nineham, Denis E. *The Gospel of St Mark*. Pelican New Testament Commentaries. Harmondsworth: Penguin Books, 1963.

Nolland, John. *The Gospel of Matthew*. New International Greek Testament Commentary. Grand Rapids, MI: Eerdmans, 2005.

_____. "The Gospel of Matthew and Anti-Semitism." Pages 154–69 in *Built Upon the Rock. Studies in the Gospel of Matthew*. Edited by Daniel M. Gurtner and John Nolland. Grand Rapids, MI: Eerdmans, 2008.

Noth, Martin. *The Deuteronomic History*. Journal for the Study of the Old Testament Supplement Series 15. Sheffield. Sheffield University Press, 1981.

Oberlinner, Andreas. *Die Christologische Erfüllung der Schrift: Eine Untersuchung zur johanneischen Hermeneutik anhand der Schriftzitate*. Wissenschaftliche Untersuchungen zum Neuen Testament 2.83. Tübingen: Mohr Siebeck.

O'Brien, Kelli S. "Written That You May Believe: John 20 and Narrative Rhetoric." *The Catholic Biblical Quarterly* 67 (2005) 284–302.

O'Day, Gail. *Revelation in the Fourth Gospel. Narrative Mode and Theological Claim*. Philadelphia, PA: Fortress, 1986.

Osborne, B. A. E. "Peter, Stumbling-Block and Satan." *Novum Testamentum* 15 (1973) 187–90.

Pagels, Elaine. *Revelations: Visions, Prophecy, and Politics in the Book of Revelation*. New York: Viking, 2012.

Painter, John. "Inclined to God: The Quest for Eternal Life – Bultmannian Hermeneutics in the Theology of the Fourth Gospel." Pages 346–68 in *Exploring the Gospel of John*. Edited by Culpepper and Clifton Black.

Parsons, Michael C. *Acts*. Paideia Commentaries on the New Testament. Grand Rapids, MI: Baker Academic, 2008.

_____. *The Departure of Jesus in Luke-Acts: The Ascension Narratives in Context*. Journal for the Study of the New

Testament Supplement Series 21. Sheffield: JSOT Press, 1987.

Parsons, Michael C., and Pervo, Richard I. *Rethinking the Unity of Luke and Acts*. Minneapolis, MN: Fortress, 1993.

Perkins, Pheme. *First Corinthians*. Paideia Commentaries on the New Testament. Grand Rapids, MI: Baker Academic, 2012.

Powell, Mark A. *Introducing the New Testament: A Historical, Theological, and Literary Survey*. Grand Rapids, MI: Baker Academic, 2009.

———. *Jesus as a Figure in History: How Modern Historians View the Man from Galilee*. Louisville, KY: Westminster John Knox, 1998.

Prigent, Pierre. *Commentary on the Apocalypse of St John*. Translated by Wendy Pradels. Tübingen: Mohr Siebeck, 2001.

Prior, Michael. *Paul the Letter-Writer and the Second Letter to Timothy*. Journal for the Study of the New Testament Supplement Series 23. Sheffield: JSOT Press, 1989.

Ratzinger, Joseph. "The Transmission of Divine Revelation." Volume 3. Pages 190–96. Edited by Herbert Vorgrimler. 5 vols. London: Burns & Oates/Herder & Herder, 1967–1969.

Reim, Günther. *Studien zum alttestamentlichen Hintergrund des Johannesevangelium*. Society for New Testament Studies Monograph Series 22. Cambridge: Cambridge University Press, 1974.

Reinhartz, Adele. *Cast out of the Covenant. Jesus and Anti-Judaism in the Gospel of John*. Lanham, MD: Lexington Books/Fortress Academic, 2018.

———. "Judaism in the Gospel of John." *Interpretation* 63 (2009) 382–93.

Rensberger, David. "Antijudaism and the Gospel of John." Pages 130–37 in *Antijudaism and the Gospel*. Edited by William R. Farmer. Harrisburg, PA: Trinity Press International, 1999.

Rengstorf, Art. *"lēistēs."* Volume 4. Pages 257–62 in *Theological Dictionary of the New Testament*. Edited by Gerhard Kittel and Gerhard Friedrich. Translated by Geoffrey W. Bromiley. 10 vols. Grand Rapids, MI: Eerdmans, 1964–1976.

Rhoads, David, Dewey, Johanna, and Michie, Donald. *Mark as Story. An Introduction to the Narrative of a Gospel*, 2nd ed. Minneapolis, MN: Fortress, 1999.

Resseguie, James L. *The Revelation of John. A Narrative Commentary*. Grand Rapids, MI: Baker Academic, 2009.

Rimmon-Kenan, Schlomith. *Narrative Fiction: Contemporary Poetics*. New Accents. London: Methuen, 1983.

Robinson, James M., Hoffmann, Paul, Kloppenborg, John S. *The Critical Edition of Q*. Hermeneia. Minneapolis, MN: Fortress, 2000.

Rowland, Christopher. *"By an Immediate Revelation:" Studies in Apocalypticism. Its Origins and Effects*. Wissenschaftliche Untersuchungen zum Neuen Testament 473. Tübingen: Mohr Siebeck, 2022.

_____. *The Open Heaven. A Study of Apocalyptic in Judaism and Christianity*. London: SPCK, 1982.

Sanders, Ed Parish. *Jesus and Judaism*. Philadelphia, PA: Fortress, 1985.

_____. *Paul and Palestinian Judaism. A Comparison of Patterns of Religion*. London: SCM, 1977.

_____. *The Historical Figure of Jesus*. London: Penguin, 1993.

Sanders, Jack T. *Ethics in the New Testament: Change and Development*. London: SCM Press, 1985.

———. *The Jews in Luke-Acts*. London: SCM, 1987.

Schildgen, Brenda D. *Power and Prejudice. The Reception of the Gospel of Mark*. Detroit, MI: Wayne State University Press, 1999.

Schmidt, Konrad, and Schröter, Jens. *The Making of the Bible: From the First Fragments to Sacred Scripture*. Translated by Peter Lewis. Cambridge, MA: Belknap Press of Harvard University Press, 2021.

Schneiders, Sandra M. "The Resurrection (of the Body) in the Fourth Gospel. A Key to Johannine Spirituality." Pages 168–98 in *Life in Abundance. Studies in John's Gospel in Tribute to Raymond E. Brown*. Edited by John R. Donahue. Collegeville, MN: Liturgical Press, 2005).

———. "Death in the Community and Eternal Life: History, Theology, and Spirituality in John 11." *Interpretation* 41 (1987) 44–65.

Schnelle, Udo. *The History and Theology of the New Testament Writings*. Translated by Eugene Boring. Minneapolis, MI: Fortress, 1998.

———. "Theologie als kreative Sinnbildung: Johannes als Weiterbildung von Paulus und Markus." Pages 119–45 in *Das Johannesevangelium – Mitte oder Rand des Kanons? Neue Standortsbestimmungen*. Edited by Thomas Söding. Quaestiones Disputatae 203 (Freiburg: Herder, 2003).

Schökel, Luis Alonso. *The Inspired Word: Scripture in the Light of Language and Literature*. Translated by Francis Martin. London: Herder & Herder, 1965.

Scholtissek, Klaus. "'Geschrieben in diesem Buch' (Joh 20,30) – Beobachtubgeb zum kanonischen Anspruch des Johannesevangeliums." Pages 207–226 in *Israel und Seine Heilstradition*. Edited by Labahn, Scholtissek, and Strottman.

Schreiner, Patrick. *Disciple and Scribe. The First Gospel and Its Portrait of Jesus.* Grand Rapids, MI: Baker Academic, 2019.

Schuchard, Bruce G. *Scripture within Scripture: The Interrelationship between Form and Function in the Explicit Old Testament Citations in the Gospel of John.* Society of Biblical Literature Dissertation Series 133. Atlanta, GA: SBL Press, 1992.

Schürer, Emil. *The History of the Jewish People in the Age of Jesus Christ.* Revised and Edited by Geza Vermes, Fergus Millar, and Martin Goodman. 3 vols. Edinburgh: T. & T. Clark, 1973–1987.

Schulz, Richard I. "The Origins and Basic Arguments of the Multi-author View of the Composition of Isaiah. Where Are We Now and How Did We Get There?" Pages 7–31 in *Bind Up the Testimony. Explorations in the Genesis of the Book of Isaiah.* Edited by Daniel I. Block and Richard I. Schulz. Peabody, MA: Hendrickson, 2015.

Schweitzer, Albert. *On the Edge of a Primeval Forest and More from a Primeval Forest.* London: Adam and Charles Black, 1951.

———. *The Quest of the Historical Jesus.* Edited by John Bowden. 1st Complete Edition. Minneapolis, MN: Fortress, 2001.

Schweizer, Eduard. "Mark's Theological Achievement." Pages 42–63 in *The Interpretation of Mark.* Edited by William Telford. Investigations in Religion and Theology 7. Philadelphia, PA: Fortress, 1985.

Senior, Donald. "Interpreting the Scriptures. The Church and the Modern Catholic Biblical Renewal." Pages 1923–949 in *The Jerome Biblical Commentary for the Twenty-First Century.* London: T. & T. Clark, 2022.

———. "The Eucharist in Mark: Mission, Reconciliation, Hope." *Biblical Theology Bulletin* 12 (1982) 62–72.

———. *Raymond Brown and the Catholic Renewal*. New York: Paulist, 2018.

Shaw, Brent D. "The Myth of the Neronian Persecution." *Journal of Roman Studies* 105 (2015) 1–28.

Shepherd, Tom. "The Narrative Function of Markan Intercalation." *New Testament Studies* 41 (1995) 522–40.

Sheridan, Greg. *Christians. The Urgent Case for Jesus in our World*. Sydney: Allen & Unwin, 2021.

Shillington, V. George. *James and Paul. The Politics of Identity at the Turn of the Ages*. Minneapolis, MN: Fortress, 2015.

Sim, David. *The Gospel of Matthew and Christian Judaism. The History and Social Setting of the Jewish Community*. Studies of the New Testament and Its World. Edinburgh: T. & T. Clark, 1998.

Skinner, Christopher W. ed. *Characters and Characterization in the Gospel of John*. Library of New Testament Studies 46. London: Bloomsbury, T. & T. Clark, 2014.

———. "The World: Promise and Unfulfilled Hope." Pages 61–70 in *Character Studies in the Fourth Gospel. Narrative Approaches to Seventy Figures in John*. Edited by Steven A. Hunt, D. Francois Tolmie, and Ruben Zimmermann. Wissenschaftliche Untersuchungen zum Neuen Testament 314. Tübingen: Mohr Siebeck, 2013.

Spivey, Robert A., Moody Smith, D., and Clifton Black. C. *Anatomy of the New Testament*. 7th ed. Minneapolis, MN: Fortress, 2013.

St John Thackeray, Henry, Markus, Ralph, Wikgren, Alan, and Feldman, Louis H. Editors and Translators. *Josephus*. 9 vols. Loeb Classical Library. Cambridge, MA: Harvard University Press, 1926–1965.

Stählin, Gustav. "Zum Problem der johanneischen Eschatologie." *Zeitschrift für die Neutestamentliche Wissenschaft* 33 (1934) 225–59.

Swanson, Kristen. *A Most Peculiar Book: The Inherent Strangeness of the Bible*. New York: Oxford University Press, 2020.

Tannehill, Robert C. "The Gospel of Mark as Narrative Christology." *Semeia* 16 (1980) 57–95.

———. *The Narrative Unity of Luke-Acts. A Literary Interpretation*. 2 vols. Minneapolis, MN: Fortress, 1986–1990.

Taylor, Vincent. *The Gospel according to St. Mark*. 2d ed. London: Macmillan, 1966.

The Bible and Culture Collective. *The Postmodern Bible*. New Haven, CT: Yale University Press, 1966.

The Pontifical Biblical Commission. *The Interpretation of the Bible in the Church*. Vatican City: Libreria Editrice Vaticana, 1993.

The Catechism of the Catholic Church. Homebush: Society of Saint Paul, 1994.

Theissen, Gerd. *The Shadow of the Galilean*. Translated by John Bowden. London: SCM Press, 1987.

Theissen, Gerd, and Annette Mertz. *The Historical Jesus. A Comprehensive Guide*. Translated by John Bowden. Minneapolis, MI: Fortress, 1998.

Thompson, Leonard L. *The Book of Revelation: Apocalypse and Empire*. New York: Oxford University Press, 2014.

Telford, William R. *The Barren Temple and the Withered Tree: A Redaction-critical Analysis of the Cursing of the Fig-Tree Pericope in Mark's Gospel and its Relation to the Cleansing of the Temple Tradition*. Journal for the Study of the New Testament Supplement Series 1. Sheffield: JSOT Press, 1980.

Tonstad, Sigve K. *Revelation*. Paideia Commentaries on the New Testament. Grand Rapids, MI: Baker Academic, 2019.

Tracy, David. *The Analogical Imagination: Christian Theology and the Culture of Pluralism*. New York: Crossroad, 1981.

Trites, Alison. *The New Testament Concept of Witness*. Society for the Study of the New Testament Monograph Series 31. Cambridge: Cambridge University Press, 1977.

VanderKam, James. *An Introduction to Early Judaism*. Grand Rapids, MI: Eerdmans, 2001.

_____. "John Meier: A Portrait of a Scholar." Pages xix–xx11 in *The Figure of Jesus in History and Theology. Essays in Honor of John Meier*. Edited by Vincent T. M. Skemp and Kelley Coblenz Bautsch. Catholic Biblical Association Imprints 1. Washington, DC: The Catholic Biblical Association, 2020.

van Iersel, Bas. *Reading Mark*. Translated by W. H. Bisscheroux. Collegeville, MN: Liturgical Press, 1988.

Vanni, Ugo. *La Struttura Letteraria dell'Apocalisse*. Aloisiana. Scritti publicati sotto la direzione della Pontificia Facoltà Teologica per l'Italia Medidionale sezione « San Luigi. » 8. Rome: Herder, 1971.

_____. « Liturgical Dialogue as a Literary Form in the Book of Revelation." *New Testament Studies* 37 (1991) 348–64.

Vermes, Geza. *Jesus the Jew*. London: Collins, 1972.

Van Der Horst, Pieter. *The Birkat ha-minim* in Recent Research. *The Expository Times* 105 (1994) 363–68.

van der Watt, Jan G., and Zimmermann, Ruben (eds.). *Rethinking the Ethics of John. "Implicit Ethics" in the Johannine Writings*. Kontexte und Normen neutestamentliche Ethik/Contexts and Norms of New Testament Ethics. Wissenschaftliche Untersuchungen zum Neuen Testament 291. Tubingen: Mohr Siebeck, 2012.

von Wahlde, Urban C. *The Gospel and Letters of John*. 3 vols. Eerdmans Critical Commentary. Grand Rapids, MI: Eerdmans, 2010.

Wagener, Fredrik. *Figuren und Handlungsmodelle: Simon Petrus, die Samaritische Frau, Judas und Thomas als zugänge zu einer narrativer Ethik des Johannesevangeliums*. Kontexte und Normen neutestamentliche Ethik/Contexts and Norms of New Testament Ethics. Wissenschaftliche Untersuchungen zum Neuen Testament 2.408. Tubingen: Mohr Siebeck, 2013.

Wallace, Daniel B. *Greek Grammar Beyond the Basics. An Exegetical Syntax of the New Testament*. Grand Rapids, MI: Zondervan, 1996.

Watts, R. E. *Isaiah's New Exodus and Mark*. Wissenschaftlicher Untersuchungen zum Neuen Testament 2.88. Tübingen: J. C. B. Mohr (Paul Siebeck), 1997.

Weeden, T. J. *Mark – Traditions in Conflict*. Philadelphia, PA: Fortress, 1971.

Weinrich, William C. *Ancient Christian Texts: Latin Commentaries on Revelation*. Downers Grove: IVP Academic, 2011.

Weiss-Rosmarin, ed. *Jewish Expressions on Jesus: An Anthology*, New York, Ktav, 1977.

Wellhausen, Julius. *Prolegomena to the History of Ancient Israel*. Translated by J. Sutherland Black and Allan C. Menzies. Cambridge: Cambridge University Press, 2013.

Weyer-Menkhoff, Karl. *Die Ethik des Johannesevangelium in sprachlichen Feld des Handelns*. Kontexte und Normen neutestamentliche Ethik/Contexts and Norms of New Testament Ethics. Wissenschaftliche Untersuchungen zum Neuen Testament 2.359. Tubingen: Mohr Siebeck, 2014.

Wilson, Stephen G. *Related Strangers. Jews and Christians 70–170 C.E.* Minneapolis, MN: Fortress, 1995.

Winsor, Ann Roberts. *A King is Bound in the Tresses. Allusions to the Song of Songs in the Fourth Gospel*. Studies in Biblical Literature 6. New York: Peter Lang, 2009.

Winstanley, Michael T. *Salesian Gospel Spirituality. An Exploration*. Bolton, UK: Don Bosco Publications, 2020.

Witherup, Ronald D. "The Bible in the Life of the Church." Pages 1615–621 in *The Paulist Biblical Commentary*. Edited by José Enrique Aguilar Chiu, Richard J. Clifford, Carol J. Dempsey, Eileen M. Schuler, Thomas D. Stegman, and Ronald D. Witherup. New York: Paulist, 2018.

Wrede, Wilhelm. *The Messianic Secret*. Translated by J. C. G. Grieg. Cambridge & London: James Clark, 1971.

Wright, Nicholas T. *Jesus and the Victory of God*. Minneapolis, MN: Fortress, 1996.

———. *Paul: A Biography*. San Francisco: HarperOne, 2018.

———. *The New Testament and the People of God*. Minneapolis, MN: Fortress, 1992.

———. *The Resurrection and the Son of God*. Minneapolis, MN: Fortress, 2003.

Zimmermann, Ruben. "Is there Ethics in the Gospel of John?" Pages 44–88 in *Rethinking the Ethics of John*.

Zumstein, Jean. L'Évangile johannique, une stratégie du croire. *Recherches des Sciences Religieuses* 77 (1989) 217–32.

———. *L'Évangile selon Saint Jean*. 2 vols. Commentaire du Nouveau Testament IVa-b. Geneva : Labor et Fides, 2007–2014.

www.ingramcontent.com/pod-product-compliance
Lightning Source LLC
Chambersburg PA
CBHW011127070526
44584CB00028B/3803